Writing the Stories of Your Life

How to Turn Memories into Memoir

by Elsa Eysenbach McKeithan, Ph.D.

Talking Stones

Writing the Stories of Your Life; How to turn memories into memoir. Copyright ©2004 by Elsa Eysenbach McKeithan. Manufactured in Canada. All rights reserved including all electronic rights. No part of this book may be reproduced in any form or by any electronic or mechanical means including information storage and retrieval systems without permission from the publisher, except for the following three situations: (1) A reviewer may quote brief passages in a review; (2) A student may quote brief passages with proper reference in his/her work; (3) A student who is the owner of a copy of the book may reproduce charts as needed for his or her own learning purposes.

If you have received this book in electronic form, you have the right to print one copy for your own use in addition to the rights given above.

Group leaders and teachers are advised that it is a copyright violation to reproduce books or portions of books for distribution in classes. Inquire of the publisher about discounts for group purchases.

We will greatly appreciate receiving a copy of any published reviews.

Requests for permission to quote, comments, suggestions, and corrections may be addressed to the author at the following address: Talking Stones Publishing Co. P. O. Box 30584, Winston-Salem, NC 27130

Cover design and layout by Christopher Goodsell (thedesigner@bellsouth.net)

Cover art: detail of a larger mural "Give it Time" by Megan McKeithan, 5' x 26', Acrylic on Canvas, in the office of Mindful Body Natural Healing Services in Roswell, Georgia. (www.VisionaryMuralCo.com)

© Copyright 2004 Elsa McKeithan.
All rights reserved. No part of this publication may be reproduced, stored in a retrieval system, or transmitted, in any form or by any means, electronic, mechanical, photocopying, recording, or otherwise, without the written prior permission of the author.

Note for Librarians: a cataloguing record for this book that includes Dewey Decimal Classification and US Library of Congress numbers is available from the Library and Archives of Canada. The complete cataloguing record can be obtained from their online database at:
www.collectionscanada.ca/amicus/index-e.html
ISBN 1-4120-3528-7

TRAFFORD

Offices in Canada, USA, Ireland, UK and Spain

This book was published *on-demand* in cooperation with Trafford Publishing. On-demand publishing is a unique process and service of making a book available for retail sale to the public taking advantage of on-demand manufacturing and Internet marketing. On-demand publishing includes promotions, retail sales, manufacturing, order fulfilment, accounting and collecting royalties on behalf of the author.

Book sales for North America and international:
Trafford Publishing, 6E–2333 Government St.,
Victoria, BC v8t 4p4   CANADA
phone 250 383 6864 (toll-free 1 888 232 4444)
fax 250 383 6804; email to orders@trafford.com

Book sales in Europe:
Trafford Publishing (UK) Ltd., Enterprise House, Wistaston Road Business Centre,
Wistaston Road, Crewe, Cheshire   cw2 7rp   UNITED KINGDOM
phone 01270 251 396 (local rate 0845 230 9601)
facsimile 01270 254 983; orders.uk@trafford.com

Order online at:
www.trafford.com/robots/04-1356.html

10   9   8   7   6   5   4   3   2

Dedication

To the memory of Frances Elizabeth Edgeworth Eysenbach

Thanks

Grateful thanks to friends, colleagues and loved ones lending a hand or an ear, for lunches and for many kindnesses. You believed in me and in this project.

Thanks to Mary Margret Daughtridge, writer, painter and true friend, for editing assistance and encouragement. Your dedication and service goes beyond imagining.

Thanks to Ann Martin for comments on the earlier version, and Carolyn Parrish for encouragement and proofreading on this one.

Thanks to Elin Eysenbach for reading the manuscript willingly in spite of your schedule, and for empowering me to become published.

Thanks to Robert Moore Allen for the use of the poem REUNION, and for gracious coaching in getting started.

Thanks to Jenny Fentress of Forsyth Technical Community College for employment, guidance and understanding as I struggled with this project. To Rebecca Fuller for introducing me to Jenny and encouraging me.

Thanks to all my students who are a never ending source of ideas through the questions you ask. I particularly enjoy grappling with the ones that have no tidy answer; but call forth from us many points of view and new ideas. Thank you for your grace and courage in sharing your beautiful, funny, frightening, poignant, moving, personal stories. You make the world a better place by sharing yourselves.

Leland McKeithan, activist, actress and singer, and Megan McKeithan, artist, seer and coach, thank you for choosing me to be your mom, and for being there for me. You are my most important legacy. I love you.

Thank you, my love, my husband, Kent McKeithan. You believed in me and in this project.

And to my readers: My heart's prayer is that you will be helped on your journey by writing your stories.

Table of Contents

The Story of Writing the Stories of Your Life	vii
How to Work with this Book	xiii
Tips for memoir writers	xiii
Tips for groups and group members	xiv
Writing the Stories of Your Life	xix
LIFE AS STORY	**1**
The Functions of Stories	2
Exercise: Getting started	3
The Need for Stories	4
Jack tales, culture and stories	4
Urban myth	7
Internet myths and legends	8
Distinguishing Story	8
A Memoir Is a Special Kind of Story	9
Fiction or non-fiction?	10
Assignments	12
LET'S WRITE!	**13**
Getting a Story Started	14
Exercise: Begin at the Beginning	15
Space Time Considerations	16
Finding time to write	17
Pacing yourself	18
Assignments	19
FINDING STORIES	**21**
What To Write About	21
Finding Your Stories	22
Where Do Ideas Come From?	22
Exercise: Brainstorm story sources	24
Example of story sources	25
Your Personal Story Sources	26
Tracking your ideas	28
Keeping a story notebook	28
More ways to find your stories	30
Whose Story Is It?	32
Assignments	34
WARM UP	**35**
How To Warm Up for Writing	35
Exercise: Warm up	36
The editor on my shoulder	38

Writing versus Editing	*39*
Howard's Thesis; A Story	40
Assignments	*42*

WRITING LETTERS– Sharing Yourself — **45**

Letter Writing	*46*
Warm up before writing	46
Exercise: Writing to different people	46
Audience	*47*
Exercise: Audience	50
Old letters	51
Sharing Yourself	*52*
Your memory garden	52
Exercise: Accessing your garden for memories	53
Secret Formula	*55*
Exercise: The Secret Formula	55
Assignments	*56*

SETTING — **59**

Change and the Twentieth Century	*60*
Exercise: Our changing environment	61
Place	*61*
Exercise: Childhood spaces	63
Time	*64*
Social Environment	*65*
Exercise: Elements of setting	66
Details	67
Assignments	*69*

VIEWPOINT (And Voice) — **71**

Narrator Viewpoint	*73*
Omniscient Viewpoint	*76*
Warm up	77
Writing exercise	77
Omniscient Narrator	*77*
Exercises: Viewpoint	*79*
Narrator viewpoint	79
Omniscient narrator viewpoint	79
Multiple Points of View and Group Projects	*80*
Voice	*80*
Voice and person	81
Assignments	*83*

UNFORGETTABLE CHARACTERS — **85**

Warm up	86
People in Stories	*86*
Exercise: My friend Susan	87

Writing exercise	89
Character appeal	91
Writing about Animals	*92*
Assignments	*94*

JOURNALING – And Making Stories — 97

Approaches to Journaling	*99*
Journaling for self awareness	100
Journaling processes for writers and artists	101
Journals for memoirists	102
Story Notebook	*110*
Keeping a story notebook	110
Developing Your Stories	112
Exercise: Plot Outline	112
Turning Journals into Memoirs	*112*
Diaries	113
Thought based journals	114
Retrospectives and recollections	115
Assignments	*116*

RESEARCH – Finding the Past — 117

Writing Strategies	*118*
Research Skills	*118*
Practical information on copyrights	120
Interviewing Skills	*122*
Listening Skills	*123*
Exercise: Listening	123
Listening for stories	124
Interviewing the People in Your Life for Their Stories and Yours	*126*
Interviewing family	126
Interviewing practice	128
Exercise: Remember the time…	129
Questions to ask	130
Memoir to Honor Someone	*130*
Assignments	*132*

STORY STRUCTURE — 133

Truth or Fiction?	*134*
Many Stories, Not So Many Structures	*134*
Story Elements	*135*
Characters, Goals and Action	136
Story Ladder	*138*
Exercise:	139
Story Formula	*141*
Shaping a Story	*142*
Third person version	142
Assignments	*144*

HOW DO THEY SPEAK? Dialogue, Dialect — **145**

Dialogue Is Not Ordinary Speech — *146*
  First, listen! — 148
  Second, Write for the reader! — 150
  Third, Make your story work — 151

Improving Your Dialogue — *153*
  Dialogue, conflict and sound — 154
  To said or not to said? — 155

Dialect and Foreign Languages — *156*
  Ways to suggest dialect — 157
  Local dialects — 158
  Foreign words — 161

Assignments — *167*

SPIT 'N POLISH – Editing — **169**

Example — *169*
  Here's the beginning! — 170

Three Phase Editing Plan — *171*
  Phase 1: Content and structure — 172
  Phase 2: Clarity and focus — 173
  Phase 3: Detail — 174

A Word about Rewriting — *175*
  Tricks of the trade — 175

Putting Together a Memoir from Different Sources — *176*
  Integrating different types of material from assorted sources — 177

Assignments — *179*

FICTION TECHNIQUES TO ENRICH YOUR WRITING — **181**

Show, Don't Tell. — *182*

Using Strong Language — *183*
  Language Precision — 184

Sensory Detail — *186*
  Warm up and writing practice — 186
  Enrich your writing with sensory details — 187
  Je ne sais quoi - that certain something — 188

Assignments — *189*

THEME – What Is It All About? — **193**

Identifying Theme — *194*
  Exercise: Identifying theme in stories — 194

Life Themes — *195*
  What's your life theme? — 196

Theme in Memoir Writing – Pulling your stories together — *199*
  Bringing your book together — 200

Assignments — *201*

AND THEY RODE OFF INTO THE SUNSET – Drawing Your Work to a Close — **203**

Finding the Right Structure — *204*
   Top down — 204
   Plots, quests and journeys — 205
   Collections — 208

Beginnings Middles Ends — *208*
   Evaluate the Flow of your Story — 209
   From beginnings to story openings — 211
   Middles — 216

Endings — *217*
   Endings from life — 217

Assignments — *218*

TO PUBLISH OR NOT TO PUBLISH – And How — **223**

Copyrights and Publishing — *224*

Publishing Options — *225*
   One handmade book — 225
   Publishing without becoming a publisher — 226
   What if you need 100 copies? — 227

Your Goal Statement — *228*

What It Takes To Publish a Book — *229*
   The publishing world today — 229

The Business of Publishing — *231*
   Study the market — 231
   Finding a publisher — 234

Small Presses and Self Publishing — *235*
   Self-publishing and print on demand — 236
   Print on demand — 237

Afterward — *239*
Glossary — *241*
Endnotes — *244*
Bibliography — *249*
Index — *255*
About the Author — *259*
Order form — *261*

The Story of Writing the Stories of Your Life

As a working writer and editor, the things in this book are the things I have taught myself how to do. I learned grammar, spelling, mathematics, and psychology in school; I am a self-educated writer. Writing is something that welled up within me, and I wrote snatches of poetry, stories, and notes from the time I was a child until I had boxes full of journals and papers. At a tumultuous point in my life, during a time of great change for my family and major upset in my work life, I decided to write a novel. Sounds like a brilliant plan for a time like that, doesn't it? I suppose it was an outlet for my emotions.

I had an idea for a story I thought would be a short story; I started it. It grew quickly into the decision to write a novel, and slowly into a finished book. I worked on "River Song" for about two years, and I finished it. It was never published, but I did it. It took a dear friend to point out to me that I had set a goal and accomplished it. My goal was to write a novel; I did. Since then I have set many writing goals and accomplished them.

When I began to write in earnest, one of the things I already knew how to do was to study. I had managed to complete a Ph.D. in psychology, and I decided to apply my study skills to learning to write well. I went to workshops, talked with writers and writing teachers and editors, subscribed to writer's magazines. I bought books about writing and I studied them the same way that I had studied my school books a few years before—carefully, diligently. I took on the exercises they provided; I did the assignments. If I didn't get much out of a book, I discarded it and bought another one on the same subject. If I found a book helpful, I kept it handy and reviewed portions of it. And eventually I showed my work to others and let them guide me.

I wrote. For a long time I wrote wherever I was, whatever I was doing, every day; I never thought I was very consistent about it, but I wrote a lot of pages. When I eventually gave myself full-time to writing, I set goals for writing a certain number of hours a day, days a week, or pages of production per day; and I learned that I often don't meet those goals. I also learned that if I don't set them, I don't do anything. Ah ha! I don't have to be perfect! Today, I set a stretch goal; if I meet it I reward myself. If I don't, I accept that I have done much more than I would have with no goal set. I congratulate myself for my successes; I look for the lessons in my failures. I check to see how I am blocking myself, and I give up self-criticism.

I learned to separate writing from editing. This was an important breakthrough for me because it helped me to move forward in my writing more freely and naturally, and more quickly. Although I am an editor, when I am writing I just write. Some people do this naturally, but most people, especially those with a lot of education, hamper themselves by thinking too much and working over the words as they write. They have been taught to write with a great deal of thought and put down just the right word. They stop and start, and never let their natural "Inner Writer" have a chance to express herself. We will address this skill in the first chapter; it is a core skill.

Over a period of years I became very well-educated in the skills of writing. I continued to write, and I began to do more editing, compiling and coaching for others. I have written advertising, marketing materials, political speeches, and stories and articles on various subjects; many published without my name on them. I have edited books, articles, and doctoral theses. Today I am a writing coach and free-lance editor. My family is important to me. I keep my coaching work to about twenty hours a week, and I teach writing classes. I especially enjoy coaching writers of memoirs. I also paint and travel and pursue my own writing projects. I enjoy my life.

I actually started this book one day in my car on the way home from my Wednesday morning volunteer commitment—painting with senior citizens in a long-term health care unit in a retirement community. I enjoyed helping. Solving compositional problems on the fly for people who thought I could paint anything was fun (not to say challenging!) but I was looking for something worth doing that was "my project." I had been a corporate editor. I had finished another novel since being downsized. I had a few editing clients. What else could I do? I seriously needed to improve my income; but more than that, I needed to make a difference for people. I did not want to return to being a temporary secretary. The next week, I called the coordinator in charge and proposed a writing class. From that class grew more classes and eventually, this book.

This book is for everybody who is interested in writing from their own experience, sharing themselves. In it I share the things I have learned about writing, stories about my life and my family, stories my students have written, and the techniques of writing and editing that are most useful for writing your stories.

Memoirs can come in many forms. They can be long or short. They can be a song, or music or poetry. You can create a collage or montage or a painting to express a part of your life. I include in this book a narrative poem "Reunion" by Robert Moore Allen, which is one of the best pieces of such writing that I have seen. As you work with this book, I invite you to listen to popular songs, to the bits of background data that accompany any type of radio music; to the newscasts and features. Listen for stories that are memoirs of one type or another. And, remember for yourself the music you loved, the foods you ate, the cars you drove. They are all bits of the picture.

Does it matter if you have no writing experience to speak of? This book is for beginners and other writers who want to share their personal stories. The people I teach are ordinary people who are willing to take the extraordinary action of writing a story from their own life experience. My students are usually a mix of people who have always wanted to write and a few who never thought of writing until something happened in their lives that changed everything. Some students have always written in their work or for fun, but are looking for some systematic coaching. They are more interested in writing their story than in learning about literature or grammar or literary criticism.

This book is for beginners and other writers who want to share their personal stories.

Intending to write something is the first step; deciding on a goal comes next. Then it's important to learn how to accomplish what you want to do. I wanted a book that would give my students just what they need, whatever goals they set for themselves. I've included a chapter on generating ideas, suggestions for improving your recollection, and ideas about organizing your stories, as well as many tips and examples that show you how to get the result you want.

You may wish to write about your own life (autobiography) or about the life of someone else (biography). If you write from the perspective of memory, either may be called "memoir." The methods in this book will help you tell your story well, whatever approach you choose. I've included techniques for writing and polishing remembrance and story, writing letters and journaling, as well as suggestions on finding ideas and collecting information, suggestions on writing habits and ways to organize your materials. I've added a chapter on publishing since some students always ask me what I think about publishing their work—and how to do it.

Oral storytellers have known for millennia that to be remembered a story must be interesting. There are certain techniques that build interesting stories. In working with various people to bring their stories to print, I have found that many of the most valuable techniques for memoir writing are fiction techniques. These can be learned.

I tried to develop a step by step process, but it can't be done. That is why all those books on writing are so convoluted. You need to know all of this before you can write well, but you can't learn any of it until you have done some writing! Learning to write well is not a linear process. There are many things you need to know, but you have to do some writing for the questions to come up. You don't know what you need to know until you have tried writing a story and you want to write better. The more you work to improve your presentation, the better your finished writing will become. But there will always be the questions.

You need to know all of this before you can write well, but you can't learn any of it until you have done some writing.

Writing can only be learned by writing. Keep writing. Don't look over your shoulder and second-guess yourself. Write, edit and go on. Be satisfied with what you create and make the next piece a new challenge.

As a writer, you will return many times to the same questions. Each time your understanding will be in a different place; consequently, what you learn as you consider the conundrum will be something new. Please don't give up! Write and learn and write some more. Get together with others who are interested in similar things and help each other.

Goals and Lessons

This book is organized into a series of lessons. I tried to make it exactly twelve. It's not, and I've realized it really doesn't matter how many lessons there are. Some classes have needed one chapter or section and some another. I actually had one class that had no need to study the chapter on dialogue, which most people find challenging! They didn't know much about writing, but when the time came to add dialogue, the whole group took to it naturally. Go figure! There is a logic to the order I have things in, but there is no right order in which to study writing skills. Use the chapters that help you when you need them.

Whether you are writing a short remembrance or a book-length memoir, this book also asks you to look within yourself, find the things you most want to share and take the risk to do it. These are my four goals for students using the book. I hope that you will:

- Learn to write without editing when you are writing.
- Learn to develop a story that works structurally.
- Learn to improve your writing through self-editing.
- Share your own truth and ideas and love through your writing.

I've provided a set of processes for writing different kinds of stories. You decide what type of writing you want to try, and do the work in the chapters that answer the questions you have. I wish for you most of all that you will come to share yourself more fully and more trustingly on the page. Therein lies the power of writing. Whatever you are feeling, someone else is feeling also. What you write resonates somewhere with someone. Take the chance. Tell your truth.

Groups

Please read the section called "How to Use This Book" whether you are working by yourself or in a class or group.

Another goal for me has been to create a book that can be used by groups of writers, adult students, book clubs or self-help groups as a self-contained course for ongoing study. If you are working in a group, read the section called "How to Work with This Book" together and agree to a plan for your group meetings.

Writing the Stories of Your Life

If you work with others in a group, you may want to agree on which chapters each one is responsible for as you work together. If you have a handle on one, you will find that you have questions on another.

I hope this book will be useful to community college and continuing education instructors, recreational therapists, program directors, scrapbook mavens and others who lead groups or teach classes in memoir writing. I have worked for several years to create a book you will find worth spending several weeks working through. All of these materials have been used by individuals and tested by classes over the past five years. I thank each person who has asked questions or given me feedback on the materials. Your success is precious to me.

In Conclusion—or—On to Beginning!

This book is about how to write a memoir, but it's more than that. I realized after I had written it that it's about me and my family. In a way it might even be a memoir. It's the sum of what I have to contribute on writing from life. I have learned a lot from writing it. Everything I learned has gone back into my work with classes and clients, and my attempts to answer their questions have contributed to the book. I am grateful.

I am always learning, and I love to share what I know. I am a person who starts with the abstract and looks for the application to bring home the truth; who also looks, on the other hand, for the profound in the every day. I am a person who restlessly seeks something new, yet often finds it in something ancient. So, I have come to value history and everyday truth, the knowledge of the people, and the profound understandings of those who have truly lived their lives and can express simply what there is to know. These are the lessons we must not lose—lessons embodied in our stories.

This book is written for my students—those I speak with in the flesh and those I will never know personally. I hope you will write a lot, hone your skills, benefit from sharing yourself, improve and shape your writing, and enjoy the exploration Let me know how it goes and what you need; I want to make it easier for you. If you wish to communicate with me write to the address in this book or look for my website on line at www.WritingTheStoriesOfYourLife.com. I would love to have your questions and suggestions and your contributions for future books.

Enjoy writing! Whatever motivates you, let yourself go, have fun. Don't try to be perfect; there is no right way to do it. Writing is about communicating and self-expression and being yourself. Work consistently, laugh as much as you can, and enjoy the process.

Let's get started.

Monday, August 30, 2004
Elsa McKeithan

How to Work with this Book

Writing is often said to be a lonely occupation—which sometimes seems odd to writers with their heads full of characters. No loneliness there! Too much going on. But it is definitely an activity that requires the discipline of applying whatever time you have in a consistent way. Do you know of any profession or hobby or skill that isn't improved by faithful efforts?

You will get the most from this book if you regularly set aside time to write your own stories and you also do the assignments and exercises. Whether you are a group member, or you are doing this book on your own, I recommend that you study the tips carefully.

Tips for memoir writers[1]

- Write something every day.
- Complete a new recollection or story with every chapter, or at least one new piece every week.
- Use a looseleaf notebook for keeping the exercises you do together with your research and ideas and the stories you write.
- Set an intention for your work.
- Set goals for yourself.
- Warm up. Just as you would warm up for sports or exercise, you should warm up for writing. It helps you get focused.
- Read. I recommend that you read and study as many stories of the type you are writing as you can.

- Keep a list of story ideas.
- When you think an idea has merit give it a separate page in your notebook. Add to that idea until you are ready to write from it.
- Write your stories rather than tell them. Read them aloud and rewrite as necessary.
- Do the assignments that work for you, the ones that will teach you what you need to know as you go along.
- Stretch yourself as a writer by trying new things; don't expect every experiment to be equally successful.
- Writing is not a linear process; revisit sections of the book that help you from time to time.
- Write a lot. Don't be too seriously attached either to your words or the outcome. Try different approaches.
- Be courageous in sharing your project with your family. You may be surprised at the results.
- Let yourself have fun. Laugh a lot.

While you are writing the stories of your life, I recommend that you write something new every day. I am not talking about editing. I want you to warm up and write daily. Warm up for three minutes and go straight into writing for fifteen or twenty minutes in your story notebook or journal. You can be on the golf course in half an hour, and you will be surprised how much you have written after a month.

- Enjoy writing

Tips for groups and group members

- Start on time; end on time.
- Foster a spirit of cooperation and tolerance.
- Take time to get to know one another and trust each other.
- Adjust the study plan to the interests and abilities of the group.
- Have a leader for the day and a timekeeper. Setting time limits for the exercises and discussions helps to keep the group focused.
- Be prepared for your meeting or class whether you are the leader or a participant.

- Keep your remarks and questions brief and on target to the discussion; give everyone a chance to participate.

- Participate fully in the exercises.

- Follow the directions carefully for exercises. There are reasons for the rules for brainstorming and other activities.

- Be willing to listen to others and to share your own work.

- Don't try to cover too much in one meeting. Find a pace that is neither too slow and minutia driven, nor too fast, hitting the high spots, but that works to keep the group interested and active.

- Listen to each other generously; don't criticize, People know what doesn't work.

- Don't help too much. Everyone has their own style and rate of learning. Only give suggestions when they are requested.

- Read some sections of the book together and discuss them.

- Review and discuss the examples together to see what you can learn.

- Give your full attention to whoever is reading or sharing. Say "thank you" when a person finishes.

- If there is discussion of a work, list the strong points before mentioning any problems to be worked on. What works is more important than what doesn't.

- Share what you learn with other people; enjoy what you are doing.

REUNION

for all those attending the Barker-Allen Family Reunion
August 24-26, 2001, Lakefield, Ontario

Tylers Close and Woodmont Boulevard—two
houses joined—improbable coincidence love crafted
well. Now four decades later we are here
within the shadow of Bendenis wall, defined in part
by those in us we can and cannot see—eye, word,

heart, hand, and destiny worked out so well in all
our lives that providence could do no better, were
it told to make a dream come true for us to live
and in its living find our treasure's share. But
now, why have we come? Do we not wish to recall

those who have died, whose lives and voices linger
in our hearts, and in our simply saying all their names
and remembering the music of their living songs
which break and mend our hearts? We now are
their most generous gift to us. Only in the vivid

language of our dreams can they tell us if they know,
but if we name and honor them with our telling
of their truth, then through our tears and laughter
we may hear their inaudible hymns of blood
and find in all our faces the oracle of their

fondest hope. Then we may recognize our
gathering for what it is and what its worth will mean
beyond this hour's telling, for another year or many,
of our truth which we have come to celebrate
by bringing all that we most truly are to share.

So let us take our pictures, raise our glasses,
and tell our stories for a larger purpose—to let
the alchemy of our blended lives transform this
time to gold. And while no one of us will eat a
hundred oysters, stand on his head for an hour, pull

a rabbit from an empty hat, or sing a perfect Lohengrin
we will talk, listen, and enjoy each other's company,
then maybe take a thoughtful walk beside by the lake,

search its calm face, and find beneath the surface of these
days and nights we share the worth of knowing better

others bound to us by blood and love–ourselves
made larger, grander, happier by the hope
that an enduring pleasure may still flow from
this weekend's reunion, blessed for what it
is beyond our grasp until we miss it, and we know.

Robert Moore Allen

Dedicated to the loving memory of Claude, Marjorie, Dominic, Clifton, Hattie Bell, and Judson

Writing
the
Stories
of
Your Life

Chapter 1

LIFE AS STORY

We're all storytellers, and we live our lives through a network of stories. Stories contain our history and our heritage, and we embed them with our hopes and dreams of the future. To know someone is to know their stories.[2]

Everyone has a story to tell, or maybe several. The stories we tell about experiences we've had may be our most fundamental method of sharing knowledge and experience as human beings. Some senior adults are particularly motivated to write their stories as part of the work of resolving their lives and fulfilling on their purposes. I have met many not-yet-senior adults who are extremely interested in telling their stories. They want to write about what has happened to them or someone in their lives. They want to share what they have learned in exploring their heritage, or they just love stories. Sometimes it is plain that they want to get clear of the past and begin again. Writing our stories can be a way of putting the past to rest and gearing up for the future. As we revisit and reinterpret events we've experienced and pass the learning on to others we make our contribution to life.

Many of my students are interested in creating a legacy. They have made scrapbooks or researched their genealogy, yet the results lack something. They need a way to organize their notes and findings, or they want a story to give it meaning. Perhaps their families have asked them to write their autobiography. Writing an autobiography is a daunting task for most people. Where do you start? What is interesting? How will you organize it? How will you even remember it all! Whatever your particular motivation, there is good news. You don't have to write it all and you don't have to take on the whole task at once. Start with your stories.

The purpose of this book is to help you tell your stories. This chapter will show how ingrained in our minds and lives stories are, and provide some background on the function of stories in life. We will begin to distinguish memoir from other types of story, and we will begin writing. As you read this chapter think about stories you have heard and loved. Think of the stories you have lived. Begin to discover the types of stories you like best and to think about what you might want to write if you had the tools.

Write the fun stories or the pieces that have the most meaning for you. Learn to develop a story well, and you can write as many as you want. Then you can put the stories together and have an autobiography that is interesting. Better yet, add in photographs and mementos to illustrate the experiences you write about.

The Functions of Stories

We operate as human beings from the stories we tell about ourselves. We say, "I'm a person who…" likes books or cars or people, who hates details or spinach; a person who can't remember what time it is, who tells the truth. And from that, people know who we are. Those who can share their stories, share themselves, and by doing that make a fundamental contribution to life. We must learn to share ourselves; it is not automatic for adults. We have learned to hide and protect and defend ourselves physically and psychologically. Writing our own stories requires us to turn within, find the hidden joys and sorrows and share them. It may not be easy, but it is worth the price. The better we share ourselves, the more joy of recognition and sharing of love we will receive from others.

It's a truism that people will tell a stranger things they won't tell their own family. Most of us have had the experience of sitting next to someone who had to tell about an experience they had or talk about their life. People often tell little stories on themselves to fill spaces in a wait or if they are nervous when seeking a service. These stories reveal a lot about the individual—sometimes. Some are just surface, the need to "vent" the moment's stress; but even that can be revealing. What stresses this individual? What does he take in stride?

In a recent conversation, my husband said, "You know, I've just realized that I'm always writing a story. When I'm doing something, somewhere in the back of my mind I'm composing how I'm going to tell it." We all do that, I think. He went on to say he might be thinking of telling me at the end of the day about what happened, or he might be planning to write the event into an article or to tell it to a friend, "but there's always a story forming in my mind. I see my life as an ongoing saga."

The uses of stories are as varied and as old as human communication. We all want to know what happened. Stories may be teaching tools, or may carry important experience or cultural values to the younger generation. Whether telling our stories is part of the process of revisiting our lives and putting our house to rights, a way of passing on experience to the younger generation, or simply meets our own need for self-

Writing the Stories of Your Life

expression, a story shared is a wonderful thing. There is room for everyone. Everyone has a story. Stories are fun.

Exercise: Getting started

- Stop for a moment and grab a pen. You might as well begin your story notebook now. Nothing I say is of value unless you write something. Do one or all of the following suggestions. Spend a short time on each. Don't sit and think for long; you already know what you want to say or you wouldn't be reading this book.

- When you start to write, write quickly without thinking about grammar or sentences. Make a list or write a note to yourself on each subject. Place each topic on a separate page. You may be surprised that when you start to write, the words will come out. Don't try to compose anything; write as fast as you can.

- Think about your day or the past week. What happened? What do you have to tell about? Write whatever comes to mind; don't censor anything.

- What do you hope to get out of this project? Make another list on a new page or write out whatever you feel will be important to you from writing your stories.

- Think for awhile about your reasons for doing this project. and write about that. How did you get here? Start with "The reason I am writing a story from my life is…" or "My purpose in starting this story is…" Write whatever comes to mind.

- What has been the focus of your life? What have you spent your time on? Write whatever comes to mind.

- What do you believe is important in life? What have you learned? What do you see yourself communicating out of your life? Write whatever comes to mind.

- This exercise is for your eyes only. It belongs in your story notebook. From time to time, you may add comments or ideas to each part of it. This exercise will help you to get in touch with your purpose for writing. From that knowledge, ideas will follow from which you can form a writing goal for yourself.

The Need for Stories

Stories provide models. While they inspire and uplift, stories also teach. They teach us about ourselves, about the meaning of being and becoming. Through the models they provide, they show us ways of coping, of overcoming, of aspiring to greatness and making it. True-life stories, in particular, can be inspiring. We pick up Guideposts or Reader's Digest and we read about how somebody beat the odds and made a comeback, how someone found their long-lost family, how a child from the slums became a successful inventor, athlete or musician; how a pet traveled for years to find its master. We learn how to cope with difficulty and never give up. We learn loyalty. We learn how to share and to learn from each other, how to ask for help. Stories teach the hidden inner truths that can't be expressed as a formula or a set of directions, but need a model instead. Stories can create as complex or as simple a model as is needed. Through a model we can learn how things work. We learn how life works. And we remember.

Jack tales, culture and stories

Remember the old tale about Jack. Jack comes walking down the road whistling. He stops when he sees a wagon overturned. It's stuck in the ditch and the horses are down. a number of people are there. They have tried to pull it out. Since they can't, they are trying to figure out what to do, trying to back the wagon out, trying to fix the wheel, etc. A lot is happening. Depending on the teller of the tale, this part can go on for quite a while. Eventually, Jack goes over and unhitches the horses to make them more comfortable. They scramble up out of the ditch. Now all the driver has to do is rig up a suitable harness arrangement and the horses pull the wagon out. Jack goes walking down the road, still whistling.

Most of the old teaching stories are rooted in an agrarian way of life. Each culture has brought to our melting pot a heritage of stories. There are similarities and differences. Another group of stories, not politically correct these days, but once well-known are the Epamanandus stories from the American South, which probably derived from Africa. Uncle Remus's tales derive from African roots. Stories such as the fairy tales collected by the Brothers Grimm were the nursery tales of past centuries in Northern Europe. These old oral stories are full of witches and evil spirits who prey upon children. The Jack tales of the Southern Appalachians derive from earlier tales from the British Isles, and are similar to the stories of Simplicissimus who wandered across Europe during the Middle Ages. The tales of Simplicissimus were tales of a wandering fool, who looked at life with a "beginner's mind" hence the name Simplicissimus. Illustrated with woodcuts, this collection of stories in German was one of the earliest books printed on a printing press.

The examples in these old tales from various cultures derive from a world where people walk and horses or oxen pull loads, a world of cattle and goats and growing things, a world lit only by fire—not a place where food comes out of a box, goes into a microwave and is hot in three minutes. While these stories contain profound truths about the nature of men and women and our relationship with the earth, they no longer speak clearly to our belief systems and ways of life. We don't understand them because the way we live seems so different; consequently, we have lost their truth as well as their beauty. We have largely lost touch with our rich cultural heritage of stories. In this country our very diversity has sometimes divided us from our stories.

There are literally thousands of these tales if various versions are taken into account; however, there are a much smaller number of different plots and underlying issues. All cultures have important stories. Some stories occur in many forms, appearing across most or all cultures; for instance, the story of Cinderella appears in Chinese folktales as the story of Yeh-Shen, or the empty pot, and in Africa as the story of Mufaro's beautiful daughters. It did not travel from one place to another; rather the fundamental difficulties between stepmothers and daughters are addressed and the story has a similar lesson. There are stories from many cultures about stone soup which is about cooperation or sharing; sometimes this story is called "the empty pot" although it is a different story from the one above. In it a wanderer approaches a village where there is little food and everyone is suffering. He has a pot, which he fills with water and places over a fire. In it he places a magic stone. Depending on the version of the story, he attracts others in one way or another to bring what they have and add it for flavor. Soon there is a wonderful soup and everyone eats.

Many cultures have a story about a magic pot or a magic tapestry which multiplies things but easily gets out of control. Usually this story is explained as warning against greed, but you could see it as being about managing resources well or sharing. In the form of the Sorcerer's Apprentice, it is about being able to manage the results of the things we set loose when we start something. If we want to understand the past and ourselves, we need to come to understand our stories. A few teachers such as Clarissa Pinkola Estes[3] have begun to point out the importance of stories and to collect and help us to reclaim our stories and their lessons.

Every culture and religion has important stories, many of which find their briefest form of expression in the maxims and sayings that people tell each other daily to explain everyday happenings. Human beings have a deep need to make sense of the world they live in. They then relate to it out of that understanding. Children ask "why" or "how" at certain ages. Parents make up stories to explain the answers. Other parents retell the tales that seem reasonable to them. Fables arise from explanations that seem to work whether they actually have any scientific basis or not. Children learn these so early that they don't realize that they are myth or superstition. Even after they have learned where Santa Claus lives, they may continue to believe cultural myths about men and women and the nature of life.

Many interesting personal stories may be found which turn on a saying learned at the knee of the old granny. Rooted in different cultural expressions, teaching stories carry along the fundamental differences in how people view life as well as understandings so fundamentally human that they appear in all or most cultural traditions. If you know such a story, write it down. If you remember being told a story or a bit of traditional wisdom, make a note on a separate page in your notebook. Head that page "Traditional Wisdom" or something that seems appropriate to you. As thoughts come to you, add them. You may find you have some very deep and interesting stories or recollections to write.

Depending on what processes adults emphasize, children learn to report about people, feelings, events or ideas. They may learn to pay attention to dreams as among the Senoi of Malaya or to treat life as a series of facts as is common in the western world. American children are taught to see cause and effect and to report facts in their stories. A friend[4] who is a speech therapist told me of attending a workshop where she learned how different cultures tell stories, what they include, what is important. She pointed out that children of African and Hispanic heritage are encouraged to pay attention to the network of people involved. Their stories of the day take the form of who said what or related to whom in what way. The stories are structured as webs of relationships rather than a structure of cause and effect, which is common among children of Northern European extraction.

In the dominant culture of the US and Europe children learn to report facts and events accurately and to distinguish fact from fancy at an early age. Even very young children may be accused of lying if they fill their reports with fanciful details–ideas which very likely are simply present, undistinguished from facts, in their more fluid, dream-like mindscape. Children are often forced to give up Santa Claus and the Easter Bunny before they are ready. With the maturational stage of readiness to separate fantasy from fact come the beginnings of adult thinking skills. Charles Shultz, the creator of "Peanuts" comic strip, had a fine sense of the "magical thinking" age and the way we carry it along into adulthood. His character Linus, the smartest little boy in the world, invented the Great Pumpkin who brings toys on Halloween. Was that a response to knowing too much about Santa Claus or not being ready to give up fantasy? I don't know. Fantasy characters are very popular with adults; look around at movies and video games for a sense of the cultural impact of these characters. Some other cultures are gentler in their approaches to childhood fantasies. Where imagination is encouraged, story telling is valued for itself in contrast to the value placed by a culture that emphasizes facts and deductions leading to scientific understanding.

Different teaching from parents embedded in different cultures leads to different types of stories. Where networks are the main interest, plot does not matter as much. Plotted stories have a linear structure—what leads to what—although there may be multiple plots in a parallel structure brought together at the end. Other types of stories; just as valid, have other structures, structures which might be described as circular, layered, or a spoked wheel. The quest plot is quite linear but often circles back to on itself to it's beginnings. Your story is likely to be some sort of a journey; you get to say how it goes.

Urban myth

Urban myth is a modern form of folktale that presents a believable story as true. Such a story very possibly was a true story originally or contains the germ of a true story. It has been honed and shaped into a spoken tale that is passed around at the office or laundromat or community center. Although it may be told about a specific person, the story has become remote from its source. Usually the teller will swear that a friend told him that it is a true story about a friend of his. The person it happened to is always the friend of a friend. Each carries a warning or a teaching or a belief about life; some are just plain funny. The story has become a kind of "Jack tale" of the city. It is about "everyman" or "everywoman"—a difference from the tales of the past which were usually told about "Jack" or "Ivan" or "Mack" depending on the location. It is about a human being trying to cope with the circumstances of life.

Some are frightening tales of stalkers, serial killers in elevators, runaway trains, crazy cabbies, and other believable and terrifying tales. These replace the ghosts and hangmen of past times.

Some stories are plainly funny, were intended for jokes in the first place, and have circulated with little change for years and years; for example, the tale about the way to check out a computer mouse or the woman shot by the Pillsbury Doughboy. There are stories about viruses, weird foods, and peculiar kinds of clothing. One that I recall hearing from time to time is about how chickens are raised so that they have only breasts, no legs, just awful cloned lumps to be served in a fast food restaurant. Not very believable the way I have told it, but every once in a while some acquaintance of mine is taken in by a more realistic and convincing version and tries to start a campaign against the restaurant chain. The joke in the story backfires on the gullible individual when the error is pointed out. You will find many of these at sites which deal with Internet hoaxes.

Usually urban myth, like the traditional Jack tale, embodies the archetype of the "Fool"; sometimes the Seeker, Orphan or Innocent. Other types such as the Warrior or Sage show up to help now and then. Occasionally, the Fool turns out to be more than a Trickster, perhaps a Sage, having some streetwise or magic way of overcoming impossible circumstances. Carol Pearson says of the Fool,:

> *The Fool is the archetype most helpful in dealing with the absurdities of the modern world and with faceless, amorphous modern bureaucracies—places where no one takes personal responsibility, rules are expected to be followed no matter how absurd they might be, and the tables are incredibly stacked against individual effectiveness.*[5]

Urban myth serves a function similar to that of the Jack tale or fable of the past. A hallmark of these stories is that each one speaks to the concerns and fears of city dwellers in much the way that fairy tales spoke to the concerns and fears of peasants and townspeople of the past ages. Such stories help us to laugh and go on in the face of continuous change and unbelievable challenges.

Internet myths and legends

Many myths and stories are circulated on the Internet today. Rudy, the cat with its head stuck in the disposal is such a tale. Rudy has chased the leftover fish down the drain and gotten stuck. It's exactly the kind of thing a cat might do; and what people do to try to get him out before they figure out the simple solution is hilarious. The story actually has the same structure as the Jack tale. The solution is simple and comes about when people stop trying to do complicated things about the equipment, and take care of the cat. This story reminds us of a simple and profound truth, put people or animals first and everything else can be handled.

Stories serve as models in living. A story, whether it is true or fiction, follows the actions of a person or persons in response to events. It shows the results of actions taken by the people involved; some tragic, some heroic, some ordinary. Most people find a story easier to remember than a list of facts. Most writers don't set out to do anything nearly so weighty or profound as to create a model; but their beliefs and truths tend to show up in the form of theme or voice. We each have a unique perspective on life. Theme is likely to be present in great measure in a remembrance, and not so evident in a Jack tale or humorous story. It is likely to show up in background of a whole collection of stories as a viewpoint or voice that is uniquely the author's. It's not so important to know what your theme is as to know that there will be one. For now, just write; put aside all the things you think you know or don't know about writing and have a good time with the ideas in these pages. If you show up, be present, tell the truth, and write something, a bit of your own special inner beauty will emerge on the pages. You may not see it but others will; and they will feel closer to you for it.

Distinguishing Story

Story is the most important aspect of any written work. There is a story behind every communication we make. Even advertisements with only one word and a picture have gone through many hours of story development. As human beings, we remember and tell stories more easily than lists and numbers. Before there was writing there was story telling. Scriptures and folktales teach us how to live. The popularity of biography remains as strong as it was when troubadours first sang the accomplishments of tribal heroes. Autobiographical fiction is the most popular form of fiction today, and memoirs are surprising booksellers by pushing celebrity tell-all and historical biography down the shelf.

What's the story here? The concept of a story varies a lot depending on the context it is used in. Sometimes the sense of "story" refers to the background; sometimes to the meaning. When a journalist speaks of the story, he is looking for the facts—what happened. Knowing what happened, he may raise the question, why? What caused this? How did this person come to this point and make this choice? Who's fault was it? What is really going on? Newspapers print the first story as a report and the second as a feature. The report depends more on facts; the feature on back story.

When someone asks for "the whole story," they want the story behind the facts. They want the background, including such things as the cultural history and motivation of individuals, in an attempt to get at the underlying meaning. As human beings, we want to dig deeper and deeper and find the "real" story.

A good novel seems to be true; an authentic breath-taking adventure story reads like a work of fiction. Nothing fascinates us like a true story, but how do we know what is the truth? We have rules of evidence in the field of law where we are interested in the intersection of facts and responsibility. In political life we attempt to create correspondence between our perception of the data of life and the organization of the society. In science we follow an algorithm designed to separate fact from perception, and we use theory (a likely story) to clarify, organize and explain what we know. Everything that we think we know is actually a theory, or a story, we invented to account for the facts as we have them.

There is a vast literature on how to write and how to write well. The new genre of creative non-fiction has evolved in recent decades. Actual events unfold in creative non-fiction as in a novel, bringing fiction technique to non-fiction. Over the past few decades this type of story and its mate, true fiction, have become major contenders for book shelf space, bringing to the fore issues of truth and integrity.

Stories help us to draw out our own inner truth. Usually when we talk about truth, we confuse the idea with veracity; we emphasize verifiable facts rather than underlying rightness or actuality or wholeness. A story can be factual and have little in it that speaks about meaning or it can be truthful and faithful to presenting an important understanding. Often it is both. Human beings are interested in the confluence of facts and morality, trying to reconcile the every day with the ideal. Such things, often the province of religion and philosophy, tend to be ineffable, difficult to explain or even express.

We use a great deal of story and imagery to communicate our understanding of the deeper, inner truth as we see it. Perhaps it would be better to speak in terms of the integrity of a story. Integrity means "wholeness, completeness." When we tell stories, we want to find and express the deeper truth, the truth that feels right somehow, the truth of our own being. A story which carries that level of truth, or integrity, becomes universal—like a folk tale or a religious teaching story.

A Memoir Is a Special Kind of Story

A memoir is a true story, but more than that, it is a recollection. It differs from biography in that it does not require objective research but it may include mementoes and research. It may be written from more than one viewpoint or in more than one voice, but it is usually written by one person writing from his or her own life or writing as narrator to tell the story of another person. It may be written to honor the memory of a particular person who has passed or an occasion such as a birthday. Most importantly, a memoir is written because it is a good story and needs to be told.

A memoir differs from a biography in its perspective. A memoir is written from the perspective of reminiscence. It is written to honor the memory of an occasion, a person, a lifestyle, a place and a time that has past. A journal entry or a book written as a diary is written in an ongoing present tense. It is always today in a diary. This can be very interesting, but it is different from the perspective of recollection. Journals or diaries can be useful in writing memoir, of course. It is possible to create a memoir in a diary style, but it is very difficult to do unless you have a good bit of material that was written on the spot.

The stories told in families carry our personal histories and our family legends. A memoir carries and individual's personal viewpoint as well as the legacy of a family. A memoir may be written for no more reason than it is a good story and needs to be told. It brings the reader a sense of rootedness, of connection with the past. It may be written as fiction or non-fiction, to serve a teaching purpose in the world, to set the record straight, to educate or simply to entertain.

A memoir may be autobiography, written by the person recalling the story, or biography—a true story about someone else. Sometimes it is edited or compiled from things written by several people. A group of favorite stories about a popular relative that everyone remembers is a nice family project. It might be done for a special birthday or anniversary. Often humorous stories are collected to be told at retirement dinners. Different people will have different views of the individual, which adds richness to the (usually humorous) compilation.

Fiction or non-fiction?

Memoirs may be offered as fiction or non-fiction. Sometimes writers know the outlines of an amazing story, but do not have access to the persons involved. If the plot is strong or the situation is extraordinary, a true story may serve as the background to a short story or a novel. The writer's imagination quickly fills in the details, creates characters who depart from the original individuals to some extent, and invents new situations. As the fictional back story develops, the true story recedes into the background. For purposes of memoir, you get to decide where you are with this strategy.

Celebrities regularly write autobiographies and fight publicly with unauthorized biographers. Such publicity, of course, boosts their careers. Their books are referred to in the trade as "celebrity tell-all." The survivor of a terrible catastrophe may write about dreadful experiences; the more shocking, the better. If the work comes out while the public is still hungry to know, it may even become a bestseller.

Survivor's tales have probably always been interesting to human beings. Sagas of bravery and survival have been told around fires since time immemorial. Today they have taken on a new urgency as we live in a world where people are both sheltered from danger and fearful of terror. People are hungry for real experience, the kind of experience where life is laid on the line for something worthwhile. That is what we are about—finding meaning in life.

Today autobiographical fiction may be fiction or may be based on real life. It is very hard to tell. The better it is, the more believable it is. Another type of memoir is written by a participant in a situation who serves as the narrator. A child may write a book to honor a parent. *Cheaper by the Dozen*[6] by Frank B. Gilbreth and Ernestine Gilbreth Carey is a classic example of this type of memoir, although it is probably more fictional than it seems. A recent book by Joyce Carol Oates, *We Were the Mulvaneys*[7], is fiction but seems so real that many people believe it is autobiographic. *Prince of Tides* by Pat Conroy is another example of the resurgence of "autobiographic fiction."

Not since Melville and Hawthorne has this type of fiction with a first-person narrator been so popular. Biographical fiction is intended to remain true to the underlying nature of the person and the times but shows them in imaginary situations. Sometimes biographers writers have a great deal of information about persons and events in history, but the material is relatively dull and uninspiring without humanizing details.

The basic premise of creative non-fiction is the same as that for true fiction: If the writer applies fiction techniques in organizing the story and supplies believable but not verifiable details for non-crucial elements of the story, it will be more interesting to read. Truman Capote created in several works a model for this type of true-life story and is credited with launching the creative non-fiction genre which is very popular today.

There is very little distinction between these types of stories. For our purposes, it is instructive to get that true stories can contain invented details that make them seem more real. If you are writing a memoir and can't remember for sure if it was scones or cookies that your mother made that particular day, pick one and stick to your story. Let us smell them baking but don't make us worry over which it was.

Stories remembered from childhood are things we understood from the perspective of a child. It is an astonishing thing to revisit them and come in contact with your child self and your sense of wonder as you tried to comprehend the world. You told yourself stories then to help you understand things, and you are still doing it.

Sometimes people begin to write as they start to sort themselves out through Recovery or Self-Awareness work of one kind or another. Many valuable books have come out in the last two decades showing you how to keep a journal, how to find your inner child, your inner artist, the writer within, etc. This is a vital process for a writer. However you do it, getting in touch with your hidden reserves of belief, personality and being will provide stories and enrich your writing.

It is not necessary to know the story to go looking for it. If your parents or any of the people who were around at the time are still alive, they would probably love to have a call or a visit from you. Sit down with them and ask questions. It is difficult to write a memoir when a person has passed on. If there is someone in your life whom you wish to honor, ask them now. Visit and bring a tiny tape recorder. Ask about their life; ask what they remember about something you remember; get it on tape and you will have some of the material in their own words. Whether it is about you or them or something else, fill it in with your understanding of it and it becomes your story.

Assignments

1. Write at least one story or recollection from your life this week.

2. Write a short piece beginning with this (or another) sentence stem: What I remember most about my parents [or put in a name] is...

3. Write a short piece about an event that happened in your life. What did you learn from that experience?

4. Find several non-fiction memoirs or autobiographies which interest you; read them and answer these question:

    - What makes each story believable or not believable?

    - What makes these books or articles work as stories?

    - What would you do differently if you were writing these stories?

5. Find several fiction works written as memoirs. That would mean that the story is written in the first person and pretends to be a true story. Read them (or at least scan each one!) Answer the following questions:

    - What do you like or not like about these books or stories?

    - What makes them work as stories?

    - Are you able to suspend disbelief; that is, are you able to believe in the memoir framework for the purpose of the story? If not, why not?

    - What would you do differently if you were writing these stories?

Chapter 2

LET'S WRITE!

Writing is often said to be a lonely occupation–which seems odd to writers with their heads full of characters. No loneliness there! Too much going on. It is, however, an activity which requires some focus and consistent effort. It is actually both a social and a private occupation. We will talk some more in this chapter about space and time and getting organized to be successful with your writing project.

Writing can only be learned by writing.

By now you have written at least one story. We will come back to pieces that you have written throughout the book; however, it would be worthwhile for you to write a number of stories or short pieces of different types to work with as we begin to edit and improve them. Keep your stories together with this book, or begin a special file for them in your computer. We will discuss creating a story notebook in the chapter on journaling.

You will learn to write by writing a lot. You will learn to write well by writing fast. In fact, it is very important that you clearly distinguish writing from editing and learn to write without giving a thought to how it ought to be done. If you practice the approach in this book, you will learn to write without restraint.

There are skills you can learn that will help you with both writing and editing. This chapter will help you get started and move along faster in your writing. Editing comes later. I recently read a passage relevant to this idea in one of Wayne Dyer's books in which he is discussing giving up attachment:

> *I feel that my writing is able to flow because I have become unattached to what anyone else says or thinks about it. I simply allow it to flow, knowing and trusting that it will all be just as it is supposed to be. I am open to improvement, but I cannot think about that while I am writing. If I do, my focus shifts to what I should be doing, instead of what I am allowing to happen.*[8]

Dyer spells out the process clearly "I can not think about that while I am writing..." because "my focus shifts" away from the writing itself. In this chapter we will learn more about turning off the thinking part and letting the Inner Writer (or natural, intuitive part of ourselves) do the writing.

Getting a Story Started

Writing can only be learned by writing. There really isn't any other way to do it. Let whatever you have to say come out.

Start at the beginning and write.

Something in the present may remind you of a story. But where is the beginning? Sometimes you don't know. Some stories have deep roots and it is difficult to tell exactly where you should begin. If you don't have a sense of the story chronologically, start wherever you are. Or you may remember some person's reaction, or how you felt. You may be thinking of several related events. Perhaps you remember the end result; you can work backwards from there.

The beginning in time is a good place to start. Write from beginning to end chronologically. What happened first? What came next? Keep writing until you have written the whole story. Your goal for right now is to write as much as you can of what happened. Get the sequence of events down and you can flesh out the details later.

You may have an interesting recollection that isn't exactly a story. You might have a person in mind; if so, tell what they did and what happened as a result. Write whatever you have to say about that person.

Some object or some event may remind you of a story. You may want to write about a particular topic or theme in your life. Just start wherever you are.

You might start by reminiscing with a friend. Perhaps you are in a conversation and you are reminded of a past event; you don't even have to think about it. You say, "Remember the time..." or "I remember when..." Write that down, write it just the way you would tell it. You can fix it up later to make it into a better story if you want to.

Your story begins wherever you start thinking of it. Start writing wherever you are and get it all down.

The best place to start writing is wherever you start thinking of it. Start writing, get your story laid out, and later you can figure out where the story should open. As you work with the idea you may decide to rearrange your story when you figure out how much of the back story to use and what else to put in or take out. You can devise a great first line later. You will have to do some rewrite, at least a little bit, to make your story better, so don't spend a lot of time getting a good looking copy on the first draft. Just go for it. Write it all down.

Write with energy and abandon. Don't stop to think, just write whatever is there for you as fast as you can until it is all gone. Later we will consider how to present it better. In another chapter we will discuss the parts of stories and how you can present your story more effectively, but for now we just want to get started writing. You should start wherever you are.

Writing the Stories of Your Life

Exercise: Begin at the Beginning

Is there something you have been wanting to write about? If so, use that idea. If not, here are some sentence stems to get you started. You can pick one and write for about five minutes.

- Once, when I was a child, I…
- My favorite school teacher (or other adult) was…
- I remember a time when…
- A pivotal event in my life occurred when…
- Stop when your timer rings.

Did you write continuously without stopping? Great! How much did you write? Half a page? A page? More? Just notice what you have done. The point of this exercise is to get you started writing, just writing.

Did you write freely or do a lot of thinking? Writing is a process. No one does it perfectly on the first draft. If you are concerned about how good your work is, that worry fills up your mind and keeps you from writing. Please let go of any concerns. Throughout this course we will work with your pieces to improve them, but you have to write something in order to play.

- Now take another idea and write a short recollection or story.
- Write about something that happened in your life, something you did—maybe a prank or a joke, the first thing you remember, something you are interested in, or something that matters to you. Don't, however, give a lot of time to finding the perfect idea. Pick something to write about and start.
- Set your timer and stop after five minutes.
- What was different this time? Were you better able to keep on going? Do you want to finish this piece? Go to it.
- If you are in a group or class, you may read these short bits aloud to begin sharing your stories with each other. Just share what you have done and give other people your full listening attention. At this point no comments should be made. No critique is necessary. What you are sharing is just ideas, first draft, or warm up. Thank each person who shares.

🖎 What can you learn for yourself from what you have written and/or what you have heard? Make some notes in your story notebook about what you have learned.

Now that we are writing, I may refer to the people you write about as characters. They are, aren't they! I think it makes it clear that I am discussing the person as you have presented them on the written page, not the actual individual. It also makes it clear that I am speaking to you as a writer. Once you have decided to tell a story, including a true story from your life, you move to a different a level of reality. What you are telling separates itself at that moment from the totality of the facts. It may be true and it is a fraction of the whole truth; it is your perspective on what happened. We will talk more about this later in the book.

Calling your people characters also serves to underscore another point: writing will draw you close to these people. Many fiction writers come to think of their fictional characters as their people. You may become so close to your characters that you know them as well or better than other people in your life, or people you were closer to in the past. For writing a memoir, this is a good thing. You have a chance to relate to your family and people you have known in a new way.

Space Time Considerations

How much time can you give to writing? Ten minutes? Fifteen? Twenty minutes a day? Set your clock and start writing. Write as fast as you can. Just write. Don't think. Don't consider your words; don't do anything but write. Don't stop 'til the alarm buzzes. Then stop.

If you stop when you still feel like writing, it will be easier to pick it up tomorrow. Whether you are a student, a group member, or you are doing this course on your own, you will get the most from this book if you set aside a little time every day to write.

If you stop when you still feel like writing, it will be easier to pick it up tomorrow.

Back when I was an administrator in mental health for the state government, I had a secretary who set an alarm clock to ring at the end of the day. She would turn it off, grab her purse and literally run out the door. If I wanted to use her typewriter after hours, there would very likely be a half-typed letter in it. Some writers stop in mid-sentence or mid-paragraph. They say it gives them a place to start and makes it easier to get going again. I often stop at the end of a section, but write the topic heading or a starter line for the next day on the top of my notes. (I seem to think of it after I turn the computer off.) This helps to draw me easily into my work. I start and when I look up, hours have passed.

Necessary Equipment for Memoir Writers

- Writing instrument
- Notebook
- Your memories
- Voice mail

Years ago I collected a comment I liked. "Necessary equipment for writers: paper, pen, your mind, answering machine." I don't know where I got it, but it makes the point that it doesn't take a lot of equipment. It takes a willingness to focus on writing and shut off other activities for a time. Show up, be present, and have something to write with.

Today I have changed that list a bit; I say that you need a notebook, writing instrument, memories and voice mail. It really doesn't take much to write a memoir: A few photos and memories, a notebook, a pen; some place where you can focus for a little while. It's good if you can find a clear time of the day when you can work on it each day.

Many people like to write in a particular place. They set up a little office where they have privacy, or always write in the breakfast room or on the patio. Being able to write in the same place regularly is good because it lowers the distraction level. You don't pay as much attention to things happening around you in a place where you always work. If you use a computer, you may want to write at your computer rather than use a pen. I do. You still need a project notebook to keep your ideas and bits and parts together, and possibly a second one for your completed sections.

Your place for writing doesn't have to be at home. Most libraries have tables where you can work peacefully and avoid the distractions of telephones and family. Some people work at their desks after hours at work. Others find a nook in a church, a friend's home, or somewhere that gives them freedom to come and go. Write in a place that suits you.

It is probably more important to gather your necessary materials together—notebook, pen, idea generators, etc. If they are portable, you have some advantages. Many students carry their work with them and use odd moments to work on it. Anywhere you have to be that you have time on your hands can serve as time for writing. Do you drive your child or grandchild to soccer or music lessons? Do you have some down time during your work day, a few minutes after dinner, one free morning a week? You can make a pact with yourself to give yourself the time for writing when it suits you to do it.

Finding time to write

Time is more difficult than space; we all have so many "important" activities to keep us busy. That's what they are, mostly. Just busy activities; not essential. My friend Rebecca Fuller[9] calls this "important busy." Important busy can run you if you let it. If you want to write (or paint or play the violin), you need to protect your time while you work at that intention.

Don't answer the phone during your special writing time. You are out, unavailable. Voice mail or an answering machine is helpful only if you are willing to let the phone ring and don't answer it. Will you take the risk? Do you dare?

Mornings before you get started on all the important-busy things you do every day are the best writing time for many people. Although I resisted the idea for most of my life, there are two advantages to early morning writing: 1) you get going before the details of life can claim your time; and 2) your mind is freshest, most creative, and ready to go in the morning. Maybe it's the dreaming; I can't imagine that having just slept would help—especially if you have to get up earlier to write! Anyway, it works. I tried it. I don't even talk to anyone at breakfast; I just have my cup of tea and get going. If you get up a few minutes early, maybe nobody else will be up and you can already be busy when they come to look for you.

Pacing yourself

Some people like to write late at night; some in the morning. Any time that you have a regular time slot in your day which you can use for writing is good. Some people write on their lunch hour. If that is all the time you have, and you actually write for twenty minutes a day for a year, you will have written for 121.7 hours. That is more than three full weeks of working time.. What can you accomplish in three weeks? A story? Several stories? A draft of a book? How many letters can you write in 121.7 hours?

If you finish a only one story a week, you can write twenty-five or so in six months, and take the second half of the year to improve them and shape them into a memoir.

Most beginners and many experienced writers will find it easier to write short pieces on different subjects. When you have a number of them in hand you can decide what the unifying theme is and pull them together. Perhaps you will write about family holidays and decide to include favorite recipes and pictures.

"I learned… that inspiration does not come like a bolt, nor is it kinetic, energetic, striving, but it comes to us slowly and quietly and all the time, though we must regularly and everyday give it a little chance to start flowing, prime it with a little solitude and idleness."
—Brenda Ueland[10]

Grandparents like to write stories for their grandchildren. How you got your name, or the day you were born, tales about your ancestors, stories of your parents, or miscellaneous memories, are all good strategies. One for each is a good strategy; you can go around again if you have more stories than grandchildren. If you don't have children or grandchildren, and even if you want to start a larger work, writing small pieces that you finish and put aside is a good strategy. After you have a number of these and have let the first ones rest a while, you can pull them out and shape them up.

Experienced writers often start a big project by writing small pieces to see what really calls to them and decide how best to present it. What if you wrote something new for one hour a day, five days a week for a year? That's over nine weeks' time. If you have written two to three pages each day, you will have five or six hundred pages. That's enough to edit into a good sized novel, biography, or autobiography.

An example of a memoir written in small pieces is *I. Asimov.*[11] Isaac Asimov, one of the most prolific writers of all time wrote 166 topical pieces, which range from one to five pages, one by one. Arranged chronologically, they provide a fascinating and comprehensive retrospective on a life which had its ups and downs. It's all very candid, sometimes funny, witty, poignant. He says what he thought, how he learned something, what he was like from his point of view, and what he accomplished. He tells what he

Writing the Stories of Your Life

learned from his foibles and failures as well as bragging about his successes. Anybody can do that. By the way, you should brag about your success—this is your chance!

Your memoir can be as interesting as you are willing to make it. Remember that by spreading out the writing to a short time every day and giving yourself a definite appointment to do it, you give yourself the extra benefit of letting the subconscious work on it in between appointments. Everything you write will be fresher and more interesting.

Some things, like books, take a long time to write; and you have to set up a schedule so that you move the action ahead a little each and every day. You will find out for yourself what your best pattern is for a long-term writing project. You may find that you need to edit portions of the work before you have completed the whole work. Make sure that your editing sessions are separate from your writing sessions. It is important to write regularly.

Allow yourself to write one new story every day, and in a month you will have about twenty stories in various stages of completion. Shift your focus to editing and very quickly you have a book.

If you have plenty of time to devote to this project, write a new story or portion of one every day. Set a maximum amount—three pages, say—and quit! Or write one story—even if it is just a page.

Make a promise to yourself or set an intention for what you want to accomplish. Explore your availability and commitment to find time for this project. Over the next couple of weeks develop a realistic plan and goals for yourself. If you miss some times on your plan, and you probably will, it's important to start again. Review your plan periodically and reschedule with yourself if your plan isn't working.

It's not important what goal you set for yourself; but that you create a structure that gets your project moving and keeps you happily working at it. It will probably take longer than you think, but if you keep at it steadily, you will accomplish it. It's all up to you.

Assignments

Read through all the assignments and choose the ones that further your work. It is not necessary to do all of them, although it may be helpful.

1. Set an intention for your writing time this week. Find a time and place that works for you. Have it be something you can actually do.

2. Write at least one story from your life, about something you did or that happened to you. Write your story beginning at the beginning; write through to the end without stopping.

3. Write a story from your life, have it be about someone in your family, or someone you have known. Write fast, from beginning to end.

4. Write a story beginning at the beginning in time. Remember to write through to the end (or at least to the end of your writing time) without stopping to think.

5. If you are in a group, bring your story or stories to the next meeting and volunteer to read one. If not, find someone to read one of your stories to—maybe your child or grandchild or an old friend. Have it be someone who will listen and not criticize.

6. Decide on a goal for yourself for this adventure.

7. Write your plan for writing in the front of your notebook or post it over your computer.

Chapter 3

FINDING STORIES

Deciding what to write about seems very difficult to some people. It needn't be, but that is what we are going to address now. If you know what you want to write about, you may benefit from additional resources we discuss in this chapter. We will also start a story notebook.

Maybe you know what you want to write about and why don't we just get on with it! If that is so, skip this section, go to the warm up for today. *Do the warm up* and start writing. Come back to this chapter later when you need some ideas on where to find your stories.

What To Write About

Usually it seems like there is nothing to write about when actually there are thousands of choices – so many that we don't see them. So many stories have happened in our lives that they are like a painting we are so used to having around that we don't really look at it any more. When we let ourselves be aware of all the material, the difficulty becomes choosing what to write about!

Choosing is only difficult if you think you have to know everything or do it perfectly. You are permanently excused from these mindsets for purposes of this course. We are experimenting with writing; doing things you don't know how to do, but have an idea you'd like to try. You are free to play!

Anything you have personally experienced is fair game for a story. Anything or anyone you care about or you think about often could be the starting point for an interesting tale. Any experience that changed you, or your life, or somebody in your life is a good bet for a story. Funny things, practical jokes, oft-told family tales make good stories. How life used to be, compared to how it is now, is a good source of material.

Anything you have thought about a lot, anything you have learned in your life and want to share may be a starting point. You may have many ideas, you may be good at some particular hobby; maybe you have a lot of recipes or you have traveled a lot.

Finding Your Stories

While outlining your life or making a timeline or resume may seem like a good way to get started, it may also prove overwhelming and yield only a few story ideas.

Another way to get at the stories you have is to follow the breadcrumbs of memory back through the winding paths of the garden of your life. Find a theme or an interest, a decision you made, a cataclysmic event, a choice, something you wanted to do and couldn't, or something you accomplished with great effort. What led you into that interest or experience? How did that experience affect your life? What happened as a result of it? Make a list of all the related events in that story line; work backwards, forwards and around it. Use a mind map[12] to help you find ideas.

Find another path in your garden and do the same thing. The goal of this approach is to uncover stories or ideas that are related to a theme or interest in your life.

> *Hence in a season of calm weather*
> *Though inland far we be,*
> *Our Souls have sight of that immortal sea*
> *Which brought us hither,*
> *Can in a moment travel thither,*
> *And see the Children sport upon the shore,*
> *And hear the mighty waters rolling evermore.*
>
> *—William Wordsworth*[13]

Wordsworth spoke of our ability to recall immortality, but the same ability applies to recollection of our mortal past. We recall it best, he says, in seasons of calm and times of conversation. This kind of reminiscing is enhanced by a cup of coffee (or something you like) and the presence of an old friend. You two can play "Remember When" or "Who Was That!" Keep a notebook handy and jot down your story ideas as you chat. Or use a voice recorder.

Where Do Ideas Come From?

A new idea is often the result of a recombination of other ideas. We build one thing on another in creative work, as we do in logical work; but the ideas on which new structures are built may not even seem related to one another. You may, in fact, have no access as to where the idea came from. Rest assured that you picked it up somewhere, mixed it up with other ideas, and out came a whole new idea—maybe a story. You can use this magic function deliberately by feeding your Inner Writer thoughts, ideas, and images; and setting a time to have new work show up. This is what novelists do when they read a lot of books and magazines, interview people, travel to new locations or do research on the background history and science of a subject. They feed the subconscious with information while they are planning a work, and they set a time to start writing. They often take a lot of notes which they hardly look at while writing. Yet somewhere the plot formed, the back story is in place, the characters seem real, and the story flows. If they need to verify bits of data such as locations or dates or historical characters, they check them later.

Now, if I tell you this, you will find me a writer who doesn't write like this or doesn't think he does. Everyone has his or her own way of feeding the Inner Writer; and each creative writer has his or her way of doing research. Some do a lot of it before starting; others write the story, then research the locations and so forth later. Some of this depends on the level of accuracy demanded by the genre; but, that is the writer's choice, too.

The Inner Writer is an aspect of the subconscious mind. I have always thought of the subconscious as the backburner. I put an idea on the back burner and when I am ready to work with it, it has simmered a while and is ready to go. When I tell myself firmly that I will have an idea or a text ready for a certain time, I have it. I don't know how. Try it; it works. Write regularly and use the ideas you get so that your Inner Writer knows you are serious about this.

Prime your Inner Writer for writing your stories. You can use interviews, research, visits to various places, old photographs, art and objects as starting points. You can visit all the places your family lived, or telephone people who knew your family. You can trace vacations you took, and see how the family grew and changed. You can ask others what they remember, and compare those memories with your own. Be sure to use a voice recorder or take notes. Take pictures now, too. You can compare them to old pictures for interesting changes, and you can illustrate your story book with them. An easy way for many people to get started is to pull out old photograph albums. Talking with the family elders is often easier if you have the book in hand (and the recorder on the table). You can ask questions about who is who and what happened.

An interesting book could be made simply from the annual trek to a summer cottage or home for a specific holiday, the annual Thanksgiving gathering, for example. All the characters have stories to tell. Whether they told them at the time or not is irrelevant; you can introduce the story in a way that shows that it wasn't known at the time, but this is what happened to Aunt Lily that year. Or, if you are writing family fiction, just go for it.

Pictures, mementos of all kinds, old tools, hand-made items, things that belonged to a parent, or a child, or to someone special are excellent sources. What do you remember when you pick up that picture or item? It may not be related to the item, but to the person. What happened? Is it just a flash or would the details come if you got started writing? Either way, the item may provide the spark for a reminiscence.

Exercise: Brainstorm story sources

This exercise will help you identify some important story sources for your stories.

If you do this in a group, have one person write and the others call out ideas. Take a minute for each person to gather their thoughts together and make a few notes; then begin. Take turns calling out one idea. The recorder should write only a word or two on the board for each idea. No comments or evaluation of ideas are allowed; brief clarification may be requested.

Group

- Everyone start a page in your notebook for "Story Sources." Take about a minute to write down your own ideas for possible places to find stories. Wild ideas are great; ordinary ideas are important.

- Share your ideas by going around and contributing suggestions quickly. Each person says one idea and the recorder writes them on the board until all the new ideas have been added. Add ideas from the board to your own list.

- No discussion or reasons allowed at this point. Brief clarification of ideas is allowed—e.g., Someone in one of my classes said "graveyards" and everyone said "What?" The student said, "You take someone with you, an older person who knows about the area." It made sense to everyone there. That's all that matters. Avoid duplicate ideas, but don't spend time trying to cull them; just keep going around until everybody has contributed what they have.

- When all the ideas are on the board, set a time limit for discussion that seems reasonable to the group. You may ask questions now. Why would anyone go to a graveyard? What would arts and crafts give you? Have your questions enhance freedom and creativity; do not evaluate ideas or make negative comments on anybody's ideas. The idea is to get a lot of idea generators and begin to see how to use them.

Writing the Stories of Your Life

- Make it personal. Which ideas appeal to you the most? Where would you go to look for that kind of material? What town? What library? Whose attic? Who could you call or talk to? If there is time, share some of these possibilities.

- Start another page in your personal story notebook for "Story Ideas." Write down any story ideas that occur to you as you work with your source list. Begin to formulate a plan for gathering data on one or more of your ideas.

Individual

Brainstorm a list of story sources for yourself. Write "Story Sources" at the top of a page in your notebook. The question you are trying to answer is: "What are some places to look for a story in my life?" Give yourself five minutes and write down everything you can think of.

- Review the list in the book and add to it. Use a few minutes for this now and add to it later as ideas come to you.

- Make it personal. Which ideas appeal to you the most? Where would you go to look for that kind of material? What town? What library? Your attic? Who could you call or talk to? Write that down with the idea.

- If you haven't already, start a special page in your notebook for "Possible Story Sources." Make it a specific list of real places you could actually look for ideas.

- Start another page in your personal story notebook for "Story Ideas." Write down any that occur to you as you work with the source list. Begin to formulate a plan for gathering data on one or more of your ideas.

Example of story sources

One class spent a few minutes brainstorming ideas for story sources. The question used was: Where could you find stories? For about three minutes each member of the class made a personal list in their notebook. Then everyone contributed ideas until all the different ones were on the board. Their list is shown in the chart.

Places to Find Stories

Trips, Travel	Reunions
Grandchildren	Concerts
Holidays, Recipes	Talk to People
Strangers You've Met	Listen to People
Children's Backgrounds	Older People
Photos/Albums	Graveyards/ Headstones – take an older person with you and ask about relatives or townspeople buried there.
Scrapbooks	
Letters	
Love Life	Knowledgeable People
Tape/Voice Recordings	Hometown
Home Movies	Reading Other Stories
Songs You Hear/ Love/ Remember	Collections (rocks, stamps, matchbooks, souvenirs, etc.)
Places You Have Lived	
Visits/ Visitors	Quilts
Schooldays	Arts, Crafts
Work/ Workplace	Gifts, Things You Own
Hobbies	Things You've Made
Neighbors	Museums
Friends	Pets, Animals
Local Characters	Teachers
Clubs/ Churches/ Organizations	Tragedy/ Major Events
Old Newspapers	Weddings/ Funerals/ Graduations
Special Events, Street Fairs	

Your Personal Story Sources

When you have a good list, select one category from the list and focus on it. Select one location and actually look for stories using that idea. If it is someplace in your house or attic where you have stored mementos, all you have to do is drag out the boxes, sit down with them and get started going through things. If it entails a trip or a visit, you may have to do a little planning. Give yourself the gift of time to pursue your interest.

It may be that the idea you've chosen doesn't really require you to find physical things. You may want to do some more personal brainstorming based on a single idea from the list. If you choose an idea that works as an organizing principle, you can use it to brainstorm a group of stories. I have chosen "Places You Have Lived" for this example.

Possible Stories and Story Sources in my Life: PLACES

Place	What Was Happening in My Life	Possible Stories
Philadelphia	Birth, Family Stories World War II, Dad and shipyards	Mom and the live chicken EE checking insulating oil Dad and Lindbergh
Beverly	2—6 years old Ed, Karl and other kids Elin	I remember knees Bobo the clown Tomatoes The candy store Starting school; Miss Reid
Raleigh	Moved to South Health and Hearing problems Too young for school in NC	Adjusting to a new environment First day in private school The day I took a cab Bubblegum story
Winston-Salem	Third grade thru high school Girl Scouts	Walking to school Mom as a scout leader Beth Tartan Dating, friends, meeting Kent
Nashville	Freshman art major	
Home again	Wake Forest	Getting married
Greensboro	UNCG & Psychology	Kevin stories
Pittsburgh	Graduate School People I knew Having twins Graduation and finding a job	Moving up there with all our stuff and no place to live Sitting on top of hill on a cobblestone street leading into the river and being afraid to drive down it. Howard, Sylvia, Gerry, Bill, Sam and Billy What to do with TWO babies?
Winston-Salem	Coming home again is not like you think it will be	Working Raising kids Getting downsized Writing Art

Keep adding to your list for a while; you will find that other things occur to you. You may find that one part of your life is more interesting or you remember more stories. Go for the stories; keep adding story ideas. When you have a list, you may find that you need information for one or more of the possible stories. Work with the ideas one at a time to shape them into stories using the techniques we are studying.

Maybe the cars you have driven represent different phases of your life, or the places you have lived have some significance to you. Perhaps you have collected plants or drawings of buildings or elephants or toys or art. Any collection can serve as a theme for organizing your work. Perhaps you know fifty ways to say "thank you" in various languages. Unusual words, slang, things you have learned from the people you have met can trigger a story or can serve to organize a group of stories.

Places work for a lot of people, especially if you have moved a lot, but there are many other ways you can find stories and organize them. Try several approaches before you settle down to work with one organizational scheme. Let your enthusiasm be your guide. If it has heart for you, do it.

Tracking your ideas

Writers keep lists or notebooks of story ideas. Are you waiting at the dentist, killing a few minutes after lunch, having a cup of coffee, or doing nothing for a moment? Have your story idea notebook handy and add to your list or jot down a key scene or first page. Just write whatever you are thinking about an idea. Setting up a small notebook that you can easily carry sets your subconscious mind to work. It will look for memories and bring them to you if you give it a chance by keeping your notebook handy.

Write your ideas down in order as they come to you. Leave plenty of margin space so that you can make notes about which project your paragraph belongs to and cross it out when you have used it. You may want to use one of the notebooks that is sold as a project notebook or project planner if you like this system; they have wide margins, numbered lines, and sometimes different colored blocks for working with your ideas.

Organize your notebook in a way that suits you. It may be effective to start a page for each idea that you are seriously planning to write and add notes, phrases, or paragraphs as they come to you. Some people use index cards. They carry blank ones around along with their calendar or tickler file. Then they file their ideas in a box where they work. Other writers prefer a running notebook that is more like a journal. It really doesn't matter how you do it as long as you do something systematic. Some people use file folders effectively; others stick to their computers.

The best system is the one you will use and keep using. Keep it simple and meaningful to you. Whenever you feel stymied or need new ideas, check through your lists and notes. You will find what you need.

Keeping a story notebook

A story notebook is a good way to organize your stories. Intended to help you stay on track, it may turn out to be useful in other ways. It gives you one place to keep things. Unless you have boxes full of photo albums and mementos, you can probably put all the materials you need for the stories you are currently working on in a few add-in pockets. I recommend using a looseleaf notebook or one of those large multi-subject spiral-bound notebooks that come with built in pockets. That way your work is portable.

Such a notebook will be a place where you can make lists, do exercises, and write drafts. You will need to do a lot of this to work out your stories. As you complete one story, move the finished version to a looseleaf notebook or the album you are creating. Remove all the junk and load up again. Keep going. Your lists can include one for story ideas. Check off the ones you have finished; cross off the ones you don't want to do; add others. You will have a record to track your progress toward your goal.

Have fun with your notebook. Make it a title page with a drawing or picture. Decorate it if you want to. Be sure you put your name and address in it and keep a pen with it.

The following tips may help you to get organized.

Setting Up Your Notebook

- If you use a looseleaf notebook, use one that's large enough to hold a lot of pages.

- Use dividers for different sections.

- Add pockets to keep things in. You can buy paper ones that also function as dividers. Clear sheet protectors also work for this purpose; get the heavy duty ones.

- If you don't like looseleaf notebooks, find a multi-subject spiral bound notebook with pockets in it.

- You can make tabs out of labels by folding them in the middle and sticking part of the sticky side to each side of a page. Or use self adhesive flags or notes.

- If you use a computer, buy three-hole drilled paper to print your materials on. Keep them in a looseleaf binder with dividers.

Inside your notebook.

- Have a place for exercises and stories you write in response to assignments.
- Have a section for story-related lists.
- When you start a list, including the ones suggested in this book, start with a bold heading at the top of the page. Add ideas freely as they come to you over time.
- Have a separate section for sequential entries—journaling—on any subject that interests you.
- When you start a story give it its own section and gather things related to that story together there.

Working with Your Story Notebook

- Date your entries.
- Write on one side of the paper so you have room to expand a piece.
- Keep lists, sketch ideas out and keep adding to your ideas.
- If you use a spiral bound notebook, you can use the pages in it for writing drafts or working things out, then type the final copy.
- If you prefer a running notebook, you may find that you want to add to your lists. Leave space. Start all lists on the next blank page, or leave the backs of all pages blank for future expansion.
- Try using your notebook for developing your ideas and using the computer for the actual writing.
- Use scrap paper for warm ups; don't keep them.
- If you get an idea while you are warming up and it's flowing, move it to the notebook or computer and keep going.

Working with Your Stories

When you start work on a story, put pictures, notes, lists, copies of old newspaper articles, etc. in a pocket—everything for that story in one pocket in your notebook. Use several pages for lists of details, research, and exercises you assign yourself to work out the parts of the story. Since most stories are likely to go through several drafts, a looseleaf may be better at the development stage. You can create a separate section for a particular story.

As your stories develop and you polish them, transfer your finished writings and the illustrations you want to keep with them to a special notebook or scrapbook for finished work. Discard the rest.

More ways to find your stories

Here are a few more ideas that may help you find interesting stories:

- Make a list of important historical events. Where were you and what were you doing? Is there someone in your life who was closely involved? What happened to them? How were you affected by the events? This would include wars, assassinations, elections, etc.

- Think back to natural events and disasters: tornadoes, hurricanes, earthquakes, unexpected storms. I remember Hurricane Hazel because of the yellow rain. My mother remembered it because it was the week of her very first camping trip; she was taking Girl Scout Leader Training. Think of something that happened to you during such a natural event. What happened? Where were you? What did it mean?

- Think of people you have known. People are the source of the most interesting stories. Was there a particular child at school, a special friend you don't see much any more, a bully, a cut-up? What happened? Who was involved? Was there someone who taught you a lesson, whether you liked them or not? Was there someone who aroused your curiosity or made you mad? Would you feel that way now? Were there interesting older individuals in your church or religious group, or a club your parents belonged to? How about relatives? Everybody has an uncle or a cousin who is famous for something or other.

- Think of being in school or of a place where you worked. Who did you know? What happened? You can start a page in your ideas notebook for each place you have spent a lot of time. Enter the names of individuals you have known; add a brief description if you want.

- Memoirs can be organized around family recipes, important holidays, places you have lived, positions you have held—anything which has been a theme in your life. Work, family, travel locations, or houses lived in are fairly popular ideas. More than one student has organized their stories by dedicating one to each grandchild, or telling the story of the child's name or birthplace. You don't have to have an organizing principle to get started, but it may help; or you may notice one after you begin.

If you are enthusiastic about the subject, the book will be interesting.

Don't limit yourself to your childhood. When people first start to write memoirs, they often think of writing about their childhood—a good place to start—but not all there is to life. One student organized his memoirs around places he had moved his family and wrote about their experiences of living in different countries. Someone else wrote about her gardens and what they meant to her. As an adult you may have had a passion for your work or an avocation or a hobby that caused you to have some extraordinary experiences, meet unusual people or do unlikely things. These stories are likely to be appealing to your family and others. Your enthusiasm is what actually makes your story interesting. What turns you on? What do you care about?

My mother was a collector of people; she could have written an absorbing book on the people she had befriended, helped and appreciated over the years, the students she took in, the concerns she went to bat for. People. My father is fascinated by trains and things mechanical and electrical; he can wax ecstatic on the subject of algebra, actually saw the first computers, and is a good listener. Yet he has other, thoughtful interests as well; I think he has read everything there is on the philosophy of religion. His thoughts on that subject might be a way to organize an interesting book. A collection of essays on his ideas and experiences would represent him best.

Most really good stories have some underlying theme; that is, they express some human feeling or common experience and make it specific and present in the telling. A good story will have something important to say, some underlying understanding that needs to be shared, even if you don't know what it is until you write it. If there is a theme in your life, write a few stories. It will show up; you don't have to consciously plan it.

You don't have to limit yourself to physical things or beings; your imagination or your spiritual life may be the most personal and interesting thing you have to share. Who are you? As Joseph Campbell said, follow your bliss. Your ideas, your thoughts, your studies may be the most important contribution you have to make. A collection of essays that grows out of your interests and thoughts is a fitting memoir for a thinker. If you are enthusiastic about the subject, the book will be interesting.

Whose Story Is It?

Someone may have said you should write a particular story, and you may or may not have a feel for it. You may think someone should write that story—but is that someone you? There are stories that are yours to tell, and there are stories that are not yours.

Think of a particular story that you might want to tell. Ask yourself the question: Whose story is it? Is it mine or is it someone else's story? Viewpoint is the perspective from which you tell the story. Is this a story you can tell from your own viewpoint? If the tale is of something that happened to you, or something you did, or that is in your head, it is clearly your story. If not, it may be or it may not be yours.

Is this story something I should tell? Does it make sense coming from me? Is it mine to tell, or am I relating something that's none of my business, something that really belongs to someone else? Don't be too tight on yourself here; if the story happened in your life, it probably is yours, at least to the extent that it had an effect on you or someone close to you, or made a difference in your life. And that is the part you should emphasize. Write a story that has heart for you. While this is not entirely an ethical or moral question, it has something of that flavor. Sometimes a story is better left to the person who experienced it.

If it is not your story, your telling of it probably won't be as interesting as something else you might write. For example, in writing about my life, what I have to say about the Vietnam war probably won't be as interesting as what I could tell about the Women's Movement of the time. I observed protests, watched TV, had opinions, supported people I knew who were fighting, and shifted away from a warlike mentality in the direction of pacifism as I began to realize that some wars can not be won, and sometimes we make things worse by waging a war. I could write articulately about what I learned from thinking about all of that, and how my ideas have grown and changed since then; but I could not tell any firsthand stories of the war. It's not my story. Neither is the antiwar movement my story.

During that same time period, on the other hand, I was close to the center of the Women's Movement in Pennsylvania. I marched and sat-in and wrote pamphlets and taught classes. I knew JoAnne Evans Gardner and Wilma Scott Heide; I worked with them and Nancy Henderson at the 1972 American Psychological Association convention. I met Flo Henderson (from New York) and Alice Paul. I spoke at an APA "Town Meeting" in front of a thousand people and was supported by my sisters. I have stories that are mine and mine only to tell from that era. And, if I took on a story that I didn't actually experience but that was within that milieu, I would have a true voice for it. It would be my story because of my experience in the field.

Stories can belong to you even if you didn't actually experience them. Do you, personally, have something to say through that story? It seems to come down to having something authentic to say on the subject, a mysterious calculus of passion, experience, and knowledge. If you have only knowledge, it's not your story. Passion alone is not sufficient. Valid experience is a part of it, and there may be more. Is it a story that should be told in your voice? How will it be received? Another way to look at is to consider whether the story is yours to write or whether you have more energy for some other story. How do you actually feel about it? In other words, don't just write a story because someone says you should unless it's your boss, or you are writing news—which has an entirely different mystique—and that is beyond this book.

Choose for yourself a story that really belongs to you, that has heart for you, that energizes you when you think about it, that leaves you shaken and enervated when you finish. Choose a story that you think, feel, and believe is important. "Somebody needs to know this," or "I need to say this," are both powerful motivators. If both are present, go for it. If not, favor "I need to say this," over "This needs to be said." Somebody else can say it if it's not yours.

If it's your story, it will hang around. You will still be thinking about it the next time you come to decide what to write, and the next time, until you write it. If you are not sure, pick something you really want to write now, and let the one you aren't sure of wait. If it is yours, it will be there lurking in the dark until you write it. Of course, if you are not sure about any of this, just write whatever you are thinking about, and whether it has heart for you will become clear as you work with it.

Assignments

1. Most important: Start your story notebook if you haven't already. Make a place to list ideas in it.

2. Make a list of memories based on the discussion above.

3. Add to your personal list of story sources. Begin to check out some of your story sources for your own stories. As you run across ideas, add them to your list of story ideas.

4. Start a small ideas notebook using one of the suggestions in the chapter or do it your own way. Carry it with you and make notes.

5. Learn more about your family, your personal past, or the story that interests you.

6. Look for mementos, photos, or other reminders of stories.

7. Visit an old friend or a family member. Take a memento or photo album with you. Reminisce together. Follow the suggestions in this chapter for capturing a story.

8. Write a story based on a photograph or some souvenir that you found.

Chapter 4

WARM UP

Warm up is so important that we will give it a chapter all its own. Just as you warm up for sports, you should warm up for writing. Learn to warm up and you are halfway there. Begin every writing session with a warm-up exercise. Throughout this book, I will give you different exercises. You will find they improve your focus and concentration; and consequently, the quality of your writing.

Actually, this chapter also includes a bit of the basic psychology of writing creatively. Get really clear about the difference between writing and editing. It is the most fundamental gift you can give yourself as a writer. Work with the processes; write freely, and enjoy yourself!

How To Warm Up for Writing

Warm up. What to write about warm up. How to warm up. I'll be with you as soon as I warm up. What I have to say about warm up is that I have been concerned that I don't have long starter sentences and good exercises ready for my students to use. I want so much to make a difference with them, and I did distill what warm up is and how to do it into a short chapter section longer one in the first one. Must work this out in the book... How to give them warm up?? different warm up experiences. Warm up suits. Me warmed up. Loved what I DID WEDS yesterday. Hit the caps by acident. Distracted. Warm up. Warm up. keep going. PeopOle warm up. Sports. Sports warmup warm up muscles. Getting behind or in front of the power. OK warm up is havin letting Warm up is letting the Inner Writer write. Getting yourself out of the way. Warm up is opening a channel better not say that what then? but it is opening a channel so that the Inner Writer is aligned to pass straight through to the fingers and do the writing without having to respond to complaints and issues from the consc or subcons or especially the Editor or Dummy on the way. No censor, just write jest right let it flow I'm warm.

Warm up is about getting yourself aligned so that the Inner Writer can pass the words through to your fingers by an easy path. The Inner Writer can offer you ideas to work with without having to run an obstacle course created by "The Editor" (also known as "The Ego" or "The Dummy"). Writing is very simple. You clear yourself; the Inner Writer, or Intuitive Writer, who is another part of yourself, writes. You wiggle your fingers and write it all down.

Warm up is letting the Inner Writer write. As you become more facile with the practice, you will find that you can explore an idea quickly this way before you write about it.

Separate writing and editing. They are different processes, using different parts of your brain.

There's nothing really mysterious about creative writing or creativity; it just seems that way to us because we are trained to be left-brained linear thinkers by our culture. The creative side of us, which generally uses the right brain, seems (oddly) somewhat less verbal and not inclined to outline and structure. It's actually only less verbal in the linear, problem-solving way, but terrific at whole, new, creative ideas. It gives you a whole idea as a picture or a feeling of something. You get your favored materials together—pen and paper, paint and canvas, clay, musical instrument, or even a computer—and get started. You get art when you draw; you get words when you let yourself go and start writing. That really is how it works.

Later you get to decide how you will use what you have. You clean it up, change it around, enhance it, slant it for your market, tune it to your reader; but first you must get it all down on paper. You can make that easy for yourself by forming the habit of clearing during your warm up. Use long warm ups (fifteen minutes or until you run down) for clearing when you really need it. Use short warm ups (three to five minutes) every time you start to write.

Exercise: Warm up

- Use a kitchen timer to tell you when to stop writing. Set it for six minutes so you will have one minute to get focused and five to write. Approximate time is good enough.

- Read the exercise directions slowly to yourself, pausing to visualize your thoughts. Then write for five minutes. When the timer rings, stop writing.

- If you can't think of something new, repeat what you just wrote until something comes. Keep your pen or pencil moving. Don't try to get your spelling right, don't cross anything out. No corrections, no changes; just write.

Option 1:

Get comfortable in your seat. Rest for just a moment. Close your eyes for a minute. Let your thoughts settle down. Notice what thoughts you have and just let them go; if they don't it's OK. Just rest let your thoughts drift. Rest just a moment. Open your eyes. What thought do you have? Start writing.

Option 2:

Get comfortable in your seat. Rest for just a moment. Close your eyes for a minute. Let your thoughts settle down. Notice what thoughts you have and just let them go; if they don't it's OK. Just rest and let your thoughts drift. Rest just a moment. Open your eyes. Fix your eyes on something in the room, on the wall, or out the window; and begin writing. Write about whatever you see. Start writing. Begin writing with, "I'm looking at...[fill in whatever your eyes rest on—a chair, a cat, whatever]" ...Keep writing for five minutes.

Option 3:

Use the same process given above with a predetermined starter sentence. Write your sentence at the top of the page. Close your eyes and relax. When you open your eyes begin by writing the starter again, and then keep writing.

- You can use any of the exercise starters in this book, or you can make yourself a list of starter sentences. Either make them up or copy ideas in the form of intriguing half-sentences from books and articles. There are also websites which provide lists of story starters. Use a different starter sentence every time.

- If you can't do five minutes at first, try three. When you get comfortable with three, work up a minute or two at a time until you can keep going without stopping for ten minutes.

- Write with energy and abandon. Don't stop to think, just write whatever is there for you as fast as you can until it is all gone.

- Start wherever you are. Write freely.

Pause when you finish and look at what you have written. Did you write without stopping? You have just done a perfect exercise. Congratulate yourself. Is it any good? Probably not. There may be an idea or two there, or it may be just gibberish. In my classes I often take these papers up with great ceremony on the first night. Then I tear them up and throw them away to show the class that this really is intended to get you warmed up and ready to start. Throw it away; this is like a sports warm up—we don't keep score.

The editor on my shoulder

Let the Inner Writer do the work.

The part of me that wrote into the first draft of the paragraph above, "Did you write without stopping for five minutes? Did you really? Be honest with yourself..." is my Editor-On-My-Shoulder, I call him "The Editor." He's also known as the Pig Parent, the Censor, or the Dummy. We don't need any of those characters in this part of our work. Oh, they have their useful functions, but not here.

My Editor is a part of myself and is actually very useful for retrieving facts, making sense, clarifying prose, etc., but when he is sitting on my shoulder making snide remarks, he is out of line. The purposes of warm up are clearing, getting focused, and learning to let yourself go. Let the Inner Writer do the work. There is no room for editing here. Since I'm in charge of The Editor, I took that stuff out. I know what works! I let myself write freely and I edit later.

Rules of Warm Up

- *Set a definite amount of time - 3, 5, or 10 minutes. Use a timer or an alarm clock.*
- *Begin with the sentence stem or idea given and write whatever comes to mind.*
- *Write fast. Write anything and everything that comes up. Write as fast as you can. Don't let your hand stop.*
- *Follow your fear.[14] If something is bothering you, write it. Just let it flow through and find out its name.*
- *Keep writing, don't stop until time is called.*
- *If you don't have anything in the pipeline, rewrite what you just wrote until something comes through.*

The purpose of warm up is to get you warmed up and going and focused only on writing. Use a starter sentence or look at an object and write about it. Get started; just start moving your hand across the page. Write as fast as you can. The object is to write as many words as you can in the time you have set for yourself. Write your fears and anger and thoughts and what's happening outside your window. Let your feelings tiptoe in, even joy and love. It's OK. You can throw it all away.

Listen only to your Inner Writer, not your Editor. If you find that you have paused to think, you aren't listening to the Inner Writer. You are trying to find the right word or make it sound good before you even know what you are going to say. Write whatever comes to mind, but don't think about it. Send The Dummy packing if he tries to sneak in and tell you how it should be. Don't listen to any voices in your head that use "should" or "ought" in their sentences. Don't even let your Editor peak at those lines—not his job! Put in what you see, what you hear, what you smell or taste, what you know or believe, snippets of description, scraps of dialogue, anything. Just write. Ideas will follow.

Writing the Stories of Your Life

Let the writing flow through your hand; don't even think about it. Just write. You will find that you get into a rhythm or a space where the words seem to flow through. This is the object: flow through, intuition; not thinking.

What do you see for yourself out of this exercise? Could you write starting anywhere? That is the point; you can always write. You can look at something, anything, and write down, *I see a house, a star, a piece of paper, anything–* and keep going after that for five minutes.

One of the things that may happen over time with this exercise is that you will find it easier to get focused so that you can actually warm up and transition directly to your writing project in a very short time. You can start wherever you are whenever you sit down to write. In just a few moments you will be clear and ready to go.

Warm up is also useful when you get stuck while you are writing. You can take a short break—you probably need one—and come back to brainstorm whatever is going on with you. Grab a phrase from your work and warm up on it. Interview yourself to find out what is hanging you up. Ask you Inner Writer for fresh ideas.

Writing versus Editing

When you are writing, write whatever is there in your mind to say as fast as you can. Get it all down. Write, write, write. Use whatever materials *you* like: pen, pencil, computer, whatever. Just write as fast as you can. Don't let anybody interrupt you and don't stop 'til you are finished or your timer rings. This is the flow writers talk about, the sensation that it comes from nowhere. The words come from yourself, your "Inner Writer." There is nothing spooky about it. It just seems that way because you let the words come from your intuitive side and you can't see and control the process while it's happening. You can't write freely at the same time that you control and direct your work. You can always discard what you have written; there is nothing sacred about pen squiggles on paper. Let go of your fears and rules, and just write.

Editing, on the other hand, is something you will do to improve something you have already written. You will organize it better, add to it, get the structure and flow of it right, adjust the pace to fit the work, take stuff out, reorganize it, add to it, rewrite it a time or two–and then attack the grammar and spelling. Don't do details until you have the structure, content and sense of the piece complete. Much later in this book there is a chapter on editing. This paragraph gives you the core of it. Get your writing on paper first, do a single fast rewrite to fill it in and shape it a little. Work the process to complete the piece; sit on it a while, then edit.

Most of us learned in school to think our way through a writing exercise; this is a mistake. It slows you down and makes you loose your way. You get focused on finding the perfect word, the right punctuation, etc. when you haven't even figured out what you are trying to say. Writing comes from a different level.

If you have a couple of small notebooks, you will soon have dozens. They multiply like rabbits or coat hangers in the dark. Pretty soon you will have to organize the notebooks and you'll be wanting a room of your own. And, oh, the books. They will be all over the house, on the floor, on the sofa, on the what-not shelf!

Writing is not editing; editing is not writing. That's really all I have to say about this.

When you write, just write. Editing comes later. Don't ever try to do both at once; and if you are already deep in the throes of this deadly habit, stop doing it. You will recover, and you will enjoy writing a whole lot more.

Do not edit while you write; editing comes later. Editing is not writing. Editing may throw you back into writing—we call this rewriting—but editing is not writing.

Writing and editing are separate processes. They come through different parts of your brain. You write from the feeling level using your intuition and creative processes. You are using your memory, your thoughts and ideas, yes; but you are using them non-judgmentally. Editing is something you do using strategy. The purpose of editing is to make writing, which has good ideas in it, sparkle. You apply rules and techniques to make your writing clearer, more accessible and more interesting. You can't do both at once.

Howard's Thesis; A Story

As I have been doing my warm ups the last few days, I have discovered myself holding the pen aloft, thinking. The first time I thought, *Oh, this is what my students are doing. They stop to think. They should keep writing.* And I wrote in the suggestions above to keep you writing during the warm up. Today it happened when a thought about "voice" distracted me. I stopped to think about my students. *I must tell them that when I'm writing and I can't think of a word, I put in "XX" and find it later with my computer.* Then I thought of Howard. When I realized I had stopped writing, I went back to writing and put down what I was thinking. It grew into this story.

Howard's Thesis

Howard and I shared an office at Western Psychiatric Institute and Clinic during my third year of graduate school where we both worked on a cultural anthropology project. He was a student in anthropology, a frustrated musician who wanted to be an orchestra conductor. I was in social psychology, a too-serious student who didn't know then how much she really wanted to be a writer. Our group occupied offices located in a dreary corner in a traditional gothic stone and concrete building – one of those turn-of-the-last-century buildings built more to impress than to be practical – the sort that ought to have gargoyles everywhere. The ceiling must have been at least sixteen feet high and the room always felt cold.

Howard was tall and a bit coltish yet. He smoked a curved pipe with a particularly aromatic tobacco. He was in his third year as was I. While I had barely started my master's thesis, he was completing his doctoral research. By spring, he had only to write the final paper, and he would be finished.

Here is how he wrote his thesis: He put violin concertos on his huge expensive tape player, and played them as loud as I would let him. He would stand for a few minutes staring at an imagined orchestra, gesticulating with his pipe, conducting the piece. Then he would sit down and start typing. He typed fast with an odd buzzing sound every so often, but never a break in the rhythm. As the music reached a climax he would end his typing and fling his hands in the air to conduct the orchestra to it's final note.

He typed in synchronization with the music, ending a section with a burst of words – finished with a section of his dissertation. He did this day after day for three months. I wondered how he kept up the pace.

When I looked over his work I learned that he used blanks. The electric typewriters we used in those days (around 1970) would make a flat line if you held down the key for a couple of seconds. That was the buzzing sound that punctuated Howard's typing. He typed as fast as he could, and whenever he couldn't think of a word, he inserted an underscore an inch or so long, like this _____. Later he wrote the right word in each of the blanks and gave the draft to our secretary to be typed into the computer.

There were many of these blanks, sometimes a dozen or so on a page, but few other changes. The secretary would ask me what I thought he had written in a blank. It was a good thing he didn't rewrite much because his writing was completely unreadable.

Howard finished his thesis, over 500 pages, in a few months. He actually graduated and found a teaching position that spring; his thesis was accepted on the first draft. The rest of us worked on.

This story is true, and I hope it may help you to learn to *write it all when you are writing and edit afterward.* His method may seem a bit cumbersome. The computer of that day was very different from today's, and the politics of getting a thesis typed would make another story. Yes, Howard was smart. I believe he was the youngest anthropology doctorate the school had ever graduated; but he wasn't any smarter than anyone else who took several years to finish their doctorate. He knew how to write, but his writing wasn't that much better than anybody else's. *He knew how to get the job done, and that made all the difference.*

Howard's method works. He used violin concertos; you can use any music you like as long as it is fast and energetic and doesn't intrude words into your thoughts. While the music helps many people, it is optional; the important part is that you keep going while you are writing. *Let your Inner Writer say what needs to be said.* Edit what you have written later; fill in the blanks, add examples, make corrections.

You can use your legal pad or do the whole thing on your computer for the same result. Whenever you find yourself at a loss for a word, put in some sign to yourself

When you write, throw caution to the winds and say everything and anything you want to say about whoever and whatever. This is your creative time. You will be surprised at what your Inner Writer will deliver.

and keep going. If you use a typewriter or write by hand, the underscored blank is a great system. I write on a computer so I use a sign that my computer will pick up and mark for me. I use *XX* or attach a couple of *X's* in front of some possible word like this *XXexample/beat/rhythm*, and I keep going. My word processor marks these notes as misspelled words. When I am editing, I can also search on *XX* and find all the omissions and correct them. You may prefer to use "??" or "George." It doesn't matter what you use as long as you know what it means. Make it something easy to type and find.

Always warm up as you begin writing.

Begin every writing session with a warm-up exercise. Throughout this book, I will give you different exercises and refer you to sources where you can find others. You can design your own exercises; the basic structure is easy. However, I suggest that you try the ones given here along with the lessons first. You can use the warm up for the week for your own writing sessions that week. At home, you won't spend time discussing the process; simply warm up and move directly into your writing. When you have found a warm up that you like, you can keep using it as long as you want.

Apply our warm-up approach to all of your first draft writing.

Whenever you write, write. Just write. Don't edit. Write whatever comes up, in whatever order. If it repeats just keep writing until you get it all down. Write like there was a time clock ticking that counts only the number of words you write, not how good they are or if they are all organized in the right order. Just write. When you get to the end, stop.

If you don't get to the end within a session but you run out of time, stop wherever you are. Pick up tomorrow at that point. Setting a clock to stop yourself is a good idea if you don't think you have time to write. It will keep you from spending too much time at it.

Most Important Rules for Writers.

- Don't answer the phone.
- Start wherever you are.
- Write like you know everything.
- Don't edit until you are finished writing.

Pick the time that is best for you. Some people like mornings; others use the late-night quiet time. Theoretically, your mind is most creative between midnight and noon, and not the other way around; but that may not suit your schedule. Don't listen to everybody else, listen to yourself. Do what works.

Assignments

1. Write something every day this week.

2. This week, warm up for a few minutes every time you write. Use a sentence starter or try the other approaches.

3. Add to your list of ideas for your own stories.

4. Take a look at your plan for writing that you made in Chapter 2. Is there anything you want to revise or add to it? If you didn't make one, make one now.

5. Create structures to support your writing habit; that is, give yourself definite times to write. Decide how much and when, and *put it in your calendar.* Keep your promises. (If you don't or can't write on some occasions, reschedule with yourself.)

6. If you haven't decided on a project to work on, make a plan with goals for the project now. Set reasonable goals for yourself, structure your work to insure your own success.

7. Write at least one more story from your life this week.

Chapter 5

WRITING LETTERS
– Sharing Yourself

After we warm up, we are going to write letters. Writing is a communication between the writer and someone else. Communication is always a two-way affair even though it seems, when you are sitting at the desk, that all you are doing is putting words on paper. Someone will read your words. Who will that be? In this chapter we will distinguish the concept of audience in writing, and that will help you focus your writing and become more comfortable with sharing your thoughts.

Maybe your family has requested that you write about your life. You've had such an interesting life, been so many places, lived through so much; or maybe they just love you and want to know you better. Or maybe it's all your own idea; you always wanted to write. Whatever your motivation and whatever you want to write eventually, letter writing is a good way to get started. Everybody has written letters before, so this will be easy.

We will start with a warm up and an exercise. Do the warm up first—I just did mine, and it helped me get focused on you, the reader. I think of you as one of my students. I write to you. Then go right on to the exercise. Read the discussion after you finish. Doing the warm up, then the exercise will demonstrate the power of using warm up as a tool for getting started. Doing the exercise will help you to have something to relate to in the discussion.

Letter Writing

Warm up before writing

Follow the directions from the chapter on warm-up. Remember to keep writing no matter what. Write without lifting your pen from the paper even if you have to write a line or a sentence over again to keep your pen moving. Keep writing as fast as you can. Don't think.

Use this sentence stem as your warm up starter: The most unusual thing which has happened recently in my life happened when…

Set your clock for five minutes. Stop when it is time. Trash this.

Exercise: Writing to different people

- Write a letter to a friend or family member about the event you warmed up on or another recent event in your life. Don't use the warm up itself, but write the letter immediately after the warm up as if you planned to send a letter to this person about this event. Take about fifteen minutes to write your letter. You are using this exercise to work on your story about the event. For the sake of time, you may need to skip other topics or chitchat you might normally put in and go directly to the subject. You can add the other material later if you want to mail the letter.

- Write a letter to a different person about the same event you wrote about in No. 1. Don't reuse the first letter, write a new one. Choose a person who is very different from the first, a person with whom you have a different type of relationship; e.g., if you wrote to your son before, maybe you would write to a woman friend now; if you wrote to your spouse, write to your boss; or a friend, write to your mother now. Make sure you pick a person who is very different from the first person.

- Read your letters aloud to someone if possible. In a group you can do this in pairs or before the whole class. Listening to other people's letters can be very instructive. Notice how different the letters in each pair are. How are they different?

- What did you do that was different in your letters? Did you talk about different aspects of the event? Did you focus on people, scenery, or technology differently? Did you leave anything out or embellish anything to give it a different slant?

Audience

The letters you wrote are likely to be different in several ways. Depending on the reader or "audience" you have in mind, you may have used different language or slang, a different style, more or less difficult words, shorter or longer sentences. You may have presented the topic differently, even made it humorous in one and sad in another. You may have written about a different topic that was part of the same event or the same trip. You might write to your boss about the results achieved, for instance; and write to your spouse about the crazy clown you met. Is your writing a brief report of the facts, or an imaginative tale?

Did you engage an interest of the person you were writing to? When I took a canal boat ride in Amsterdam, I took pictures of tiny automobiles parked along the canals because I knew my husband would be interested in them. I took pictures of boats and flowers and people because I was interested in them. One way to engage your reader is through an interest of theirs such as cars, history, or gardening; for example, a trip to Brookgreen Gardens in South Carolina could easily produce a letter about the environment, one about horticulture, another about the sculpture, a different one about the history of the park and its original owners; or a letter telling of a family picnic and detailing the birds and other wildlife, depending on the interests of the reader. Did you tell about the background and reasons for the event, share your own thoughts, tell about the history of the area? Did you make one letter funny and not the other?

In this example, Darlene has written to her daughter and her sister about a trip to Phoenix. Notice the differences.

Darlene's Letters

Story Notebook Entries

09/15/03

Trips –

Several years ago I decided to take a very special vacation trip. I searched and searched and searched through the Elderhostel catalogs for several months to find the right trip at a time I could go. I put so much time and energy into this and cross-referenced information with my AAA trip guide book and narrowed the choice down place by place until one day I said to a friend as I threw up my hands in frustration, "Phooey, I think I'll just stay home because I'm exhausted from all this research and decision making!"

After a few days of mental rest, I got back to it and narrowed my choice to Sedona, Arizona and the Grand Canyon, whenever I recall any of that trip, I smile and glow...

09/22/03

Dear Sheri,

My vacation has been triple wonderful. As the plane neared Phoenix I was totally puzzled by what looked like very little sticks here and there on the hillsides. As we landed, I could see they were Saguaro Cactus, very large and impressive as if they were standing guard. I just looked and looked and looked!

Arizona, at least the Phoenix, Sedona, Scottsdale, and Grand Canyon part is so beautiful. The last evening and the next morning I spent at the Phoenix Botanical Garden. I kept wishing you were there too to see the hundreds of different Cactus plants and succulents. Since you made me realize the beauty of shapes and differences in cacti and succulents, I really can't wait to get my film developed and share the pictures with you.

Love, Mom

09/22/03

Dear Joyce,

I was remembering our conversation about my trip to Arizona and it brought back such nice memories. As the plane approached Phoenix, my excitement increased at the realization that I was entering a new world. I had never seen anything like it.

The red rocks near Sedona with their incredible formations were stunning. I still don't really understand it all. Also, the Grand Canyon left me speechless with awe. I wish we could spend a couple weeks just enjoying the wonders of nature there some time. I also learned that dry Arizona heat is much more tolerable than good old Southern humidity!

Talk to you soon.
Love, Darlene

The first is a letter to Darlene's daughter; the second to her sister. He daughter is interested in horticulture; she writes to her sister about the rocks and the grandeur of the place. Darlene automatically adjusts her approach to be interesting to the reader.

The term "audience" is used by writers to talk about the person you have in mind as your reader. Your idea of who your reader is will make a difference in how you write your story. You will write differently for men and women, for children and adults; people you know well and people you do business with. The problem is that we become uncertain if we don't know who we are writing to.

Shaping your writing to present a certain viewpoint is called "slanting" it. There is nothing wrong about slanting something. We all do it all the time; in fact, it is a good thing to be able to do it consciously and to be able to identify the slant in someone else's writing.

We do a lot of this "slanting" towards our audience unconsciously. You know what to write to your friends and family because you know who they are. Sometimes you just write what you are interested in because you want to share yourself and you know they care, but you still write it differently depending on who you are writing to. Try writing more letters to people you know. If you study what you have written, you will discover the techniques you already know for making a letter interesting to a particular audience.

The audience for a memoir is likely to be your family, although it could also be a wider audience. It is a bit more difficult to write to an unknown reader. If your book may have a wider circulation, or you hope that future generations will read it, consider who that audience is likely to be like. What are they like? Make a list or notes on the characteristics of that audience, pay particular attention to their interests and what they might already know and not know. What questions will they have? In writing this book; for example, I keep my students in mind; not always the same one, but a variety of them. I think of the questions they have asked and what they needed in explanation. I write to my students. They are the best representation I have of my typical audience.

Imagine the audience who will read your stories. Is it your children, grandchildren, the ladies of the club, your church? You may be very clear who your audience is. If so, make a note in your notebook listing and describing the characteristics of your audience. Whenever you start a story draft, you may want to write down the name of the person you see as most typical of your audience.

Think about the story; what is it about? Who would be interested in that? Who else? Who else? And so on? First you might think of your family and some of your friends. Which friends? Why would they be interested and not others? What kind of people are they? Who else might be interested?

For example, suppose the story is about a cat who found his way home. First you think of your daughter and your grandchild. They like cats. You think about some other relatives who hate cats and don't have pets; they probably wouldn't be interested. Who else would be interested? People who like cats. People who like animals. People who like stories about unusual events and animals with unusual abilities. Is your story a children's story? Or is it a story for all ages? What else is in the story that people might relate to? Make a list of different kinds of people whose interests might intersect with this story. Those people are your audience for that story. Describe that audience. What are they like? What are they interested in? What questions do they have?

Sometimes your audience is much more extensive than other times. The audience for a memoir will include family, friends, and people with interests similar to yours, people with the same degree or career commitment as yours, people with similar experiences and hobbies. Sometimes a memoir connects because of a place, a time period, another person in the story, a shared interest. The possibilities are nearly endless.

Exercise: Audience

Think about the stories you have in mind to write. If you are like most of us when we start writing a new piece, you are not very clear about who your audience is. Do the following exercise in your notebook for each story you have already drafted.

- Think about just one story. Put the name of that story at the top of a fresh page. Who can you imagine reading that story? List those people. Now imagine readers you don't already know. Ask yourself: What kind of people would be interested in this story? List people using the form "People who..."

- Now, think of a real (or imaginary) person who might read your story. What is that person like? How old are they? Male or female? Make a list of their characteristics. This is your "typical reader." His or her name is "Reader."

- What is your Reader interested in? Make a list of Reader's interests and preferences. Pay particular attention to the questions Reader will want answered.

- Now consider your story and relate the story to your Reader. What would your Reader need to know to understand and enjoy the story? Rewrite your story with that Reader in mind.

Put several of your stories through this process. How are the readers you envision for your story similar? What did you learn about that Reader? Construct a "Typical Reader" from your research. Use this Reader as your target reader throughout your work with your stories. Take the idea for a spin; write something new with your new-found Reader, your audience, in mind.

If your audience is your family, there may be many assumed bits of knowledge that you would have to fill in for a more general audience. Take a look at your work after you have completed several stories to see if there is sufficient explanation for someone who was not there, or who is of a later generation. Better yet, share your stories with someone in your family, probably someone of the younger generation, and let them ask you any questions they need to have answered. Don't ask for an evaluation of the story; just ask what questions they have. Take note of the questions and use the ideas to improve your letter or story.

The things your Reader would need to know are important points of connection with him or her. Your communication will not occur unless you fill in those gaps. You will not catch the reader's interest unless you engage some interest of his. This does not mean you have to spend a lot of words on connecting. You do it with a nuance, the use of one term instead of another to describe the same thing, a quick phrase providing explanation, or a bit of background. You can do it with style.

Is your Reader your children or your grandchildren? If you are over a certain age and writing your recollections for young people, you may want to explain terms and technologies they are not familiar with. Nobody uses slide rules or ice boxes any more. Eight-tracks and coal scuttles are things of the past. Remember not to talk down to young people in your explanations; write to them just like you would talk to them. Pictures are helpful, too.

Your Reader may be a different person for different writing that you do. Check in with yourself to see who your reader is for a new project. Run this process on the new project. You may have to do some research on that person's knowledge and interests. Don't assume that you know just because you have labeled the type of reader you want to reach. They know what they are interested in, you want to reach them. You may also find some people who will surprise you with their interest that you wouldn't have thought of if you didn't explore it.

Old letters

Crafting an interesting letter takes skill. Like all skills, it is a learned ability. Time was when people wrote letters when they went on trips; kids wrote home from camp or school. People wrote to a company with a complaint or to a professional asking for an appointment. Today, we do most of that by phone or on email, and the record of our day-to-day lives is lost. That may not be a great loss, or it may be the reason for the current interest in scrapbooking and journaling. Who knows? A good place to look for stories from the past is in people's letters.

Find old letters and read them. Are there any stories in the letters or between the lines? Is there something you would like to know? If you wrote the letters or were present for the events, is there anything else you remember? Do you have a different take on the events from the letter writer, or from your present perspective? As we work through this book, there will be many opportunities to use material from sources such as letters. We will work with viewpoint, story crafting, research and interviewing. Hold on to your letters and they will be useful resources.

One possibility is to arrange the letters in some meaningful order; i.e., chronological, or by sender, or as a correspondence—if you are so lucky as to have both sides. You can add bits of narrative to them to fill in what was going on in your life or the life of the sender at the time. You might write your reactions to finding them or add some photographs, drawings or other items to create a little book. Make sure to distinguish between the narrative and the letters in some appropriate way.

Sharing Yourself

Writing the stories of your life is actually pretty easy. All you have to do is write in your own words what happened to whom, what the outcome was, and how you felt about it. And this is exactly what is hard about it: You have to be willing to write freely and not worry about how the words come out or what you say on the first draft. We get in our own way; we second guess ourselves, we try to make it come out pretty. It doesn't. Writing is not editing. Writing is just writing. It comes out however it does, however you have access to the ideas. No matter how it seems when you first write it down, you can edit your writing to improve it. We will spend time on that part of the process later.

You have to be willing to let people know who you are. At the same time, you have to know that whatever comes out can't hurt you. It's just words on the warm up page. You have all the power. You can throw these words away, shred them, burn them, do whatever you want to do to get rid of them! Sounds silly? But that is how our unconscious works. We are afraid of things that we think we don't have power over. Once long ago someone gave you a grade for writing down the right word on the first try. Forget that! You are a real writer now and you don't have to try so hard. All you have to do is access your memories and write whatever is there. You can polish it up later, but the more you are willing to let yourself shine through, the better your stories will be.

Dig a Little Deeper

- *Is there anything you are not saying?*
- *Is there something you are censoring, holding back?*
- *Are you thinking? Or writing?*

Sharing yourself in writing means turning off your inner censor, your editor. We have talked about this already, but it bears emphasis here. Is there anything you are not saying? Is there something you are holding back? I say the sentence, "Dig a little deeper." over and over to my clients. Do you stop to think while you are writing? Do you feel your breath catch or does your pen hesitate for a second? There is something you are censoring right there. What is it? You may not be able to get at it directly, but if you keep writing fast and pass again over that spot it may come up. Keep writing during your warm-up as if your life depended on it. There is a tiger after you and you have to keep the pen moving to prevent the tiger from reaching you.

Your memory garden

Getting access to who you really are and who you once were requires giving yourself time to remember and reminisce. We mentioned the idea of looking at your memory as a garden of ideas in an earlier chapter. Give yourself a sunny afternoon or an evening in front of the fire. Have your notebook and pen handy. Follow the threads of memory like paths in the garden. Lean back in your chair and relax. Daydream a bit, and visualize this with me.

Writing the Stories of Your Life

Your memory is like a huge garden of ideas; it's so big it's like an arboretum with indoor greenhouses and outdoor areas with plantings and lakes. It's a huge park with all kinds of terrain. The stories are there somewhere planted in the garden, all the forgotten stuff that you want to share. The paths of the garden are long and winding; you will need time to enjoy it. Now imagine that you cross a bridge and find a path down the side of it to a river. There's a boat. You get in the boat and ride on it. The river is quiet and you realize that it is really a canal. Since it is a canal, you can ride on it in your boat or you can ship things along it. There are canal boats to take the cargo.

The canal reaches from deep in your memory garden to your pen. The canal connects directly to your pen. Each canal boat has only so much room in it; you can ship a lot of words to the pen, but not all at once. The boat goes under a bridge. The canal twists and turns and the channel narrows. It goes into a tunnel. The boat just fits the channel now. Only the words that are on that boat can get into the channel. If you don't let those words out through your pen at the end of the channel, nothing else can get into it. Even if you don't want to actually use something you have written in the final story, you have to let those words flow out of the tube so that something else can come through on the boat.

Of course, this is a model to help you think about how all that stuff gets out of your memory and into your writing. It really does seem to function like a boat on a canal that has to be emptied and sent down the back channel for more. Thinking of your memory as a garden path, or a river, or a tube that connects to your pen lets you connect to the flow of ideas. If you don't let what's in the channel flow through, nothing else seems to come up.

Use what you are given and more will be added.

My memory path winds and twists. I don't see everything at once. The path goes around a lot of things and finds the material I want; it doesn't bring me things I really don't want to talk about or things that are off the subject. I have to trust the path; I created it after all. So I follow the path to whatever is there. I let it come out in my warm-up or my first draft writing. I just keep writing. Later I edit whatever I have written. I pick and choose among the flowers in the garden. I choose the flowers I will pick for my bouquets. I arrange them to work the way I want them. If I want pretty, I pick pretty flowers; if I want fierce, I pick up sharp rocks and rough logs. I get to say what comes up. And the deal is: I have to trust the process for it to work.

Exercise: Accessing your garden for memories

Have a paper and pencil ready by your chair. Put on some music from the past if you like. Sit back, relax, let your mind float free, daydream. Take time to savor the process. You can use any image that appeals to you, a boat or a tube or a memory ladder, even an airplane. If you find yourself thinking, notice what you are thinking and let it go. Let your mind wander. Try one or more of the suggestions that follow.

- Reflect on the image of a memory garden. Walk down the path, and begin to review the memory plants in your garden. When you have found one you like, move it to your canal boat and let it come up to your pen. Write freely for fifteen minutes or until you have exhausted that idea.

- Imagine that there is a string attached to your pen and that it reaches back as far as can be into your memory. The string really is a ladder; memories can climb up the ladder and come out through your pen. Who is climbing the ladder? Describe the memory. Write freely for fifteen minutes or until you have exhausted that idea.

If you are looking for a particular memory, or more detail to add to a memory, have that event in mind. Read what you have written, review your lists; then sit back, relax, and use one of the techniques to wander around in the event and see what else you can see.

- Let yourself use all of your senses. Perhaps there is something you heard, or smelled or touched at the time. What was it like? How did you feel? Ask yourself these questions one at a time, and give your mind time to wander around on the paths a while. Write down anything that comes to you (even if it doesn't make sense) and go back to the garden with the next question.

- If nothing comes right away, let it go; your "editor" may find it in a day or two and bring it to your attention.

Some people access memories through their feelings and will be reminded of people and places by times when they felt the way they do now. For that purpose it is useful to simulate a particular feeling or use a concrete object, such as a picture, that might bring the feeling up. If you are a visual person, you will find daydreaming an easy way to find ideas. Music may help you if you are looking for something pertaining to a particular time. If you tend to connect events to sounds and words, just relax, listen. Don't think, just be there. When your mind is really quiet pick up your pen and start writing.

Smells accidentally encountered can suddenly bring up a long forgotten memory—even one from a childhood long out of mind. Odors are particularly good for stimulating childhood memories. The smell of spaghetti cooking may mean home to you. I will never forget the smell of a balsam Christmas tree, though they are a rarity in the South where I live now. How do you feel about roses, or honeysuckle? Certain soaps can bring up a particular person. English Lavender makes me think of my grandmother. We all use all of our senses but some of us rely on one more than another. See what you can find by bringing the senses you don't usually rely on into your reverie.

Secret Formula

As we work through the chapters of this book, we will discuss the strategy and structure of stories from the back story to the epilogue; and it may seem like there is an awful lot to it. There is always something to learn about writing, but there is a lot that you already know. It's more important to write than to know a lot about writing. Take it a bit at a time. Use what you can and don't worry about the rest. There really is a simple formula for writing a story from your life. I will give it to you here.

I call this simplest formula the express version. Answer the questions on the left, and you have the story part on the right. Put them in a workable order, not necessarily that given, and you have a story. Not only that, this story is about something that changed you—maybe a little, maybe a lot. It is about something you learned and how you learned it.

Write Your Story—Share Yourself
(Secret Formula, Express Version)

Question	Story result
Who was I at the time?	Necessary Background
What happened?	Action
What did I learn?	Outcome
What am I like now?	Result

"Who was I at the time?" means what was I like? What kind of person I was can be suggested in just a word or two: young and eager, Daddy's princess, a spoiled child, a serious student. But take time to think about it; make a list or write a description of yourself. Were you young and shallow, hungry, hunted? Were you naïve, idealistic? Smart? Silly? How did you feel? How did you approach life? Descriptions such as, "…we were young and always had our way;"[15] "Yon Cassius has a lean and hungry look; such men are dangerous;"[16] are memorable because they say in a few words something that is significant about the person and relevant to the story. You get the picture. Pick a few words from your list that draw the rest of the picture along with them. Use them in your story.

Spice "what happened" with who and where and when as necessary. Finish with who am I now or how am I different. That's the formula for writing down your personal stories, one by one. It actually works for writing a book, too. Does this remind you of any published or classic works? This formula is like a magical pot. The more you use it, the more you will have to give away and the happier you will be.

Exercise: The Secret Formula

Following the formula above, write a short narrative or story.[17]

1. First answer each of the questions separately. Write as much as you need to thoroughly answer the question.

2. Then work your answers into a story or narrative piece using material from your answers to the questions.

3. What did you learn?

The secret formula is actually a blueprint for sharing yourself. It will work for stories you tell, stories you write, sermons, and just letting people know who you are. It will help you to realize how you change and grow. The more you use it, the more depth of intimacy you will have in your life.

As you shape this story, remember your audience. Who are you writing for? A favorite trick among writers is to imagine a specific individual who will read their book. Keep in mind a person and write your story to them.

Assignments

1. Write a long letter to a particular person about some recent event in your life; tell the story of what happened, how and why, in your letter. Include the people who were important to the story and their roles in it. Share what you learned.

2. In your story notebook, list the people whom you see as your audience or the Reader for your memoir project. What are their similarities? What questions might they expect to have answered by your story?

3. Focus on one person in your audience for a story and write so that your story will be meaningful to that person. You may want to continue doing this throughout the course.

4. Write several letters to a real or imagined correspondent (all to the same person). Is this the style for you to tell your stories in?

5. Start a correspondence with someone by mail or by email.

6. Find several fiction works written as letters. What do you like or not like about these works?

7. Find several non-fiction works which are, or include, collections of letters.
   - What else does the editor include?
   - How do you feel about the letters? Are they believable?
   - Do they tell the story? Is there anything else you want to know?

8. Write an essay discussing your findings and opinions based on one or more of the exercises in this chapter.

9. Write several email letters and traditional letters. Have at least some of them be on the same topic. What differences do you see between email and traditional letters, if any? Check for differences based on audience, also.

10. As always, add to your list of possible story topics. Visit your list when you are ready for a new idea, write something using one of your ideas.

Chapter 6

SETTING

Traditionally, setting equals location in place and time. Setting helps your reader to appreciate the story by understanding the background of the story in terms of its location in time and space, but there is far more to it than that. Social location is equally important. This chapter addresses time, place, and social environment. How people might have thought, what they knew or had, or what would be significant to them may be conveyed indirectly by the setting; for example, water is valuable in the deserts of the Southwest in a different way from the way it is important in the bayou country of Louisiana. People understood the world differently before televisions and computers.

Setting equals location in time, place and society.

Setting can have a major influence on the story or only a small one. Some stories could only happen the way they happened in a particular time and place. Other stories could happen anywhere. If yours seems universal, it will still benefit from specificity of location. Location provides possibilities and limitations. Your use of the setting in your story is one of the ways you have as a writer of communicating something about the people in the story. Would "Casablanca"[18] be the same in some other setting? You can enrich your story remarkably by deft use of setting to convey feelings.

Setting is not just an address, but a window into the time and culture of the place. Setting involves the reader or viewer in the space, the time, and the lives of the characters. A setting limits some activities and requires others. You can't give a party for two hundred in an eight by ten room. You can't read a book if you don't have one. Marie Antoinette's famous remark, "Let them eat cake!" illustrates (among other things) a lack of understanding of the social implications of the setting. For her, bread or cake was always an option; for the common people of France, the most basic of necessities was missing and they were ready to take action. This remark, whether she actually said it or not, illustrates a major difference in the social environment for two groups in the same city.

Change and the Twentieth Century

May you live in turbulent times![19]

Both the particulars of a certain family or social location, and the possibilities of the times themselves play an important role in twentieth century memoirs, as they do whenever times are turbulent. Change is an ever-present backdrop. In any given year for the last century or so something new became possible, and life changed because of it. Life has changed more in the last two centuries than in thousands of years before that. It may be important in your story to point out what is not available in the setting as well as what is. Life before antibiotics had different possibilities.

In times past much more time and effort went into providing necessities and cooking. Think of the American frontier in the late nineteenth century. Even in the early twentieth century, a time within memory for some of our parents and grandparents, many places lacked electricity, running water in the homes, and other amenities we now take for granted. Fires had to be stoked, clothing washed by hand, meals prepared from fresh foods. It wasn't all bad. Life was different. Most people spent their days doing the chores of survival and production. There was little leisure for anyone—including, perhaps, the very rich who spent their days managing large groups of people managing their homes and estates. On the other hand, leisure was not programmed electronically; people made their own music and fun.

Using an outhouse, having to feed an open fire, or drawing water from a well is not necessarily so much of an impediment as you might think. If everyone else is in the same boat, the situation seems normal. To our electronically wired, centrally heated, and microwave fed lives, the prospect of doing without indoor plumbing, automobiles, and kitchen gadgets seems daunting. To the Bantu family coming from Africa to the United States for the first time, the gadgets themselves are beyond the scope of imagination.[20] People who live in major cities such as New York, London, or Berlin may go their whole lives without learning to drive. People living in rural areas or smaller towns and cities in the United States find it very difficult to have a life without a vehicle of their own.

I have pointed to a few, very obvious differences. Many of the ways environment affects us are much more subtle. Most depend on how we have set up our lives – our space, our time, and our relationships. Think about it; how does your environment affect your life? Where is your home located? Is it convenient, or a project to go shopping? What is your environment like today, and how does it differ from the way your parents grew up or the way your relatives live now? How is it different from what it was like when you were young? Did you have to spend time shoveling coal or chopping wood? Maybe you do that now by choice. Think about how your choices affect your life. How has your life changed with your personal environment or setting, and why?

Exercise: Our changing environment

Before we go further with this discussion, grab your story notebook and write something about your changing environment, how it has influenced you, and how you have related to it. Here are a few more questions to get you started:

- What chores did you once have to do that no longer matter?
- What did you do for entertainment when you were younger?
- What entertainment did you once create that you no longer do for yourself?
- How has life changed in your lifetime?
- How have environmental changes made a difference in the way you live?
- How have you changed the environment for yourself and others?

Place

The setting has a special role to fill in a memoir. You want to convey to your reader how the world was for you or your characters in those days. Bringing in aspects of the environment as your characters relate to them will give a richer picture than merely cataloging the location. If you use the physical environment in the story as a part of your story, it will be easier for you to remember it than if you try to describe it all at once.

Elements of the spatial aspect of setting include things, animals and people, not just buildings or fields and woods. A railway station at rush hour is different from the same place at other times. Grand Central Station is extremely different from a small town station anywhere else in the country. Railway stations in Europe are generally very much more integrated into the life of the area than they are in the United States. A barn full of animals is different from an empty barn. Did the cows have names, or were they a large anonymous herd?

Setting can contribute tremendously to the emotional impact of stories. Things contribute possibilities for action; they also carry emotional connotations. Ghost stories are set in graveyards and old dark country churches for a reason.

The things people furnish places with are significant. They may be simply functional or sophisticated, comfortable or overdone. Specific items may figure importantly in your story. People become very attached to particular items. Saying something about the furniture may say something about the people who lived there. It can be either a major note or a sub-text. Were your characters just like their furniture, a little worn around the edges but comfortable and friendly? Or were they sophisticated in contrast to the impression they chose to convey through their setting? It is just as interesting to note a contrast as a similarity. The similarity carries a feeling of congruence and helps to explain the people. The contrast sets up a conflict or a question in the reader's mind. The reader wants to know why.

This example comes from Jim E. Lewis's story about his math student, more of which is included in Chapter 7. Jim holds the identity of his student for the end of his story, so I won't tell you here. Prior to this excerpt, he has mentioned the locations in which the tutor and student worked. The contrast between the private spaces and the public persona of these people is intriguing.

> *While he was taking the test, his parents gave me a guided tour of their home. The public part of their home had been designed and decorated by the mother. She had the home built using parts of old log homes she had purchased in Western North Carolina. It [the main part of the home] was furnished with furniture she had purchased from private homes and antique dealers. The private part of the home was very modern.*

The feeling of the public spaces, the entryway, living room, etc. represents a fit with a certain culture. One assumes that in the private spaces the woman has done what she personally prefers in her decorating.

What is the weather doing? Is it raining, five below zero, or 90° and humid? Weather patterns affect human behavior and limit our possibilities for action. Is the hero riding the current in a lifeboat under a broiling sun or tucked away in an air conditioned high rise building?

Location, location, location!
—Real estate saying

Sometimes it is enough to begin by mentioning the setting, especially in a very short piece. The old schoolhouse, Grandma's farm, New York City, a battleship in the Pacific, for example, may be sufficient to orient the reader, especially if you are writing for family or friends who were there. If you are writing for the younger generations, for example, or for a wider audience, you will need to devote more space to showing them your setting.

In a collection of memories, you might devote one piece to providing a full sense of the place. Grandma's farm, for example, could be described along with a discussion of the crops, the people, and maybe a favorite vignette or short tale. If you describe a city, like New York, you will need to talk about the locations and the people, the smells and the activities within it. Try to focus on a particular area or on your reaction to your first sight of the place—whatever place it is. I will never forget driving out of a long dark tunnel and catching my first sight of the gleaming skyscrapers of Pittsburgh at the same time that I was coping with a cacophony of traffic changing lanes on a major bridge. It was all new to me, and I would spend the next decade living and studying there. I fell in love.

Writing the Stories of Your Life

What a battleship was really like from the inside would be interesting to your readers, as would any kind of military transportation or location. Just because you know what it is like, doesn't mean that your reader knows. He or she is eager to imagine what you are living with, what you are or were facing daily. Making the reader aware of the setting involves more than description or lists; it includes giving the reader a feeling for the heat or the snow, the routines, the responsibilities, and the nature of the human interactions. Be sure that this chapter or piece has some action or people in it so that it is interesting in itself.

Once your audience is familiar with the setting, you probably don't need to describe it again in detail, but refer to it instead. However, as you move along in your story, adding the perfect detail here and there will help your reader to smell and hear the place as well as to visualize it. It depends on your purpose. If your memoir is for future generations, do not assume that they will know what you know. Tell them about the setting. Tell them in a way that they can get the feel of it.

If you have space for only one crack at it, describe your setting in a way that contributes to the feeling of the story you are telling. A bright sunny day, or a rocky driveway, or the smell of cabbage cooking can make a difference in the feeling of the place as well as the action potential. How does the character walking up the rocky driveway smelling the cabbage feel? There are many possibilities. She might feel nervous, annoyed, anxious, glad to be home, or concerned that cabbage is still boiling after two hours—what happened to Gran? The feeling of a place can help to build the tension in the story. It can also build nostalgia or disgust. It is up to you to interpret the feeling for the reader. Connect an element of setting to whatever is going on in the story. If the smell of cabbage reminds you of home, say so.

Some of us love setting; we want to decorate it in detail, paper every wall and report the whole list of objects d'art. Don't. Use the setting to support your story. Don't just list the details; use one or two and have them enhance the mood. Make the details work for you. The trick is to find one or two specific details that serve as touchstones for the feeling of a place. I remember visiting my Aunt Naomi's home when I was about six. The living room of this three story house on a narrow New Jersey lot was full of overstuffed furniture and little ceramic pieces. There was no room to move around. I remember being as careful as possible and actually frightened by it. Can you relate to this feeling? I think the tension was broken when I did knock something off but it didn't break, and I survived.

Exercise: Childhood spaces

Think of a place you visited as a child. Make a quick list of things you remember about it. Were there stairs or an elevator? Did it have antimacassars on the furniture? Were there things you shouldn't touch? What happened? What was it like? Was there a woodstove with an old hound in front of it? Was it comfortable and safe for children?

How did you feel when you were in this place? Name the details, and relate your feelings to them.

If your story moves from place to place, make sure your reader stays oriented. When you all go to church or you take a walk in the woods, tell the reader so he can follow along. You don't have to put in every step, but let your reader know where your characters are.

What kind of woods? A walk among the oaks of Pennsylvania smells different from one through a stand of pines along a southern tidal creek. Use a word or a sentence to catch the feel of the place.

Time

Knowing when something happened is as important as knowing where. Walking into a church in the middle of a Sunday service is different from opening the church door in the middle of the night. We orient ourselves in the world by knowing where something is located in time and space. Some traditional writers have in the past not used time-relevant information in their writings as if to say "This story is a universal truth." Setting a story in "anytime" worked when things didn't change much. Today, things change so fast that a story that is not rooted somewhere seems to float in an unreal space. Universal or underlying truth will be there even if you anchor the story in time.

There are many ways to connect to time in a story. You can use a "time tag" that tells the year or the month, or the exact date. You can tell how old you were when the story happened. Tell the age of the main character, tell what the world was like at the time; connect the story to a significant historical event or a relevant family event. Unless there is a special reason, you do not need to be exact about dates, but it is helpful if you give the story some time setting; e.g., "the summer when I was sixteen." In a short piece where your setting of place could be as simple as "my grandmother's kitchen, full of wonderful smells," your setting in time might be the grade you were in or the job you were given to do.

The reader of your memoir will be interested in both the time and place that a particular story happened. There are as many ways to label time and space as your creativity will provide. Setting it in time and space gives your story the necessary

---

Examples of time tags:

- *He must have been about thirty...*
- *On the first day of the sixth moon...*
- *When I was seventeen...*
- *In 1814 we took a little trip...*
- *I was nineteen in the summer of '42...*
- *December 12, 1998...*
- *Just before the world was irrevocably changed by the death of your father...*
- *A story told around the campfires...*
- *Our first child was about to be born...*
- *I heard this story when I was a child often enough, but I have no idea how long ago it happened...*
- *The day that Kennedy was shot...*
- *Before 9-11 became a concept...*

grounding. Sometimes you can combine time and space, as in "The summer when I was sixteen we moved to an old house in Lancaster..."

If your story is a recollection or an appreciation of a person, you may have a wider perspective. You may write comments that summarize the meaning of a lifetime or a relationship; however, the more specifically you can ground a particular story in realistic detail, the more real it will seem. If you do not know exactly when and where something happened, you may simply say so. Describe what you do know; for example,

> "I knew him in high school, but this story happened later than that. I can't say exactly when except that it was after we both moved to New York. I didn't know he was living there, but one day I ran into him in the Chinese restaurant around the corner from my apartment."

By grounding your story in time and space this way, you have given your reader a sense of reality. You have also dropped in an important bit of back story and made your reader wonder about your prior relationship with him. Your reader is happy to hear about the event or relationship that followed.

Social Environment

The people who inhabit a setting are an important aspect of that setting. When I did research in the relationship of the young child to the physical environment, I was surprised to find that most researchers up until then had looked only at the social characteristics of the environment, not the physical. They were asking questions like: Is the environment conducive to learning? Does it facilitate healthy development? The variables they were studying were aspects of the parent-child relationship or the teaching style of personnel in the daycare setting. Even there they did not pay much attention to the kinds and numbers of toys or what was done with them. Without going too far into all of that, let me assert that the physical environment stands in a give and take relationship to the social. It is at once a reflection of who we are and an influence on who we can become. The people who inhabit a setting, such as day-care workers or teachers mediate the effects of the physical environment on children.

Physical environment, which is a repository of resources, provides options, opportunities, and limits to our daily activities. A real-world example that we've already talked about is setting up space and time to write. A place of one's own to write in seems to be every writer's dream. But it is more than a place; it's a plan for relating to other people who share your space. Creating such a plan involves relating to the social environment by informing others about the needs we have as writers.

How people relate to space has a lot to do with how their lives run. A space that requires a lot of maintenance takes a lot of one's time; whereas, one that is simple gives freedom. Time and space are related, and both are related to the expectations we have and that others have of us. Some of us are run by our schedules (or other people's schedules) more than others, but in the twenty-first century our lives are very, very different from those of the past.

The social environment interacts with the physical to facilitate or limit our success as individuals. As writers we have the power and the responsibility to manage the setting for our work. Our characters also have or had that power. The extent to which they were successful at it is related to the outcomes of their lives.

Exercise: Elements of setting

It is important to explore your setting and relate it to your story. There are three important aspects of the setting that you will need to explore: physical space or location, time or the times, and social environment and culture. Working on your own or after class, this may be something you will give attention to over a period of time.

This exercise is designed to integrate the three major aspects of the setting and help you relate them to your story.

- Think of a story you have written or are planning to write.

- In your story notebook divide a sheet of paper into three columns. Head these columns: Space, Time, Culture. Spend a couple minutes brainstorming each list. Write down aspects of the setting—details and fundamentals—as fast as you can.

- Now use a different color pen and write down things you don't know about the setting. These items may be important. If they are, you will probably have to research them.

Group:

If you are working in a group, share your ideas as you would in a brainstorming session. The leader will call on people in turn and someone will write the ideas on a board. Do one section at a time: Space, Time, Culture. Remember to contribute your ideas quickly with no discussion until everyone has passed or time is called. Then the group may discuss their ideas and findings. See how much overlap there is in the fundamentals, how much difference in details. Someone else's ideas may spark an idea for you.

- With your partner or writing buddy, discuss what you have listed to figure out which items represent the most important aspects of the setting for your story. Pick out a feature of the setting which underscores the emotional tone of your story.

Writing the Stories of Your Life

- Next, write a description of your setting using the ideas which reveal it most clearly. Include aspects of the setting which set the tone for your story. Is there something you can use as a metaphor? Is there a change in the people as a result of the events which might be reflected by the setting?
- Share your descriptions with your group or writing buddy.

On Your Own:

- Do the first group of activities above; remember to address space, time and social environment.
- If there are details you need to research, do it.
- Move on to writing a description of your setting.
- Review the setting as you have it so far. Write a description of each aspect of your setting. See which items from your list you actually use in your writing. Is there anything missing? Is it important.
- How can you use the physical setting to give a solid grounding to your story? What does your reader need to know about time? How can you integrate the social setting into your story?
- You might want to discuss your setting and related symbols with your writing buddy.

Details

Pick a specific aspect of the setting that conveys the feeling of the place and let the reader know how that one thing affects the character—you or whoever you are writing about. A few words to characterize the setting in the moment will be sufficient, but those few words are very important. Don't leave them out!

Your description should not be too detailed in a short piece. Instead, find a few words that completely characterize it in the moment. A word here and there will be sufficient, but those few words are very important. Don't leave them out!

If your story is long, you can add a descriptive tidbit here and there as the characters come into contact with it instead of completely describing the setting all at once. Your setting should work with your story. You can talk about how people relate to it; you can show them interacting with details. You have written an extensive description, or at least have a fairly extensive list of setting aspects, by now. However, in your story, you will probably find it better to apply this knowledge in ways that show your characters interacting with the setting–once you have set the mood.

Details are the most usual way that people relate to settings. People interact with the details of life. People worry about the exact time and run for trains. They make lists and go shopping. People remember the smell of Channel No. 5 or sauerbraten years later. These details contribute to the feeling tone of the story. They are important. One detail, say the smell of a woman's perfume, used as a motif, can carry a whole story along. Specific details help your story emotionally and visually.

Your description should not contain too many details in one paragraph, nor should you use long lists of items in a single sentence. You can get away with one long list one time, but not list after list of what you had for dinner in a memoir. Save that list for one special event; call it a chicken dinner if it happened most Sundays.

Continuing the exercise above:

- Find details that your characters will have to interact with. How can the details of your setting be used effectively to enhance your story?

- Write a description of your setting using the ideas and details which reveal it most clearly, including aspects of the setting which set the tone for your story. Is there something you can use as an ongoing metaphor? Is there a change in the people as a result of the events which might be reflected by the setting?

- Review what you have listed to figure out which item or items represent the most important aspects of the setting for your story.

- Pick a few details that convey the feeling of the place and let the reader know how they affect the characters—you or whoever you are writing about.

Your setting should work with your story. If your story is long, you can add a descriptive tidbit here and there as the characters come into contact with it instead of completely describing the setting all at once.

- Pick out a feature of the setting which most strongly underscores the emotional tone of your story. Use that or another detail as a sort of signal in the story to let the reader know something important is about to happen, or as a symbol for the events. It may be any type of detail; often it will be the sort of item that can carry a lot of meaning, such as a treasured vase, a piece of art, an antique mirror. You can embed such a symbol into a story, or you can use it as a starting point.

- Try writing a piece using an important physical object or characteristic of the environment as a starting point. Edgar Allen Poe did this in several of his stories and poems. More recently, the movie "Close Encounters of the Third Kind"[21] comes to mind where Devils Tower National Monument is featured as the location for contact with aliens.

One important detail may be used several places as a tag for a character to help identify him. This is effective if there a lot of characters and a minor character is important. It might be a cap he always wore, something he said or a gesture.

If you are writing a memoir about another person, apply the exercises and assignments in this chapter to that person and his or her setting. Do a little research into social and medical realities of the times, typical homes of the period, educational and career opportunities, relevant political and cultural events. You may find that setting has a great deal to do with what happened in your story.

Assignments

There are a large number of assignments offered with this chapter in addition to the exercises you have done. Remember to choose the ones that further your work, not necessarily the easiest ones. It is not necessary to do all of them.

1. Find a book or a story that you like. How did the author handle the elements of the setting? Is there a section or paragraph where the setting is specifically described? How much are the various elements of setting worked into the story? How well does the setting support the story?

2. Pick several memoirs, autobiographies or biographies. Notice differences in the handling of setting in different stories. Which is more effective in your opinion?

3. Write about something that happened in a particular location. Have the place be an important factor in the story. Find a way to anchor the story in time. Use the setting to support the story.

4. Write a story beginning at the beginning chronologically. Pay special attention to the effects of time on this story.

5. Write a story that you anchor in time using only secondary information—not a specific date or time reading.

6. Use one of the time tags you have developed to begin a story.

7. Think of a time when the physical or social setting made a difference for what happened in the story. Write your story.

8. Write something that happened to you. You, of course, are the protagonist in your personal memoirs. How did you interact with space and time and the social environment?

9. Review a story you have written, paying attention to how the characters interact with the setting. See if you can strengthen the relationship of time, place, and social environment with your protagonist.

10. As always, add to your list of possible story topics. Visit your list when you are ready for a new idea, write something using one of your ideas.

Chapter 7

VIEWPOINT (And Voice)

Are you telling about something that happened to someone else, or are you telling something that happened to you? Either way, are you telling it from your own viewpoint, or from some other perspective? Your reader can tell what he is seeing more clearly if he knows where you are coming from. Understanding viewpoint will give you some options for telling your story in different ways. There are only a few things you really need to know about viewpoint to write a good recollection, story or memoir.

Viewpoint gives a story context. Having a sense of viewpoint is important—mainly because once you choose one, you must stick to it. Using one viewpoint gives your story logical consistency. Your reader knows where to stand with regard to the story.

The kind of information to be conveyed makes a lot of difference in what viewpoint you choose, and ultimately, how you tell the story. Using a different viewpoint also gives the story a different feeling. Many stories or recollections are lent an air of authenticity by the use of a narrator. In other cases, there is a lot of information that needs to be integrated and being close to the action is not as important. In a memoir that is more like an essay, the omniscient viewpoint will serve you better.

Writers use the term "viewpoint" to distinguish the point of reference from which a story is told. The meaning is very close to the everyday use of the word, but specialized. How you tell your story depends on the viewpoint you use. How you want to tell your story determines the viewpoint you choose. Is the story told through one of the characters? Are you the narrator? Is another person the narrator? Is the story told from a distance as if it were written by an anonymous editor? Viewpoint determines whether you use first or third person pronouns.

Whose eyes are you looking through?

How you tell your story depends on the viewpoint you use.
How you want to tell your story determines the viewpoint you choose.

Depth of viewpoint refers to the perception the reader has of how close he is to the story. If he can see, feel, and taste events, "smell the blood," right along with the protagonist, he is close in. If the feeling of the piece is dry, pedantic, or just factual, the viewpoint is not deep, no matter what viewpoint you use. Usually a story is more lively the closer to the action you take the reader. A "narrator" who glosses over things and thinks too much is less effective at presenting the emotional aspect of a story than an "omniscient editor" who includes the close details and feelings of his characters. Choosing the right viewpoint helps you tell the story at the depth that you want it—scholarly, friendly, personal, intimate. The deeper the viewpoint, the closer the reader is to the action and emotions.

Frequently the story you have to tell in a memoir is a recollection; it doesn't have a full-blown plot; it is more like literary fiction, the kind that gives you a flashlight view of something. It is still possible to take this viewpoint in deep. Readers respond emotionally to depth of viewpoint because they feel that they are present in the action. If the reader feels so close that he feels like the action is happening right before him, he will usually feel that the story is exciting. We can't help but get aroused when we are close to the action. Details, present tense of verbs, short exciting sentences, feelings, and a little suspense all help you to unfold your story at a greater depth. But it is the knowing—knowing and feeling—that you communicate from inside yourself that truly creates depth and intimacy. To fully communicate with your reader, you must let yourself go, tell the real truth, speak from your passion, find ways to express your emotions and your personal perspective. Don't gloss over things or leave hints; say what you really want to say.

While a number of different viewpoints are possible in fiction, and writers spend considerable effort on learning to distinguish them, two basic viewpoints will be sufficient for most memoirs and everything you are likely to write as a part of this course. The two basic viewpoints for memoir writing are the narrator's viewpoint and the omniscient viewpoint. If you are fictionalizing your story, if you are writing true fiction or narrative non-fiction that reads like a novel, you will probably use one of these two points of view. The omniscient narrator is a hybrid which is especially useful for memoir. I can think of very few uses for it other than memoir.

Figuring out which point of view is best for your story is not difficult; it is more likely a matter of becoming aware of something you would do anyway. The question that distinguishes one viewpoint from another is: Who is telling the story? Other questions derive from that, including: What is it possible for that person to know about the story? What could a person with that viewpoint not know, and will that help or hinder the story? Is the story going to be more interesting told in the first person or the third? How close to the action of the story do I want my reader to feel?

Narrator Viewpoint

A story told from the viewpoint of a narrator is said to be in the narrative, or narrator's viewpoint because it has a person who is a character telling the story. You can usually recognize the narrative viewpoint by the presence of the word "I" in a sentence that is not dialogue. In fiction the author is not actually the narrator; the narrator is a character or persona the author has made up. The narrator may be presented as the author or as a character with a name and dossier. Such fiction reads like very good memoir writing and may serve as a model if you have a story that could be unfolded that way.

One of my favorite authors, who writes very believable and poignant narrative fiction is Adriana Trigiani. [22] Her trilogy: *Big Stone Gap, Big Cherry Hollar* and *Milk Glass Moon* are among the most personally moving novels I have read in a long time.

Andrew Greeley's Blackie Ryan mysteries are written with Monsignor John Blackwood Ryan as the narrator. *The Bishop and the Missing L Train* actually has multiple narrators, as several of the players get to tell their own versions of their story. Bishop Blackie Ryan is a generally invisible person who solves the mystery and takes care of the players; he is, of course, deeply embedded in Greeley's fictional world of the Irish Catholics of Chicago.[23] Although Greeley denies it, it is not hard to see Blackie as an extension of himself.

The line between fiction and fact is often merely a choice of the author's. An interesting autobiography and well written, but sold as fiction is Virginia Holman's *Rescuing Patty Hearst*.[24] I have met Ms. Holman and am assured that this book is definitely autobiographical. Telling it as a story provides certain advantages, however. It is such a strange story that it becomes more believable as fiction. As fiction, it also requires less justification and discussion; the writer is able to focus on a particular narrative line of her story. The narrator, a skilled writer, is able to move into the child's point of view and back to the present very smoothly. She is able to tell a painful but true story in a believable way and let it stand on its own as a story.

Take a trek to the local library or your favorite bookstore. You will find shelves of memoirs and biography ranging from narrow escapes and celebrity tell-alls to historical accounts and contemporary business instruction. Fictionalized memoirs, unfortunately for our purposes, are shelved with the rest of the novels, but a knowledgeable librarian should be able to help you identify a few to read.

Some memoirs or autobiographical accounts are written as stories, unfolding almost like a novel. Usually these are written using a narrator, yourself. As the writer of your own stories, you will generally have been present at the time you are recalling; you would, therefore, naturally be the narrator. Tell your story in the first person. "We heard a noise in the hall, and we hid behind the couch… " If you are writing about something you observed, you would put that in the third person. "Aunt Hattie reached up and got something from the shelf. She carried it to the table. We tried to be totally quiet, but I knew Bertie was going to sneeze from the dust..."

If you want to write so that your reader sees the story unfold, tell it like an eyewitness account. The narrator functions as a character, and must be present for all major events; however, he may tell about things as well as participate in them. Strictly speaking, the story narrator can not tell things at any particular point in the story that he could not have known at that point. If the narrator is not present at an event in the story, the writer will have to have the narrator explain; e.g., "Now, I don't know if this is true or not. It's what old Pete told me..."

If you want to write directly to your audience, use a letter format. This is an example of a student story in narrative viewpoint where the writer holds back some information for a surprise ending. I have shortened this story considerably for our purposes. Mr. Lewis includes some interesting vignettes about the family in the story.

My Most Famous Student

by Jimmy E. Lewis

On a beautiful spring day in 1968 the school year was fast coming to a close and I was looking forward to the summer break from the everyday activities of the classroom. As I was finishing my second period Algebra I class, the school secretary called me on the intercom speaker and said the school principal wanted me to come to his office when I had a break. I said to myself, "What have I done now?"

...[My principal, Mr. Lytle] said, "Mr. Lewis I received a phone call earlier today from a prominent citizen of our community and he has asked me to recommend someone from our staff to tutor his son in Algebra this summer...

As I drove up a very narrow mountain road for this interview, I met a car coming down the mountain. I pulled off in a wide place on the road to allow the car to pass. When the driver pulled up beside me I recognized him from having seen him on television. He rolled down his car window and told me he had just delivered the family their evening meal and suggested that I turn around and not bother them. I explained that I had an appointment. He was satisfied with that explanation, and I traveled on up the mountain...

At first glance, their home appeared to be a very modest, rustic looking house composed of wooden logs and clapboard. It had a porch with a magnificent view of the mountains. There were three white baskets filled with pink geraniums hanging from the front porch. Much to my surprise, this modest looking home opened up once inside and was much larger than it appeared from the outside...

Their son, my future student, was introduced and... plans were made and agreed to as to when and where I was to tutor their son.

My first session was a time of getting to know about my student and what he knew about the subject of algebra. Mr. Lytle... had said he would be looking for a friend, as well as a teacher. So, I let the boy talk freely about himself, his family, and his private school experience...

For ten weeks, I visited my student's mountain side home twice weekly.... When he wanted to talk about something other than algebra, I listened but kept coming back to algebra, the reason he was being tutored...

The last session was test time. I opened a sealed envelope and administered the test sent from his school. While he was taking the test in his father's study, his parents gave me a guided tour of their home...

Every year around Christmas time, I am reminded of my "famous" student when I see him on television asking Americans to fill a shoebox full of toys, personal items, and a five dollar bill. My famous algebra student was William Franklin Graham and his father is Billy Graham and his mother is Ruth Graham. Franklin has a bright future as leader of the Christian organization started by his father, as well as the ministry he himself started. I feel honored to have known this family, and I would like to think that in some small way I was able to make a contribution to this extraordinary individual's life.

By the way, the man I passed on my way up the mountain was George Beverly Shay.

There are other narrative threads in this piece which I have omitted. I have shortened it so that it not only shows you the narrator's viewpoint but shows you how one particular thread of narrative runs through the story raising questions and answering them.

Using narrative viewpoint strictly, the narrator character can not tell things he would not have known until the point in the story where the narrator would learn these things. While this rule works particularly well for unfolding a story as it happened, it can present some problems for the writer, especially the writer of memoir. If you were a child when the events took place, if you were out of the loop, if you want to tell the whole story in retrospect, strict narrator point of view can be limiting. If the story is complicated by different involvements, the solution might be to use another person, perhaps an adult who would have known more about what happened, as the narrator. Or that person can be the viewpoint character if you tell it in the omniscient viewpoint.

If a story has been passed down to you, think about who told it to you; you may be able to put it into their mouth, tell it in that voice. If a story isn't working from one person's point of view, you might try writing it as another person saw it. Then you decide which one is more interesting. Or, if you are very adventurous, you can try using both and cut the two stories together, going back and forth between viewpoints.

In writing a memoir, you can not effectively withhold too much information because the reader knows you already know the outcome. You are alive, aren't you? The reader knows you know, and the story may seem contrived if you withhold anything obvious. If you want to withhold some bit of information to create a "twist" ending, staying strictly in narrative viewpoint may work well. Assuming you are the narrator, it will be easier if the twist is something you did not see coming at the time. Get as close to the action as you can. Try using the present tense for your verbs. Add a little dialogue, just snippets of conversation. Have it seem that the story is unfolding right in front of your reader's senses.

The narrator is supposed to be a player, and too much explanation from the narrator distracts from the story. If your narrator spends too much time discussing the story background or meaning, it can get boring, especially in a long narrative. If there are a lot of "off camera" events in your story—events you, or your narrator, were not present for, consider using the omniscient viewpoint or the omniscient narrator. Some stories just get too complicated when you try to unfold them in close up as they happened. Explanation from various perspectives may be needed to have it make sense. It's all about balance and interest.

Omniscient Viewpoint

Pretend you are God, or at least Wonder Woman. You fly over the landscape and see everything. You can look into the secret places where reasons are kept and find out why people do things. You can tell what people are thinking. And you can do this for everybody in the story, as much or as little as you choose. This is the omniscient viewpoint.

A fictionalized account using the omniscient viewpoint will almost always be written in the third person. Third person means the characters will be referred to by name or as he, she, it, they, etc., in case you have forgotten. If you, the writer, include an opinion, you can usually state it as if it were true; don't use the "I" word. In a recollection, you may have wished to distinguish opinion from fact, but in a story the facts are as they are presented, true or not, for the sake of the story. Talking about meaning slows the story down.

In telling the stories of your life, you are likely to be the narrator, the one who tells the story; however, there may be times when you find it useful to tell a story with more information than you would have had as the narrator at the time it happened. It is also possible that you want to include more than a narrator would have access to now. If you want to look into several people's heads and tell us what they are thinking, you are using the omniscient point of view. Put the story in the third person. If you are comfortable with the storyteller's voice, you will likely use the omniscient viewpoint more often.

Writing the Stories of Your Life

Omniscient Viewpoint and its several variations can be very useful if you are writing in an essay format, if you are telling about something that happened to somebody else, or if you just don't want to write in the first person (I, me, we, us). It's also useful if there is a lot of explaining to do that doesn't seem to fit the narrator's character. However the need for a lot of explaining in a story may also mean that some action scenes need to be written to bring the reader closer to the material.

Warm up

Set your timer for 3-5 minutes and keep writing for the whole time. Just add words or repeat if you can't think of anything. See how many words you can get down in a short time.

Use this sentence stem: One day, when I was a child…

Writing exercise

After your warm up, turn to a fresh page in your notebook and go right into this writing exercise. As always, do this exercise in your class notebook; you may want to come back to it. Work on this exercise for about fifteen or twenty minutes. The idea is to do quick rough drafts that give you a sense of each viewpoint.

- Look back on your life and pick any incident from your childhood. Use whatever pops to mind first.
- Write a brief account of the incident telling it from where you sit now (omniscient narrator).
- Rewrite the incident from the child's point of view.
- What differences do you see or feel in the different tellings of the story? Circle or highlight words that are different in the two stories. Do they contribute in any way to your getting something different from the story?

Omniscient Narrator

A variation of these viewpoints is the omniscient narrator where the story narrator is given the power of the omniscient viewpoint. This works particularly well for memoir since you, the narrator, do know everything now, whether you knew it then or not. You definitely know everything that needs to be known to tell this story. This viewpoint is inherently retrospective. Since we all have "20-20 hindsight" we tend to end up knowing the explanation and the missing pieces of the past. Often we learn things from others after an event of significance. The omniscient narrator is a hybrid viewpoint created for just such a story. The story is told in the first person as you remember it, and you get to tuck in thoughts or feelings belonging to different people, or background explanations and reasons, when you need to.

Let's say you are the narrator. You must write in the third person about other people; you write yourself in the first person. Most people automatically do this; but you must also avoid using the second person (you and yours). If you want to write directly to your audience, use a letter format. In an omniscient viewpoint you can't talk to someone outside the story; you have to stay inside the framework of the story. You can say, "Johnny was thinking it would be a good idea..." You can put in a character's feelings or motivation and the audience will believe that it is true and know that it is as you recall it. You have good reason to know because you are telling the story.

The omniscient narrator viewpoint is a good way to tell family stories of the "I remember when..." sort. You are combining story with recollection, past with present. Balancing essays with vignettes, ideas with action, thoughts with story makes for good memoir writing.

A sensible approach for many memoirs is to write your book as a recollection, firmly grounded in the present. From the here and now you dip into the past in different ways depending on the nature of the particular scene you are including. If there is something you couldn't have known at the time, you have several options. You may want to tell how you learned about it–only do this if the matter is an important one. You can put the words you need into someone else's mouth. You can explain in the present with snippets of story from the past. You may occasionally have to explain how you know something, or you may simply assert that it is true. You have plenty of room for stories, vignettes, essays, and whatever you want to write. A good way to do this is to pick an organizing principle such as we discuss in other chapters and work from that. An organizing idea or metaphor gives you a place to stand, something to come back to.

First person narration will be more interesting if you let your reader see who you are and how you feel about the story. Despite the difficulties, the omniscient narrator's viewpoint is a very good viewpoint to use to tell your own stories. Every viewpoint has its advantages and problems. In first person narration it's important to think about what the reader needs to know to understand the story. Since you are remembering the story, and already inside your own head, you may fail to notice or mention things you are used to looking at that the reader needs to know. The exercise below will help.

If you are not sure of the viewpoint in a story you read, ask: who is telling the story? Depending on who is telling the story or (having the story told through him or her), certain information is made accessible or not accessible. Only information which would reasonably be available to the viewpoint character can be included in the story. If the viewpoint seems to jump around, it is probably a variation on the omniscient viewpoint. It might be better to put the story solidly into the omniscient viewpoint.

Writing the Stories of Your Life

Most people will naturally write using the omniscient viewpoint even if they put the story in the first person. It really isn't terribly important what viewpoint you use as long as you are consistent about it and the story works when told that way. If you are trying to do a limited viewpoint, keep checking to see if that fact would be known by that person at that time in the story. Otherwise, just go for it! Use the omniscient first person viewpoint variation. Readers don't care about viewpoint as much as English teachers do; readers will make room for your current knowledge and listen to the tale however you tell it if you make it fresh and interesting and accessible for them.

Whatever viewpoint you use, keep it consistent. If you pair two viewpoints; e.g. hero and heroine, be sure that you shift only at logical points of change. Make sure your reader knows you changed viewpoint characters.

Exercises: Viewpoint

- To find out what viewpoint you naturally use, write a brief story from your life. Start wherever the story starts and tell whatever there is to tell. If you can't think of anything better, write down something that happened the last time you got together with a friend. Apply what you know to determine what viewpoint you are using.

- Is your viewpoint consistent? If you shift around a lot, use what you have learned to select one viewpoint and rewrite the piece using that approach.

- Did you feel restricted at any point by this viewpoint? Would this story be better written from a different viewpoint? Rewrite the story from a different viewpoint. You can usually tell in a few pages whether it will work better that way or not.

Narrator viewpoint

- Think of a story you are planning to write.

- Write a description of the setting of your story. Write a paragraph or two about who you were at the time the story happened. Don't add these pages directly into the story. Alternatively, you can do both of these preparation steps in list format. Put them aside.

- Write your story with those ideas fresh in your mind.

Omniscient narrator viewpoint

- Think of a story you are planning to write.

- Write a description of the setting of your story. Write a paragraph or two about who you were at the time the story happened. Don't add these pages directly into the story. Alternatively, you can do both of these preparation steps in list format. Put them aside.

- Begin your story in the present. Write your story with those ideas fresh in your mind.

    Because you are looking back on the story, your viewpoint is not the same now as it was when it happened. Did this cause any problems for you? How could you solve them?

You can find additional information about viewpoint in almost any good general text about writing fiction.[25]

Multiple Points of View and Group Projects

Are there several important players in your story? Perhaps there were some events you were not present for or could not be present for. Consider using multiple narrators, each telling his or her own story. Sometimes there are multiple versions of a single story in existence. Different people in the family are known to have different takes on the facts, or experienced the event in different ways. When John gets through telling his story, Mabel always says, "Now, how it was for me..." That's a story with two different viewpoints told by two narrators. You can take the materials from each narrator and cut them together. Make sure you use a heading or an introduction that clues the reader as to the change of viewpoint or who is speaking.

Off camera stuff: If there are a lot "off camera" events, events you weren't present for, consider having multiple narrators, each telling his or her own story. This is a difficult fiction technique—if you do all the writing. However, for a memoir project with several people involved, it may be the natural place to go.

A word to the wise: When collaborating on memoirs, get clear who has what responsibilities and set a timeframe for completion. There is more material on putting together a group project or a project with several sources of material in the chapter on editing called "Spit 'n Polish."

Voice

Voice is simply who you are, talking.

Voice is another of those mysterious constructions devised by writing teachers and literary critics to confuse students. In the last section, I alluded to the concept of voice several times, so I figure I may just have to say something about it. Voice is simply who you are, talking. It's the whole constellation of things you would say or wouldn't say, words you would use or not use, the sounds of your part of the world, your Weltanschauung, your worldview. It's your personal viewpoint on everything, that leaks through the cracks into your work. It's called voice, because it is the voiceprint of who you are. It's who you sound like—your voice.

Your "voice" is the sound and feel of who you are. It really isn't necessary distinguish your own voice when writing your own stories because it will show up on its own. It's always there, the way you think and handle language. The more you write, the more consistently it will appear.

The reason that you need to think about voice at all is because your story will be thousands of times better if you let yourself show up as the storyteller. If you write impersonally, as you were taught to do in business or school, the magic of memoir writing will be missing. This is your one opportunity in life to say whatever you please.

The magic of your personal story lies in the feelings. Sharing emotion brings intimacy with it. If you show up to write, and really show up, let yourself say whatever comes through, you will take risks—risks to your privacy, risks of being misunderstood, risks around ideas or interests that you have. Other people have the opportunity to get to know you—perhaps for the first time. Who are those other people? Your loved ones, your family, people who know you and like you. They probably know who you are better than you know yourself already. They may or may not know certain facts—but be assured they know you. You may be surprised to find that they always knew something or other and are relieved to know you know, or glad to finally have a chance to discuss it with you. You can never be intimate with other people unless you take the risk of showing who your are.

The underlying voice that repeats from one story to the next is your natural style.
—Orson Scott Card

Voice and person

I write, I coach students and clients on their writing. I sometimes write out the talks that I give, but not often. I teach from topic notes; I speak directly to my students, often responding to their work or questions. I decided to write this book in the first (I) and second person (you), the way I talk when I coach. The pace and rhythm is more like talking, but not quite as informal as a conversation. I am careful to avoid some slang words I might use when speaking, but I put in others. I find myself occasionally explaining a phrase that I wouldn't explain when speaking because I would know right then how it landed when I said it, whereas I can't know for sure that everyone will get it from the written version.

Parts of this book are written in a rather directive way, do this, do that. I am explaining facts or concepts, telling you what to do, and encouraging you. I give you a non-technical explanation that is relevant to the type of writing we are discussing. I use contractions and informal speech patterns, but if you analyze it, you will find that the voice is a bit more formal than spoken language. To be sure that you know what I am referring to, I put in references and other details that I probably wouldn't actually utter if I were talking. All in all, however, this book is written in an informal, teaching voice.

I think this voice is closer to the storyteller voice that you will use in most of your life stories than the voice that is present in most books about writing.

Be yourself, tell the story.

Find your voice—was it ever lost? Your voice will appear if you let it. Be sure to include yourself—your passion, your energy, your beliefs and foibles- in your story. Let your reader feel your feelings and know your thoughts; tell your reader your "take" on things. Use your favorite metaphors and similes. Let yourself go; say whatever you like. Have a glass of wine today; put your feet up, get in touch with your childhood, dance to your favorite music. Do whatever it takes to loosen your tongue a bit. Be opinionated. Talk like yourself. That's your voice; that's what makes your stories yours.

You will probably write at least some of your stories in the first person. You should let the flavor of your own speech and ideas creep into your work, and bloom and spill over in glorious color! You may have a specific audience in mind; in which case, you may write directly to them as I am writing to you. If you present your stories as letters, you may find that you use a variety of persons (first, second and third). Offhand, I would say avoid second person in stories, but consider using it in narrative such as letters. If you use second person in narrative, make sure that the person who is "you" is clearly defined; e.g., your grandchildren, and the writing is directed to them. Name names, make it personal, or stay away from second person.

You may actually have several voices; they are the different ways you are with different people. I've written this book in my teaching voice. I started to say I don't use that voice much in my personal life—unfortunately, I do! It's my natural voice for me. But I have a different sound in my novels, other aspects of my work life and with my family. For a thorough discussion of voice and character, study Orson Scott Card's *Characters and Viewpoint*.[26]

One final reminder: In allowing yourself to write freely, remember that you always have the power to tear it up. You don't have to show anyone your work. My request is that you do the writing first and then decide whether you take that risk. I urge you to try it. Pick someone you have a safe relationship with and show them some of your writing. See how they react. Don't ask for criticism; just share.

Storyteller voice

Stories that begin with "Once upon a time..." clue us in to the timeless voice of the teaching tale. Oral storytellers find a certain rhythm; they repeat words and they use simple sentences or clauses that build to a climax. These things make a story easier to remember, to tell, and to understand from hearing. Each storyteller has a particular voice. This exercise is intended to help you to connect with that tradition.

Wander through the garden of ideas and find your inner storyteller. Be as corny as you can. Write a fairy tale or a jack tale or any sort of story you like.

Use at least ten minutes for this exercise or write until you have at least five sentences. Keep writing; don't spend a lot of time thinking or correcting. Just write, echoing the words from the sentence before in the next sentence.

- Set your clock or timer for ten or fifteen minutes. Write a new story from the old one.

- The rules are: You must repeat several words, at least three words, from the sentence before in the second sentence. And again in the third, and so on until the bell rings. Let the story take you wherever it will; it doesn't have to make sense. Just free float with it. Repeat a few words, turn them around, play with the words.

Do this exercise periodically for your warm up, maybe every day this week, or once a week to loosen you up. Do it without thinking, let the words flow. Your will find your storytelling voice.

Assignments

1. Study some stories you have already written. What viewpoint have you used? Would the story be stronger if told from another viewpoint?

2. List and look through a number of published stories and categorize the viewpoint. Notice any differences in closeness to the action depending on the viewpoint. Do you feel differently about the story if it is told by a first person narrator?

3. Pick a story, preferably one of your own, and rewrite it using a different viewpoint. How is the story different when told from a different viewpoint?

4. Write a short narrative from another person's viewpoint. Write as though you were inside their head looking out. Make sure you include their feelings as well as what they see, hear, smell, etc.

5. Make a list of words that describe feelings. Look them up in a dictionary.

6. Reread the stories you have written in connection with this chapter. Could you express yourself more fully? Pick a particular story. How do you really feel about the incident you have written about? Find some words for your feelings and add them to the story.

Chapter 8

UNFORGETTABLE CHARACTERS

In this chapter we are going to talk about people—not gossip, but talk—about writing so that the people in your life come alive on the page, your reader feels like she knows the person, and you've managed to get across the real heart of your story.

People like to read about people, they like to look at people, they even prefer to dream about people. Advertisers know that more people will pause longer for the picture of a person than for any other picture or graphic they could use to catch attention. People look at pictures of disasters, wrecks, and other news events longer if people are present in the picture.

Psychologists have found that babies prefer human shapes as early as four months of age. They also appear to remember people they haven't seen in a while. We shared a house with a friend and her daughter at the time our twins were born. They were three months old when Gerri remarried and left on a honeymoon. A few weeks after that she came to see us. Megan practically jumped out of my arms reaching towards her friend as soon as she saw her.

Stories have beginnings, middles, and ends. People must be present in some form throughout, or there is no story. Think of *On the Beach* by Neville Shute[27] The story simply ends where it is left, and you know that the last person has died–a haunting, almost lyrical ending for a story that presents some hard-to-face realities about atomic winter.

Stories are about people. Sometimes the people are disguised as dogs or raccoons or bunny rabbits; especially, but not exclusively, in children's stories. Sometimes they are mechanical devices. The cyborg in *He, She and It* by Marge Piercy[28] is a good example along with the robots R2D2 and C3PO in *Star Wars*[29] Occasionally a personality is assigned to a country or a flag as in a piece called, "I am the country," which has been floating about on the Internet for some time. At the very least, the person of the narrator is present in the story.

Warm up

Think of a person, any person. Write the person's name in your notebook. (If you've forgotten their name but remember the person clearly, just call them "Susan" or "John.") Write for five minutes as fast as you can. Write everything you can remember about that person.

People in Stories

Now that we are writing, I refer to the people you write about as characters. They are, aren't they! I think it makes it clear that I am discussing the person as you have presented them on the written page, not the actual individual. It also makes it clear that I am speaking to you as a writer. Once you have decided to tell a story, including a true story from your life, you move to a different a level of reality. What you are telling separates itself at that moment from the totality of the facts; it is your perspective on what happened.

Writing will draw you close to these people. Many fiction writers come to think of their fictional characters as their people. You may become so close to your characters as you write your stories that you know them as well or better than other people in your life, or people you were closer to in the past.

Every character has a flaw. Usually the writer of a novel will include the character flaw early in the story, but the reader may forget it by the time of the climax. This flaw may be a hidden dark streak or only a lack of experience, ability, some knowledge, or anything else that the protagonist needs to solve the story problem. It can be an inner or an outer motivational issue. This flaw is the character's challenge in life; he has to take steps to overcome it to achieve his goal. Otherwise, no story.

Think about people you have known. Everyone has a flaw or a challenge. Some people have very obvious ones, but everyone has something they have to overcome in life. Some make it, some don't. Sometimes we don't really know what challenges a person. Sometimes it is hard to put it into words. As you think of the people you want to write about, be alert to the things they have had to overcome, have yet to overcome, things that might motivate them or cause conflicts for them, things and people they love, their lifestyles and choices, their careers, and preferences as well as their physical and statistical characteristics.

Writing the Stories of Your Life

Exercise: My friend Susan

This exercise is widely used in writing classes for many reasons. If you are working alone, keep reading; there is a version for you, too. It teaches you to notice details. It shows you all the things there are to notice about people. It loosens you up; I use it in classes because it gives students a chance to work together and find out that everybody else is just as good at it (or not) as they are. I got it from Lawrence Block[30] who made sure that his book got to my husband several years ago in time for him to give it to me for Christmas!

What you do is very simple. Pair up; one person does the exercise, and then you switch and the other does it.

Think of a person you know, but don't see often. Have the person be a real person, someone you know or knew. It can be anyone, any age. You will call the person you are thinking of "Susan" or "John," not their real name (unless it is one of those names).

Person One starts off by saying "My friend Susan…" and adding some detail or fact about the person. Person Two simply says "Thank you." Do this quickly; picking up the beat as the other person finishes speaking so that there are no pauses in your process.

So it goes like this:

"My friend Susan is tall." "Thank you."

"My friend Susan travels a lot." "Thank you."

"My friend Susan just came back from Paris." "Thank you."

"My friend Susan is a civil engineer." "Thank you."

"My friend Susan has dark curly hair." "Thank you."

"My friend Susan has blue eyes." "Thank you."

"My friend Susan has the most amazing computer you've ever seen." "Thank you."

"My friend Susan is married to a therapist." "Thank you."

"My friend Susan has two cats, but her husband has to take care of them a lot of the time." "Thank you."

"My friend Susan loves children's books." "Thank you."

"My friend Susan doesn't have any children, but she has several grandchildren." "Thank you."

Person Two: Pay close attention to whatever the other person says. You want to really listen so that a picture of the person starts to form. Say "thank you" quickly each time they come to the end of a sentence. As the other person talks, a sense of who "Susan" really is may evolve for you. Don't say anything but "thank you." You may nod and smile if you like; you don't have to be stiff or somber, but listen and say "thank you." Don't take notes or doodle. Listen well.

Person One: Describe your person with a long, quick list of facts. If you get stuck, give a juicy detail about the last thing you said. But watch out—don't start telling the story. This is the time to get all the details up to the surface one by one; they don't have to make sense. Just keep surfacing another detail; don't be concerned about whether they're in any order, or logical or consistent—people aren't logical and consistent—just keep giving another fact as fast as you can.

Group Process

- The leader sets the timer for five minutes; and all the pairs start together.

- When the bell rings, Ones and Twos trade, and Ones describe someone they know.

- After everyone has had a chance to do the exercise, individuals can share how it felt and what they got out of listening or describing someone.

- Spend a few minutes writing. Use a page in your story notebook to make notes on the character you have recalled. Write something using the character recalled to mind, for that is what you have done. You have fixed that person clearly in your mind for the moment. You have remembered some details and others are available right behind them.

- If there is time, the group should discuss what they see from the exercise that could make a difference in their writing.

Individual Version

If you are doing this by yourself, use your notebook.

Writing the Stories of Your Life

- Set your timer for at least five minutes, ten is better. Write the sentence stem, My friend Susan... and follow it with a fact about the person.

- Write the stem again and write something else about the person, and so on. Alternatively, you can write the person or character's name at the top of the page and list the thoughts and details, but it will ground you in the feeling of the person to repeat the name each time. Write as fast as you can.

- Don't get distracted to writing paragraphs yet. Write down as many details, facts, and ideas as you can about the person in the time allowed. If you are still moving along well at the end of your time, write some more until you run out of ideas.

Writing exercise

When you finish with "Susan," you should have a long list of details and ideas about one person. Write a story or essay using the character you have recalled to mind, for that is what you have done. You have fixed that person clearly in your mind for the moment. You are "close" to this person's point of view. You can see things their way. It is a good time to write about them. Follow these directions:

- When you have finished your "Susan" list, write a short piece describing the person you described as "My Friend Susan." Take about fifteen minutes and write freely about the person. Write anything that comes to mind. Explore the further reaches of this character's strengths, flaws, challenges, preferences, relationships, etc. Get as many details as you can. Stop in fifteen minutes and go on to the next item.

- When you begin to think of things the person did or said, or events they were involved in, choose one thing. Follow that thread and tell the story of what happened on that occasion. Stop after five minutes.

- Look over what you have written; have you started to tell a story yet? Or are you still describing the person? If not, think of something the person did and write about that. Or, think of something the person said; what were the circumstances that led up to it; what happened? Write as much as you can about this event.

Both types of writing, character description and story, have value. I call them to your attention so that you make a clear distinction between writing about a person and telling a story. Human beings want to know what someone did, not just who they were. Events and action make your writing about people more interesting. Decide how much of each furthers your goal for the piece you are working on.

Repeat this exercise for various characters, real or imagined. It is a good idea to use the exercise each time that you start to write about a person. You can use it effectively before you write about someone, or after you have roughed out a piece to improve it.

For your main characters you will find that the more detailed information you have available, the easier it is to write them. You won't need to use all the detail, but to the extent that you have all that detail available, you can get closer to your people, you can know what they would do or think in a situation and how they sound. You can pick and choose among the details so that your work is fresh and appealing.

On the other hand, if all the characters in a book are fully rounded, it may become overwhelming—like certain novels of Dickens or the classic Russian authors. You do not need a total background dossier on every waitress and cabbie in the story. In fact, in the stories you write from your life, you probably won't know all the background of many of the characters. Even more reason why you will want to pick one or two details that say a lot about the person, their style, and reason for being in the story.

This exercise is extremely important. It is the model for a process that will help you in many ways. It helps you see things you might not think of if you start off "cold" on your story. It not only helps you notice things, it can help you track things. You can easily add to a list in your notebook. Make one for each person who is featured in your stories. Add details from time to time. Check it whenever you start to write about that person.

Before you revise a story or character study, or vignette, repeat the My Friend Susan exercise for each of the main characters. Make lists of their characteristics, clothes, behaviors, flaws, relationships, favorite foods, etc., whatever you know about them. Dig a little deeper; think of things you didn't think of before. Follow the rules for the individual version.

Here's how to do it: Put each character's name at the top of a separate page in your story notebook. First put down the facts and details that are already in your story; then add everything you know about this person. Do this for each character in the story. For the main characters you will have rather long lists, sometimes several pages. For some characters you will have very brief lists. Use your lists to find the one telling detail, the important description or fact about that character that makes him or her real to your reader.

I did this exercise after I wrote the first draft of my story about Howard's Thesis. (See Chapter 4) I found the detail of the pipe and remembered him conducting the concertos, things I had missed in first writing.

Character appeal

Your story will have more appeal to your audience if your characters have a strong appeal to your reader, that is your reader likes or is interested in your characters. Your stories are better when your people seem real. Think of the books you have read that you liked. Did the people seem alive? Could you relate to them? What made them seem alive?

Refer to your own feelings to measure character appeal. Is this person you are writing about "simpatico," emotionally appealing? Is he or she attractive in some way to you? Make notes about how you feel about your main character.

Would you feel comfortable or scared or sexy or strong around that character? Nobody is all bad or all good. Rounding your characters means looking at the dark side as well as the bright. Even if you don't like the person, there probably is something about them that intrigues you and holds your interest. Maybe they are the most villainous individual you have ever known and you want to know why or how they got that way! You want your reader to feel how scared you were around that person.

Maybe this character is a wonderful individual. Your reader needs to see and feel that for himself. Details help you connect the reader and the character. They provide a visual experience and a sensory experience. They give the reader things to relate to from their own life. How well do you know your character? Can you see, feel, hear and smell that character? Can you feel what they are feeling? Your reader will be appalled or entranced with a person based on the description you provide. The reader wants to come away feeling that they know the character well, or at least understand their motivation and actions in the story.

A Writing Challenge

Writing the people to full rounded glory means including some of the particulars of their lives, some details you can touch and savor as you think about the person. In a brief piece about a person, you do not have room to tell the whole story of their life, but you can make them come alive in that instance for your reader with just a few words. To do this, you must first bring them fully into your own mind. Let yourself ruminate and reminisce about this for a few days.

- Write a very short character sketch. Start by making a list; add to it as details come to you. When you actually sit down to write, have that person fully in mind. Pick a detail or two; pick a particular experience that was typical of your relationship with that person. Write that. Hone it; have it be a short, exciting piece of writing.

Writing about Animals

Stories about animals succeed or fail on their interest for another person—your reader. They must not read like: " Oh, Precious was such a wonderful pet. I'll never forget her because I loved her." You may feel that way, but you haven't told us anything about Precious. We don't even know whether she's a dog, a bird or a ferret. The story so far is about you. You have to write about the animal herself, her style and looks, her own personality. to make it appealing to the reader. It will be most appealing if it also shows your relationship with Precious rather than describing it.

Like writing stories about people, writing about animals requires getting in touch with their personalities, which is to say, their motivations and goals as well as their interests and abilities, and their idiosyncrasies.

Start with the facts. Use a page in your notebook to list the details—all you can think of in five or ten minutes. What did Precious like? What would invariably attract her attention? What did she hate, loath or fear? What did she look like? Who did she like? How did she show affection? What was she like when she was tired? What were her favorite foods, smells, toys? Did she love or hate grooming? Was she shy or friendly? Did she fear or love the car or your boat? Along the way you may notice stories poking their heads up. Jot them down in a word or two and keep going. Get all the data you can think of into a list. Put in a picture of Precious.

When you start to write, give us a vignette—a verbal picture of Precious. If you want to say she was beautiful, tell us what she looked like and what her fur felt like. Try to look at things from Precious's point of view. What was her sense of herself and her role in life? The sense of smell is extremely important to animals. Did she find her way around by smelling things? Did she disguise her scent by rolling in the garden mint? If spunk and personality were her forte, give us a quick action that embodies her behavior at the beginning of your story. Then tell a story about something she did.

To find a story, play Remember When as we have in getting in touch with memories of people. Find another person who remembers Precious and sit with them and reminisce for an hour or two. Use a recorder and/or a notebook to jot down ideas. If there isn't someone who remembers her, find a pet lover who will listen to you reminisce for a while.

Successful animal stories often seem to turn on the human-like qualities of pets; for example, Lassie, who rescues her human charges over and over, appears to think. We like to read about St. Bernards who sniff out avalanche victims, working dogs who help the handicapped or round up sheep, and rescue dogs who find and protect children. Stories of bravery and going beyond the call of duty are always popular whether the hero is a dog or a person, male or female.

Other stories are funny; they turn on the differences between the way animals think and evaluate a situation and the values humans apply. Sometimes these are tragic stories. When a dog perceives a danger that a human doesn't see, the results can be dramatic and terrible instead of sweet and pleasing. A lot then depends on the relationship of humans and pets or other animals.

What has Precious done that amazes to you? Or is endearing? Or funny? What she did endeared her to you because it communicated something to you; it reminded you of something important. Perhaps it communicated one of the basic values. Animals take care of business as they see it. Life for them is lived constantly at the level of life and death. Such values actually are the deep values for humans also.

I think that there is a hidden current in this stream. Successful animal stories capture the true intentions and real-world behaviors of those fascinating creatures who share our space on this planet. It is inherently interesting to human beings to learn what animals do. From zoo tales to Pi,[31] we want to know about that world of animals. And we do anthropomorphize them. We make up meanings that are more human than animal. Yet, the simplest intentions–taking care of a child, discharging one's responsibility, bravery in the face of danger, taking care of life's basic needs for shelter and food–lie at the core of truly inspiring stories about human beings. The simple stuff is the deep stuff; and the relationship of human and animal friends is a deep well for stories. Animal stories have us get in touch with our emotions in a basic way.

It isn't all seriousness, however. Animals don't make everything mean something heavy; they just go with the flow, learn what they can and stay present. Living in the present gives one the power to play, to enjoy the sun, to take grooming seriously, to explore, and to know when to find a place to hide. They seem to be happiest when they know where they fit in their group and they don't have to hunt too long for dinner. After such needs are met, their quirky, personal individualities show up. I'm no expert on animals in general, but I've had a number of cats over the years—all different. I've been friends with a few dogs, but never managed to get close to a guinea pig or a fish.

A Brittany Spaniel of my acquaintance sits on your feet facing you if she likes you. It really feels like a personal recognition when she does it; I suppose, because she gets much closer than the normal personal space distance. Many dogs will sit on your feet, but they do it facing out—like they are guarding. Even when you pet a dog, they usually keep some space between you, as do humans when you hug them.

My young daughter had a silky all-black cat who went for walks about the neighborhood with us. There was no turning her back, and no having to carry her home when she balked at an invisible territory line like most cats will. No, she just paraded along the sidewalk, tail high in the air, dancing beside us. In fact, she liked walks so much that once a neighbor pushing a baby carriage sent her older child back to tell us that Erin was going for a walk with them.

The best stories are the ones that have love and humor in them even if your pet never actually saved someone's life or did anything dramatic. Show the animal's personality in the things he or she does. Give your reader details of size and color and likes and dislikes – something distinctive so that particular animal stands out from all the similar ones. Glue in a picture and you have honored your animal friend.

Assignments

Choose assignments that let you experiment with different types of characters. Groups: One way to cover some of the more time consuming assignments is to divide the group up to work on different assignments. Each person or mini-group can work on a particular assignment and share the results with the whole group. On assignment No. 6 everyone could do one story and combine the work into a single chart.

1. Write a story about someone you have known. Do the "My Friend Susan" process before you start to write. Have a clear intention in mind to show this person in a particular light. Pick details that enhance your viewpoint. Show your character in action.

2. Write a story about a pet you have owned or loved. Show the animal's distinctive personality and show how your pet relates to humans. Be sure to use the "My Friend Susan" process to gather details.

3. Pick a story (novel, biography or memoir) you have read. How did the author characterize the main character? Make a list of specific words that characterize the individual. What kind of words does the author use to make you feel like you know the person?

4. Pick one of your stories from a previous chapter. How could you improve the characterization of the person you are writing about? Use the "My Friend Susan" process and any other techniques you have learned in this chapter to help you.

5. Find a story you like and evaluate it for the function and appeal of the characters. Are all the characters fully rounded, or are some of them one-dimensional? How well does this work? What would you do differently? Try rewriting the story so that you make the characters more or less appealing. You can learn from either approach.

6. Find at least six stories of one type or genre. You might use novels written in the first person, autobiographies, adventures, or romances. You might find a collection of stories or interviews. Study the characters in each piece. What techniques does the author use to have you feel that you know these people?

Writing the Stories of Your Life

Use the chart at the end of this section or make one in your story notebook. Remember to make copies before you fill in the chart. List the main characters from each book along with their role or function in the story. Find some words the author uses to describe each character. Use the comments column to evaluate the appeal or effectiveness of the character.

7. As always, add to your list of possible story topics. Visit your list when you are ready for a new idea, write something using one of your ideas.

Character Study Chart

Story Title, author, reference

Character's Name or Role	Character's Part in Story	Descriptive Words about Character	Comments

Chapter 9

JOURNALING
– And Making Stories

If you have kept a journal in years past, you have a great resource for your stories.

Someone always asks about journaling at the beginning of every course I teach in Writing the Stories of Your Life. I include this chapter to answer those questions. Journaling is an excellent exercise for writers, but not a requirement. You may prefer to use a story notebook while you are writing your stories. I have already described my approach to keeping a notebook for the purpose of writing life stories and putting a book together. Old journals, yours or someone else's, are a gold mine. Let's look at journaling and its uses in memoir writing.

Keeping a journal is a good way to find out what's in your psyche, to keep yourself writing, and to prepare for any future writing you may want to do. I recommend it. Don't get too hung up in how to do it; do what works for you. Haphazard or diligent, your journal is a great place to write ideas and notes, to make running notes on projects, try out stories, write bits of description or trap sudden inspirations or ideas. There is no right way to keep a journal.

A journal is as much an intention to record and save as it is a physical form.
—Alexandra Johnson[32]

I journal, yes, but I don't do it daily. Sometimes a lot, sometimes intensely. Sometimes I go for weeks without writing in my journal, but I rarely go for more than a few days without writing something. I also keep notebooks on various subjects and have kept many notebooks that I made when I took courses in self-growth and various academic subjects. Every book or major project gets its own notebook.

Truthfully, the subject matter in my notebooks tends to get jumbled together because I write notes to myself as they happen to occur to me. My brain doesn't stay fixed on one topic steadily; it's always got a couple of tracks going in the background. These things pop out when "reality" is not demanding my attention at the moment. I use a sheet for clearing myself in the middle of a boring meeting. I draw rocks and flowers and faces in the margins. I think of a story idea and write it down. In spite of my intentions of order, there is a great chaotic disorder to my notebooks.

There is a solution: duct tape! Actually I rip out the sheets and tape or staple them into the appropriate notebook—if it matters enough. Glue sticks are useful, too. I set up a separate story notebook for each book that I write or edit. These notebooks stay pretty focused. I include the current draft of the writing, notes and research materials. Usually, I use dividers for chapters or sections. Eventually, a large project grows into a notebook for materials and one for finished chapters.

Yes, you can use your computer. Set up a file to be your warm-up file and another one for your journal. Discard the warm up stuff regularly. A couple suggestions about journaling on the computer:

- Date your entries within the file. Your computer will redate your file every time you save it. You may want to find things by date or just to know when an entry was written.

- Don't edit in your computer journal; leave it like you wrote it when it happened. When you want to work with a story, lift ideas out by copying them.

- Back it up and/or print your journal regularly.

I have kept my journal on my computer. I see some problems with using the computer for my journal. First, I can't scribble and draw in it. Second, the stuff I write in my journal is terrifying in print—not so bad in longhand. Third, I tend not to print out my journal files and file them. When I change computers, which happens every few years, I lose those files. Fourth, I may save them on the backup discs, but I don't have easy access to them. I can't flip through and find something trivial, or just get interested in what was going on at a particular time. If I've fooled around writing this way and that, or writing things over, or later written a note in the margin of a longhand journal, I can see how I resolved something. There is a hardness, a finished edge to print that is just too much for me in a printed journal. It seems too complete, not fluid and changeable (although it is more easily changed). No longer personal, mine, private.

Don't lose heart, however, if you don't have a journal and don't even want to keep one. There is an excellent alternative: the story notebook! Let me review some approaches to journaling first, then we will talk a bit more about the story notebook. If you have worked through this book starting at the front, you are already keeping a story notebook. This would be a good time to expand it.

Approaches to Journaling

Basically a journal is a book of writings or a notebook in which you write things. I had kept one for decades before I discovered that there were any specific systems for doing it; in fact, I think that the elaboration of systems in the later part of the twentieth century is a function of our cultural need to know exactly the right way to do something and exactly what leads to what. There isn't any right way. You will get different results depending on what you do. Try things. Find a way that makes you happy.

There is no right way to keep a journal.

Usually the entries are sequential and dated. They don't have to be daily; they don't have to be consistent. There is no special requirement that makes one notebook a journal and another one not a journal.

"Journal" and "diary" are parallel words from different languages[33] (a common event in English). The core concept of both words is writing something daily to track it, whether it is your life, a trip, or a scientific process.

Your journal can include anything you want it to. People keep diaries listing the things they do each day and call them journals. People keep journals restricted to specific topics. Journals can be used for self-growth, clearing, getting started (e.g., morning pages[35]), or they can contain story starters, thoughts and notes, even pictures. Some people carry a journal around and use it as a running notebook, mixing personal thoughts with career events, taking notes at meetings, and describing a flower and starting a novel all in the same book. Others reserve their journal for private, personal ramblings or poetry. It depends on you. What kind of journal do you want to keep?

What's it all about, Alfie, when you sort it out...[34]

If you go to the Internet and put in "journaling" and "writing," you will find hundreds of websites eager to help you use their approach. There are many journaling systems and workbooks available on the self-help shelves of your local bookstore. I will review a few of them. I will also show you what I do.

There are courses in journaling—as if there were a right way to do it! These are available at many writer's conferences, colleges and universities in the English department and as continuing education—often taught at community colleges and other local venues. Some of these courses are helpful because they teach you a system that you can use for self-growth or self-expression. A workshop or a teacher may be able to guide you to getting more value out of the journal you keep. I suggest you try various approaches and pick whichever appeals to you. Work with it consistently over time. If you take a course and like it, get the books the leader uses.

The real reason for keeping a journal from a teaching point of view is to keep you writing regularly. Journaling keeps you in touch with your Inner Writer; or perhaps more important, it gives your Inner Writer a means for communicating with you. It gives you a way to track what you do. You can see changes in your writing, your issues, and your interests over time.

Journaling for self awareness

At their core, journals are about sharpening consciousness...[36]

If you are interested in journaling for personal growth, there are many approaches. Ira Progoff was probably the first to teach a specific therapeutic system for using a journal. His approach, Intensive Journaling, "a structured method of journal-writing for personal and spiritual growth,"[37] invites the journal writer to work from deep inner layers outward. Many people have found it freeing. Progoff founded an institute to forward his work[38] and wrote several articles and books on the subject.

People must be honest with themselves as they do their journal work. Otherwise, they will only be deceiving themselves and will attain false results. I know that it may not be easy.
—*Ira Progoff* [39]

In one exercise I remember doing, you write whatever is there for you about a situation—let's say you've argued with your spouse. You then take each side of the argument and write back and forth from one point of view and then the other. If the two sides are inside you—competing motivations or different voices—you write from one voice and then the other. Argue with yourself. Sort it out. Find your inner truth. Of course, there is more to it than that, but you get a flavor of the approach. Such a dialectical process has you see your own conflicts and presumably resolve them. This is deep and difficult work. Working with a therapist or teacher is helpful.

Recovery

Based in the Recovery (12 Step) movement, *The Artist's Way* by Julia Cameron is more than a journal; it is a whole set of processes and ideas which includes journaling. A valuable course, it is very difficult to do on your own. In my experience, people, even when working with a leader, tend to start the course several times before they finish it. It will get you in touch with your own creativity, teach you the habits you need, and help you to become more productive. To accomplish it you have to be (or become) comfortable with the Recovery approach and you have to persevere to complete it. Joining a group with a dynamic leader is a good idea if you want to do this one.

Find a teacher you like who will encourage you to become more creative through working in your journal.

Cameron has also produced a book on writing called *The Right to Write; An Introduction to the Writing Life,*[40] which contains a number of useful suggestions on writing and getting through the self talk that keeps you from writing. Many exercises and writing tools are provided.

"Inner child" workshops and workbooks are usually based in the Recovery approach also. There are several of these and they can be valuable, especially if unresolved issues from your childhood keep you from writing or are what you need to write about. *The Inner Child Workbook* [41] by Cathryn L. Taylor is quite good. I would not recommend doing this kind of work alone; it is better done in a group with a qualified leader. You will go deeper and get more out of it if you do it with others.

Women's Authentic Self

I like Sarah Ban Breathnach's *Something More; Excavating Your Authentic Self.*[42] Her related volume *The Illustrated Discovery Journal; Creating a Visual Autobiography* of Your Authentic Self[43] provides a preset format to help you work on your own to get in touch with your true self. It contains guidance for filling in attractively decorated blank pages that encourage you to explore various aspects of yourself and your journey. A nice feature is several bound-in deep pockets for storing pictures and materials while you work on the book.

Breathnach's writing is addressed to women in a general way, not to writers in particular. You may or may not find it is for you. If you like having a plan ahead of you with detailed guidance, you will find that you can follow through and get a lot from the Discovery Journal. Doing this project in a group is going to be more fun, but it isn't essential. You can manage this one on your own. Breathnach also provides many useful, supportive ideas which will help women to discover themselves in her daybook, *Simple Abundance.*[44]

A trip to a bookstore will find several books you can fill in as journals, some of them topical, some mostly blank. You may also find a number of approaches to self discovery. I have listed a few in the bibliography, but there are new ones all the time.

An important principle to take from this section is that your journal or diary is a private thing; a place for your private thoughts and opinions, even your personal trash if you want it to be. It isn't anybody else's business. It doesn't have to be factual, it can be a place for stories. Have it be a place where you work your way to your own inner truth, your personal authenticity. And share it only when you are ready with people you trust. In fact, there is no reason for you to ever share it. When and how is your choice.

A journal is a private world.

Journaling processes for writers and artists

Most writers keep journals of some sort. A journal can be a place for practice, for disciplines or exercises one sets oneself, or for personal clearing. The original idea behind a diary or a journal was probably to have a place for a daily entry in a logbook. One might write a daily note while on a trip for a report to be given later. Lewis and Clark's journals[45] of their 18th century exploratory trip across America are an example of that sort of journal.

Many, if not most, well-known writers have kept journals, The journals of Samuel Pepys, James Boswell, Virginia Wolff, Katherine Mansfield, and other well-known writers give a picture of life as it was for them. Are Robert Fulghum's books[46] journals, are they stories he once told in sermons, or are they books edited from his journals? They are honest, funny and healing to read. I could go on. Go to the library, a bookstore or the web, and you will find many published journals and many books on writing them. I've included as examples a few references to books that I have benefited from.

Sheila Bender is well-known among teachers of writing for her writing exercises and for her approach to journaling.[47] Of all the books I have discussed, Bender provides the journaling process which is most focused toward beginning writers. As she points

I just started a new journal using a big sketchbook with the intention that I can stick anything into it that I want to – pictures, ideas, and notes. I can write from where I am in my life; I can write life experiences, stories, ideas. I wonder what I will do with it?

out, it does not matter what type of book you use or if you use the computer. Whether you write long entries periodically, or short notes frequently, or keep daily lists is your choice. Your book is a journal if you say it is. *A Year in the Life...* provides prompts and exercises which can be very valuable for jogging your Inner Writer into being more creative and letting the writing flow more freely. It is, however, a book of exercises for people who are studying to write fiction, poetry or even non-fiction works, people who would consider themselves "writers." It is not necessarily for memoirists; but it's worth looking at. You may find it useful.

As a student at the Art Academy of Cincinnati, Elin Eysenbach learned to keep a running sketchbook-journal. She uses a big spiral bound sketchbook in which she pastes pictures that inspire her, takes notes, diagrams ideas, makes sketches, and tracks the progress of projects. She does this by writing or pasting the project description in with its due date, collecting resources and pasting them in, doing sketches and preliminary drawings. Along the way she adds photographs of the work in progress at various stages. She puts in random pictures that interest her as well as notes as idea starters. She fills all the pages on both sides as she goes. It is an artist's running notebook, visual as well as verbal.

Many writers are very visual people. I think Elin's approach is so effective that I highly recommend it to you even if you never draw or paint a thing. It may work for you. Pictures have a different effect on your subconscious than words; they prime your Inner Writer and get you going. If a photo or picture appeals to you, stick it in your journal and write about it. In my Creative Writing classes we adapt this idea and do various exercises including collages and writing from pictures. Students also use their notebooks for story starters and draft stories. People come up with different ways to do it. Anything that loosens you up and helps you stay organized at the same time works.

I teach journaling in my creative writing classes because it is the best way I know for ordinary people to get in touch with their creativity through writing. I recommend using drawings, pictures and readings as starters to get you going. Write about pictures, make lists, and so on. Getting in touch with your Inner Writer, letting your muse out of the box, and getting something on paper is essential. No one can help you with your writing until you get something on paper. Do whatever it takes. You can find books with creativity exercises[48] and do them in your journal or story notebook.

Journals for memoirists

If you are a person who is ready to write, you probably could benefit from keeping a journal. You may want to start a it now as you begin to work with your family history or to create a memoir. Start wherever you are and with whichever method appeals to you. Buy a notebook or sketchbook you like and feel comfortable with. Carry it around and use it.

Writing the Stories of Your Life 103

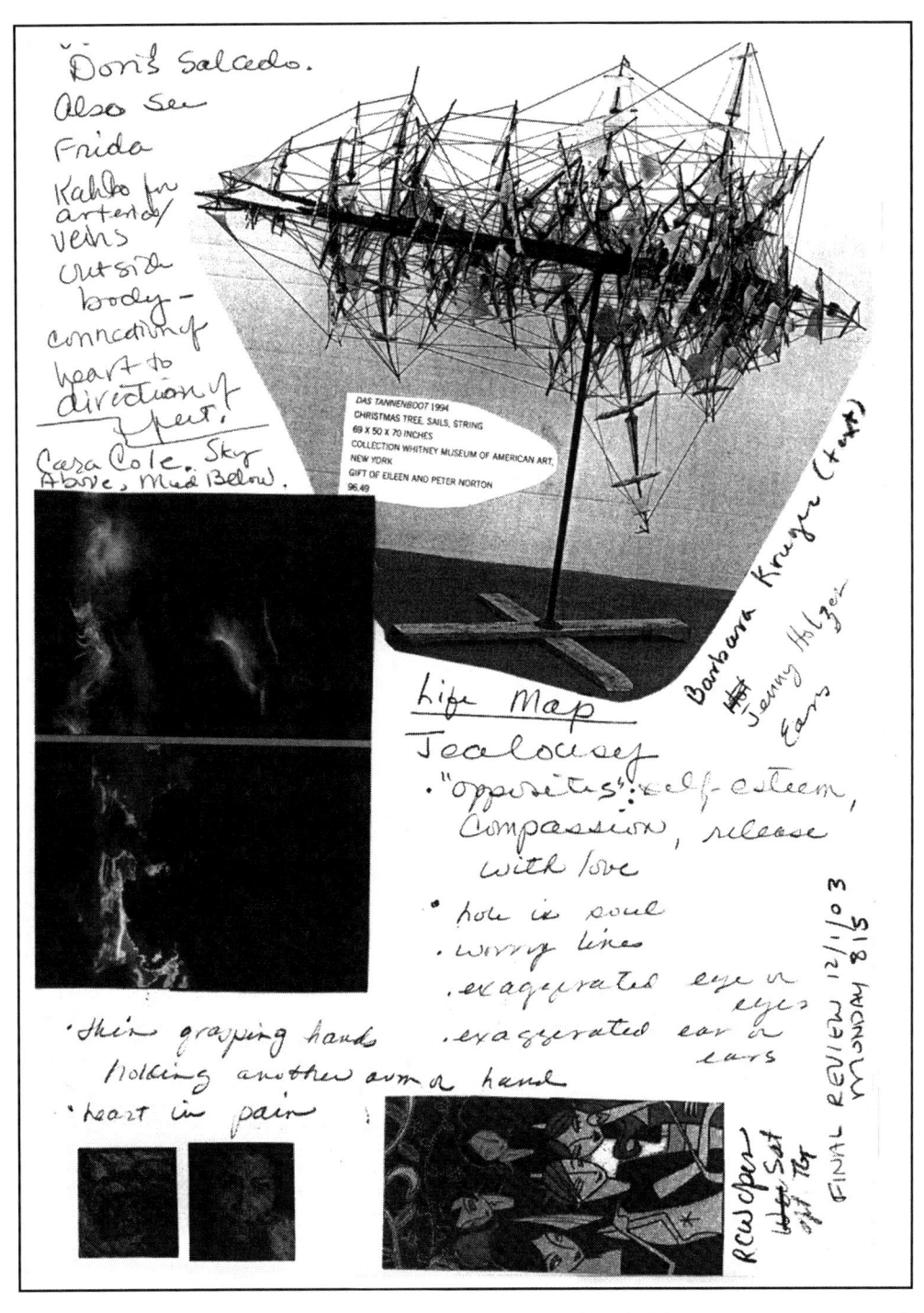

If you have difficulty getting access to your emotional side, you may want to work with one of the systems designed to further self-awareness. Anything you learn will be useful in your writing.

At first it's enough just to record surface facts. Yet the moment they're put on the page, a deeper movement of the mind is set in motion. As any seasoned journal keeper will attest, one quickly learns to trust that a different, more supple kind of intelligence or memory bank is being tapped.[49]

Journals you have already kept are very important for memoirists. However, if you have not kept a journal, do not despair, your story notebook is sufficient for accumulating all the material you will need for your memoir. There are many sources of historical material which can serve in lieu of a journal. Although it is focused on writing from journals, this section may be of interest if you have any old material to work with.

Go to your journal or story notebook to work out story ideas. When you have ideas, your Inner Writer is telling you to write. The logic of it is not the usual linear logic of A leads to B leads to C, but a logic of the creative, intuitive side which gives you vignettes or ideas in some order of its own. Writers often find that these ideas are not as random as they seem, but have a story logic of their own. However, you often don't see it at first. Writing in a journal is one way to capture these bursts of creativity.

If you are stuck in your writing at any time—not just for a minute, but really stuck, go to your journal and write about it. Just write about being stuck or discouraged, or whatever it is that you are up against that is keeping you from completing your writing task. Or assign a space in your story notebook for this purpose. Writing for clearing is somewhat like warm up; you can do it on scratch paper and throw it away if you choose or just leave it there as evidence of your progress and overcoming.

Your Old Gold

If you have kept a journal or any writings from your past, whether they are school papers, letters or notebooks on various subjects, mine them for stories as you work with this book. A seemingly insignificant phrase or a sentence that you wrote years ago may bring to mind the whole picture or the whole story as it unfolded. You will see it in front of you, you will hear the voices. Gradually the names and details will tune in if you let them. An example of a published memoir written from such journals and scrapbooks is Frances Mayes's *Under the Tuscan Sun*,[50] which has since been made into a movie. Reading the book may be valuable for you. It is written largely in the present tense, as if the action were happening right in front of you, as if it were an actual story unfolding—yet the tone is dreamy with memory. If you are a lover of words, lush prose and poetic detail, this is a model for writing your story.

While much of your old journaling may be too private or repetitive to use in your memoir, there will be gems hidden within it which will get you started on your stories. Take an hour, or a day, to look through them. Grab a highlighter and mark memories that might be worth writing up. Rip them out if you are throwing the rest away. If you have boxes of photos, notebooks, or any other such "junk," take time to go through them. Put "sticky note" tags on or near the photos in old albums that remind you of something you want to write about. Use a different color for things you have always wondered about. You can label on the notes to help you find things again.

Sharing Your Story

Your journals can be a wonderful resource for writing your recollections. Sharing yourself is never easy. Psychologists know that people very quickly forget how they were before they changed. Whether they actually manage to confront and change an important belief or a core philosophy, or simply learn a different way to handle a problem, people very quickly forget the old version. Journals are very helpful for bringing home to you how you were in a different time—your attitudes, beliefs, interests and tastes. Some of these may embarrass you now. You don't have to show them to anybody, but confronting them yourself may be instructive.

Refer to the chapter on writing letters for the basic formula for sharing yourself. Use the material in your journal to construct a fair statement of how you were at that time. Use an excerpt or two if you have a good one. You don't have to use quotes, but you can if you want to say "this is what I wrote in my journal at the time…" Tell what happened; tell what changed you. Tell how you see the situation now and how you feel about it. If you like, you can write about what you would do differently, what you think would make the world a better place, or add any opinions you have. Don't harangue your reader on the same subject over and over, but say what you have to say. It's your memoir.

The selection which follows is an article I wrote using an experience I had recorded in my journal. It's about writing, but it's also about life.

Telling the Truth About Our Lives

> *Our authenticity is found hidden in the small details of our daily round—home, family, work, pleasures …big moments of happiness are just the punctuation marks of our personal sagas. The narrative is written every day in the small, the simple, and the common.*[51]

> *Transformation may be, as Sarah Ban Breathnach tells us, "a slow process," but all that painstaking process of uncovering and piecing together the bits of our past and the substance of ourselves leads inexorably to the moment when everything comes together and we see our path with clarity. Settled on that high point with its breathtaking view we can see past and future, we see the truth of our hidden inner self, and we know where to go from here. Writing from inside one's own life is one of the ways of uncovering that genuine nugget of clarity. Like archaeology, writing is occasionally thrilling; and plodding--maybe even tedious--work at other times. Most of us struggle with the conditions of writing more than the writing itself. We struggle not against wind and weather, but for space and time to work, the patience, persistence and confidence to do it.*

It takes discipline and determination, and a willingness to share ourselves that is often beyond what we are consciously willing to give. Of course! The ego (or executive function, sometimes called "the dummy)-- our self as we know it " is doing its job, shielding us from digging around for a new understanding, protecting us by preserving the status quo. It sends up all kinds of questions and concerns and ideas of other things we need to do to keep us from looking deeper into ourselves, finding our inconsistencies, scratching old wounds, rubbing a magic lamp of memory.

When we have, for however short a time, put aside our concerns about what people will think, how we will look, what will happen, etc., and written what there is to say about something in our lives, we will be rewarded with a moment of clarity. It may come as a feeling of satisfaction, a thought, "Yes, that's it!" or a mental view of the scene or the road ahead. It may be small or large. It is important to stop to savor that moment, smell the roses, if you will.

Sense the satisfaction. Feel pride in uncovering something new and fresh, still sensitive, or old and beautifully polished, something of yourself. You can decide later who gets to read it. This you have written for yourself. Savor the joy of doing it and the satisfaction of having accomplished it. And then, we move on.

The moving finger writes, and having written moves on
-Omar Khayyam

Have you ever climbed a hill or a mountain, just to enjoy the view? Recently, my husband and I drove to Cone Park on the Blue Ridge Parkway in search of exercise and respite from our lives. This was to be an easy hike, so we took the carriage path from the stable. We love the view of the meadow and the mountain from the family cemetery, so we set out for that spot. Once there, the meadow called us; but more than the meadow, the lure of the mountain beyond captured us. We set out again on the path across the meadow. It's not a hard climb, but it was a very hot afternoon and my recent walking had been limited to brief strolls around the block we live on—a very level location. I found even that easy walk challenging, and he started urging me on, putting his hand at my back to help at the steep places.

Soon we were in the woods again, climbing the mountain. I wanted to stop, and we did, to look back at the meadow and the ridges of mountains behind it. From there we must have climbed for another mile slowly, stopping often. The tree-lined carriage road rises steadily through a series of switchbacks, running between ancient trees and huge rocks to a place where we sat on a wall overlooking the valley far below. There the mountain falls away with a breathtakingly steep drop. There is a view of a lake with a manor house (probably a resort) mirrored in it. Gentle mountains surround that small valley and lope off into the blue distance beyond.

I had no interest right then in continuing up that trail. I wanted to stay there, and we did for a while, resting and drinking some water. Soon, however, the idea of reaching the tower at the peak of the mountain became more powerful than the need to rest and return. "It's just a few more turns," he said. "There's a great view from the tower."

That clearing at the top was not just around the bend, and there are only a few places on that mountain with vistas. It's a couple of miles from the cemetery to the top. Along the way there are huge old trees, wild flowers, the beautiful leaves of galax, Virginia creeper, and running cedar; interesting fungi, trees that have grown in strange and wild shapes from being bent early by storms or other fallen trees now long gone from the scene. A mysterious but friendly place. Several times along the walk I wanted to quit, but I also wanted to keep going. The lure of the view from the top called us on.

When we eventually reached the tower after a much longer climb than we expected, we hung around in the clearing awhile before taking the stairs. Only the fact that there was no view at all from the small clearing had me hit those open stairs and climb up several flights to the top landing of the fire tower! From the narrow platform at the top of the quivering tower we gazed over the mountain to the meadow and the manor house and lake we had seen on the way. We could also see the Cone mansion and other park buildings. We could see mountains for 365°! We saw fields; here and there farm houses, a small town and a water tower.

We peered down on the gleaming backs of birds as they cruised to a perch in the sunlight on the trees directly below us. We watched a pair of hawks soar, and gazed at thunderstorms coming across the mountains right at our level—until it occurred to us that sitting on that open platform at the top of the world might not be the best place to be in a lightning storm. The walk back was easier, of course, though damp. We made it back to the stable just as the sun sank. We drove home, had dinner on the way. A good walk, a lovely day.

Writing is like hiking; it's a process. There are many times when the best you can do is to put one foot in front of the other and keep going. There are times when you don't want to go on, and plenty of times when what you have accomplished seems small and insignificant compared to what you think others have done. On our hike we were passed by many other walkers, even by a couple of guys walking up and jogging back down. Yet for the hour we spent at the top of the tower, there was no one in sight. Our joy in being there was all that mattered.

But what made it really worth it? If we are climbing a mountain, and stop for the view, the lure of an even better view has us get back on the road. The road is where the breakthrough lies. Though there is clarity where there is a view, it is the clarity of having insight into our lives. Getting back on the road and reaching for another view has us put the insight into action. Just as it takes many steps to walk a mile, it takes a lot of putting one word after another to write a story or a book. Don't fret about whether it is the perfect word, just keep doing it and your work will become stronger from the exercise; that is, more interesting and more powerful. Sharing the experience we have had and what we learned provides the breakthrough in writing. The next peak view may be higher or deeper, have greater clarity, greater joy, a new experience.

And we move on. The next view, even if the same scene can be seen is a different view. So with life, when there is a new view, a new perspective; there is a new experience from a different perspective, there is a new truth. My new truth that afternoon was the experience of serenity at the top of that tower. I sat there watching the hawks fly and listening to crows call and small creatures move around. Occasionally, we heard a twig or an acorn drop to the forest floor. We saw clouds come across at the level where we sat. I learned that I could walk a six-mile hike on a hot afternoon and have it be worth it for the incredible peace of the mountain. All my griping on the way up had not helped at all, better I had welcomed the experience.

Writing is like that, it takes something to do it. Sometimes it requires steady effort, sometimes you can stop and enjoy the view. I love the sound of words, the feeling of the sea or the wind in my fingers as I hear and visualize what I type into my computer. My writing is rarely profound or beautiful; mostly it is pragmatic, useful. That is my truth. But the occasional feeling of "Yes, that's it!" is enough.

The difficulty we experience does not lie with the process of writing, but with our concerns about it; our concerns about finding out who we are and sharing our truth. We are often afraid to risk closeness, and writing is an intimate experience. We fear that if we let someone else in, they will know us better than we know ourselves. First we must risk coming to know ourselves without the rose-colored glasses; then we have the opportunity to let others see us as we see ourselves.

When I've got something written the way I want it, I almost always want to share it, but I don't have to. I have to tell my truth for myself. I have to dig into something until I get its kernel, learn the lesson; but what I do with it after that is my choice. Unfortunately, there is no magic in the written word itself, only in the sharing of it. Risking the sharing magnifies the potential for joy. There are so many people feeling the way I feel, waiting to hear it put into words; wanting to know what I have learned or figured out. Not because I know it; it really has nothing to do with me. They are interested in themselves, and they are hungry for the way to understand.

Many times I have put aside my writing, I have thought it was not good enough, or not worth continuing – that it had been useful, but time to go back to other things. Really, I was afraid, afraid to have others see what I have written. They might criticize; they might not agree, or even reject me. So what? Chances are they won't; and if they do, they may be engaged in a dialogue which gives rise to another interesting learning experience, a different perspective around another turn in the trail. What I have learned is that my book deserves to be finished, to have the insight wrung out of it, the view achieved, and the serenity experienced of walking back down the mountain knowing that the job has been completed, the vision shared.

Writing from your life is a great way to get complete with that story—whatever it is—enjoy the view and be ready to move on. If you do not keep a journal, get a notebook—get one that you like and are willing to carry around with you. Write in it often. Jot down stories from the past as they occur to you. Write notes or stories about things that happen. Sketch out an interesting character. Write notes and thoughts and scenarios; don't worry about doing it any particular way, just write. A journal can be a valuable source of writing ideas and data later on.

Writing from your life means digging into yourself and being willing to tell the truth. The story I just shared does not contain any material that is truly embarrassing, but I was extremely tempted to gloss over the part about my inability to walk very fast in the heat. I want you to think that I'm young and strong and beautiful just like everyone else! I'm not. I don't walk fast; I weigh too much and I never exercise enough. That really doesn't make me very different from most people, but I'm different from our shared ideal of how people ought to be! We think we are different and we hide when sharing ourselves might bring something valuable to others..

Tell yourself the truth and others will tell you their inner secrets.

Social scientists call these ideas that we have about how people are, norms or stereotypes. You might say they are generic or stock characters. Don't write about stereotypes. Write about the real character in front of you, sweaty, bitchy, fat and all. Write about the real person, write about yourself. It is our differences that make us interesting, our weaknesses that make us loveable, and our willingness to tell the truth all the way to the bottom line that makes for good writing. So write what there is to say; write it for yourself.

Tell yourself the truth and others will tell you their inner secrets. Soon you will find that your own secrets are not so awful. Others have faced things that are even more challenging, or that required more courage. Or maybe not. It is not about making comparisons, but learning to appreciate each experience for the gift it brings, and developing the ability to be with and even enjoy the full range of what life has to offer that matters. The more we share ourselves, the less need we have to protect and defend and fight, and the greater our capacity to be compassionate, to enjoy life, and to become wise.

Story Notebook

As a memoir is a special kind of story, a story notebook is a special kind of journal.

If you want to get your life stories written, I believe you will get more from developing a story notebook than from studying the process of journaling, or even from beginning a new journal. While there is a lot to be said for tracking new happenings in your life, a story notebook will help you to write the stories you have already lived through. This approach is intended specifically to help you to get your stories written.

As a memoir is a special kind of story, a story notebook is a special kind of journal. It's a journal focused on your life stories. You will use your notebook to write stories that you have found, to shape them and get them finished. You can add whatever journal writing you do in a sequential fashion to a special section of your story notebook if you want to. Writing about the experience of writing your stories may provide some interesting insights, which you can use or not when it comes time to put it all together.

Keeping a story notebook

A story notebook is a good way to organize your stories. Intended to help you stay on track, it may turn out to be useful in other ways. It gives you one place to keep things. Unless you have boxes full of photo albums and mementos, you can probably put all the materials you need for the stories you are currently working on in a few add-in pockets. I recommend using a looseleaf notebook or one of those large multi-subject spiral-bound notebooks that come with built in pockets. That way your work is portable.

Such a notebook will be a place where you can make lists, do exercises, and write drafts. You will need to do a lot of this to work out your stories. As you complete one story, move the finished version to a looseleaf notebook or the album you are creating. Remove all the junk and load up again. Keep going. Your lists can include one for story ideas. Check off the ones you have finished; cross off the ones you don't want to do; add others. You will have a record to track your progress toward your goal.

Have fun with your notebook. Make it a title page with a drawing or picture. Decorate it if you want to. Be sure you put your name and address in it and keep a pen with it.

The following tips may help you to get organized.

Setting Up Your Notebook

- *If you use a looseleaf notebook, use one that's large enough to hold a lot of pages.*
- *Use dividers for different sections.*
- *Add pockets to keep things in. You can buy paper ones that also function as dividers. Clear sheet protectors also work for this purpose; get the heavy duty ones.*
- *If you don't like looseleaf notebooks, find a multi-subject spiral bound notebook with pockets in it.*
- *You can make tabs out of labels by folding them in the middle and sticking part of the sticky side to each side of a page. Or use self adhesive flags or notes.*
- *If you use a computer, buy three-hole drilled paper to print your materials on. Keep them in a looseleaf binder with dividers.*

Inside your notebook.

- *Have a place for exercises and stories you write in response to assignments.*
- *Have a section for story-related lists.*
- *When you start a list, including the ones suggested in this book, start with a bold heading at the top of the page. Add ideas freely as they come to you over time.*
- *Have a separate section for sequential entries – journaling – on any subject that interests you.*
- *When you start a story give it its own section and gather things related to that story together there.*

Working with Your Story Notebook

- *Date your entries.*
- *Write on one side of the paper so you have room to expand a piece.*
- *Keep lists, sketch ideas out and keep adding to your ideas.*
- *If you use a spiral bound notebook, you can use the pages in it for writing drafts or working things out, then type the final copy.*
- *If you prefer a running notebook, you may find that you want to add to your lists. Leave space. Start all lists on the next blank page, or leave the backs of all pages blank for future expansion.*
- *Try using your notebook for developing your ideas and using the computer for the actual writing.*
- *Use scrap paper for warm ups; don't keep them.*
- *If you get an idea while you are warming up and it's flowing, move it to the notebook or computer and keep going.*

Developing Your Stories

When you start work on a story, put pictures, notes, lists, copies of old newspaper articles, etc. in a pocket—everything for that story in one pocket in your notebook. Use several pages for lists of details, research, and exercises you assign yourself to work out the parts of the story. Since most stories are likely to go through several drafts, a looseleaf may be better at the development stage. You can create a separate section for a particular story.

As you develop your stories and you complete them, transfer your finished writings and the illustrations you want to keep with them to a special notebook or scrapbook for finished work. Discard the debris.

Exercise: Plot Outline

While we are looking over stories you have started and story ideas, try this exercise for fun:

- Pick one of your stories that has an event in it—something that happened, an event that had an outcome. Or make one up quickly.

- Now, Write the whole story into one long sentence. Make your sentence at least twenty-five words long; but more importantly, make sure that every step of the story is included. Take 3-5 minutes to do this. Don't worry about the grammar. It will probably be a run-on sentence. Getting it exactly right isn't important; the idea is to string the core of the story together into a single telling.

- Share your one-sentence stories with your group or your buddy.

You have actually written a brief plot outline. Expand on that core plot to create a new story. Write several of your stories into one sentence, then read the results out loud to yourself or someone else. Pick out one to work with.

Develop your plot outline for that story into a full story. Review your results. What have you learned? Is this a useful technique for you?

Turning Journals into Memoirs

Get out your old journals, type the relevant pieces, correct the spelling and you have a book! Sounds good, but it doesn't quite work that way. When you wrote in your journal years ago, you weren't who you are now. You were writing about something as it happened, not a story that is completed and possibly even forgotten.

If you are the type of writer who has thoughtfully recorded many incidents and experiences with commentary as you went along, the type of writer who has personal balance in the time of crisis, who writes down the facts as well as your feelings; you have a journal that is priceless as a resource. If you also have a naturally gossipy, funny, or chatty style, you may have a diary that is interesting just as it is. Go back to the first line of this section, and my apologies!

You probably did not put in all the background you will need on people and places. You just wrote what happened. You wrote in the present at the time; now you are in another time. What was present is now past, possibly deep past. You may feel differently about it than you did.

You may have written for purposes entirely other than making a track record of your life. If you wrote to clear yourself, you may have written all the junk and none of the good stuff. You may have omitted important facts that you knew but others will need to understand the stories.

Your journals are a gold mine for getting you in touch with yourself and things as they were. Make no mistake about that; but they may be better retained for your eyes only as resources for your stories rather than becoming "the book." It depends on you. Most of us won't find a consistent flow of useable writing in our diaries and journals. A book which may help you work with your journal to produce stories is Alexandra Johnson's *Leaving a Trace: On Keeping a journal; The Art of Transforming a Life into Stories.*[52]

Diaries

One possibility is to present your writing as a diary. (There's a whole subfield of literature in which people referred to as "diarists" are studied.) You would do pretty much what I have suggested above, as Frances Mayes has done in *Under the Tuscan Sun*[53]. Use your journal. Keep your own mind in the space of "Whatever time I am writing about is the present;" in other words, write (or rewrite) from your journal as if the story were happening now. It is right in front of you, fresh. Keep the work in the present tense or near past. Frame your story fore and aft, with recollections or some current time commentary. Fill in missing information in your commentary so that the meaning is clear.

Diaries work especially well as a memoir form if most of the material is in place from the crucial incidents—times that were difficult, harrowing, or especially exciting in some way. *The Diary of Anne Frank*,[54] *The Hiding Place* by Corrie Ten Boom,[55] and the recent film "The Pianist", give us a window on the Nazi occupation of Europe that is all the more harrowing for the telling by an eyewitness.

Another possibility is to present journal entries as letters, and link them in the same way. Or perhaps you have letters from some time periods and journals from others. You could turn it all into letters or all into journal entries to tell your story, but letters often can be presented in context of a journal—as if you had placed them between the pages of your journal at the time. When you publish the manuscript, you will want to use different type fonts or page layouts to indicate the letters and journal entries. This can be a very happy marriage if you have a good collection of materials. You can always write some narrative to explain whatever needs clarification.

If you don't have diary entries from the significant times in the story, it might be better to write the book as recollections than to try to recreate the diary entries. You are a different person now. What you remember will be stated differently, will have a different flavor than it would have had at the time. You have processed the experience and the feelings that were crucial to it. You may remember these feelings, but not with the power they had at the time. You may have been concerned about something that you have entirely forgotten now. That's OK; it shouldn't stop you from writing about the event. Write it as a recollection from the perspective of who you are now. Use excerpts from your journals if there are well-written or otherwise interesting paragraphs, lists, poems, or what have you.

Thought based journals

Perhaps you are a person whose life has been full of inventions, or who has dwelled in some particular realm of knowledge. Your journals or diaries may be interesting for the thoughts and ideas in them, and possibly for the people you have met or known and the studies you have made. One way to prepare journals like these for sharing is to follow a thread of reasoning through the books. Make chapters out of different inventions or stories.

Answer questions like: Where did a particular idea come from? How did it come to you? How did it develop? What was going on in your life? How do you usually get ideas? What have you done with your thinking? Excerpt relevant portions from the journals and string them together with story. Share your feelings and concerns, your joys and sorrows as well as your thoughts. Let your reader see who you are as well as what you have accomplished and how you did it.

Discard endless ramblings, angry tirades, terminal processing. Emphasize stories or appealing essays. If your reason for writing about your life is to share your thoughts in relation to your work, you could very well write a fascinating book based on ideas you have explored in your journals. This is the stuff of who you are.

Many retrospective books are published in the areas of religion and social sciences, not to mention writing and exploration. How a well-honed scientific mind works is of interest to others in the field as well as to people in general. People want to know how you got to where you are now, what you have learned, and how you changed as a result of what you did or thought. You may know of examples in your field, or you may find some in the biography section of your closest bookstore.

If there are illustrations, consider copying them for the final version. Add outcome information to your thoughts. If you think this idea is one someone should research, present your ideas and say so. Your life of thought may make fascinating reading.

Retrospectives and recollections

The most usual way to write a memoir is to start at the beginning and tell about your life. I do not recommend it. I have emphasized writing individual stories or pieces one by one because I believe you will come up with a more exciting result if you start with the most memorable events. This gives you the opportunity to select stories based on a theme, or to tell a particular story that had a defining influence on your life.

Look for ideas or recurring concerns that link your stories. A good way to write a memoir is to write a number of short pieces on important events in your life. Figure out what you want people to know, what your theme is; or just choose an important recurring event–like moving to different houses. Write up the important events and the ones that show how life was for you. You might not, for example, want to write about all the moving days themselves. You could write up one event from each place, or a profile of a particular person you knew at that time in your life.

You can choose an activity or hobby which has heart for you, such as cooking or traveling or gardening, and write stories which grow from those activities. Who you are will emerge from the process.

Using your journals, you may be able to identify certain turning points in your life, times when you made important choices. You may or may not have realized how important those choices were when you made them. Write those stories. Surround each story with some current time commentary. Fill in missing information in your commentary so that the stories make sense. Link them with a thread of meaning. Let yourself as you are now shine through.

An interesting writing strategy is to present an excerpt from your journal and follow it with a comment on the event or the idea from your present perspective.

You don't have to be a celebrity to be interesting, but you may need some help editing your ideas and materials. We will cover the general strategy of editing your work in a later chapter; however, one chapter is not all there is to it. While you have some perspective on your journals from your present viewpoint, they are your writing. It is very difficult to be clear about what is good (or not) and what is useable among your papers or your writings. Sharing the burden with someone else can be clarifying and helpful and the first step towards putting a memoir together. Or you can select some materials and have someone else edit them.

In summary, journals are gold to be mined—your gold. There are many ways to use your journals and writings or those of other people effectively, as many ways as you can be creative. The best approach for most people is to find some organizing principle, write a group of stories, and arrange them logically according to what you want to show. Don't try to do it all at once; have a limited goal. Write six stories on the six places you have lived; get that done and do something else later, for example. Write on what is important to you; don't bother with things you don't care about.

Assignments

1. Find an old journal and write one story from your past. Use the strategy of presenting the journal entry and writing a commentary or current perspective to go with it or as a contrast.

2. Update your project plan and goals in your story notebook.

3. Work in your story notebook regularly. Update your lists.

4. Use your story notebook to draw together materials for stories you plan to write.

5. Write a story as a diary entry or entries; try to get into your mindset at the time. Write the same story as a recollection from your perspective now.

6. Write a story using photographs or other memorabilia as a starting point. Write what you remember; if a story comes to mind, write it.

7. Write an imaginative story or poem based on a passage from your journal.

8. Find a journaling style or method that suits you and begin a journal. Comment on why you chose it and what you learned from this chapter.

9. As always, add to your list of possible story topics. Visit your list when you are ready for a new idea, write something using one of your ideas.

Chapter 10

RESEARCH—Finding the Past

There are many kinds of research. The research you may need to do for writing your stories can be as informal as a chance meeting or as careful and detailed as a science project. It's up to you. You may need background, setting, cultural information about the times, and many other details as well as verification of facts, names with their correct spelling, and dates.

Even if you are writing about things that happened in your own life, you may need to clarify facts and dates to get it all straight. Research is going to be necessary if you are writing about relatives or events from childhood. Memory is notoriously incomplete and biased, especially one's own memory from childhood. Consensual validation—agreement between people—is a time honored way of getting the story straight. Consensus can be erroneous, of course, when everybody thinks one thing and the truth is something else. This makes digging into the past fun, sort of like a treasure hunt or a mystery trip. You always have a chance of finding something unexpected!

A visit is a good idea if you are writing about the older generation, your ancestors or the town your family came from. It could be fun to trace their migrations and travels. There are many ways to get the data you need. I hope to give you a feeling for the process, a mindset to get you going and some possible sources.

The research you probably need to do is the type that journalists, anthropologists and ethnographic researchers do—more naturalistic than what we usually think of today as scientific, which is experimental or controlled research. As a journalistic researcher you look into the different facts and viewpoints surrounding a particular story. You are looking for back story. You want to understand what happened and why. You are always thrilled to come across illustrations and more stories, and people who know or knew the person you are researching.

Ask a lot of questions, mull things over. Don't go crazy if there are unanswered questions. There probably will be. It is likely there will be some stories told from irreconcilably different viewpoints, also. You have the option of reporting all or none of these. It's up to you.

Balance your natural tendencies, stretch yourself a little and do the best you can. You will learn a lot.

Along the way you will learn a lot about yourself, your strengths and liabilities, the type of choices you make, some of the reasons things are as they are. You will get to know yourself at least a little better; I promise you. Enjoy the journey; don't get hung up on the details. Include what seems right. If you don't know or can't find something that seems important, say so and work with what you have. If you are not a detail person, I say to you, have patience with the details. The picture you are looking for may emerge from the specifics. Take your time enjoy the journey.

Writing Strategies

Depending on your writing goals and your writing style there are two main ways that writers work from research: 1) Many writers, especially fiction writers but including feature writers and biographers, first rough in the story, then do research on anything and everything they need to enhance it and rewrite powerfully. 2) Other writers research first, allow the whole story to emerge from the data they collect, organize it and write it. In both cases the final step is to check details against facts.

In actual practice your personal strategy may be a bit of both, but you will lean toward one approach or the other, depending on the type of work you do. I'd argue for the first approach generally, because even in the case of a scientific thesis, you will usually have a general idea of what you want to say before you begin your research. You create some sort of hypothesis and look for information on that idea. Write a draft or make an outline or mind map to find out what want to write about and what you need to know. Later you refine your hypothesis and clarify your questions. You keep working on the idea. However, along the way a whole new story may emerge and that will be the one or one of the ones you want to write.

Resources

In "Finding Stories" we looked through the attic for letters and photos. Now we have a few stories written, but we aren't sure of the details. What to do? Study the letters, the journals, and the photo albums for clues, and make a list of questions. Interview family members with the photos and other material in hand. Often the item itself brings up the memory a hundred times clearer than any description or dry question. And make a list of questions. Take the item with you when you interview older people.

People are likely to be your best resources for this sort of thing, whether they are your family and friends or the librarian at your local library. You may need many different kinds of help to find everything you want to know and to get it together the way you want to. If you have done any genealogy work, you may have learned that it is not the charts but the poking around for information that makes it fun. Libraries, court houses, churches and many kinds of volunteer organizations keep records. Some even have long memories. Other places to go to do research include the census bureau, various military and social organizations, old neighborhoods, small museums. Review the list of story sources you made earlier and the list in Finding Stories. There are many organizations that may be helpful.

Graveyards mark the birth and passing of individuals and families. A lot can be learned from them. A distant relative of mine tells a story of arriving at a cemetery in his mother's home town late in the day, finding the tombstone, and getting that empty "OK, so?" feeling. He and his wife stopped, however, at the office. The woman who kept records was just locking up. She invited them in to their surprise, and looked through her files. These were not computerized files, but old journals carefully filled in over a hundred years. With a tiny bit of information from him, she was able to tell him several interesting things about his family and who to go see in the town. They went as directed to an old café and found the person they were looking for! Sometimes a lot more can be discovered by asking the people who work in the place to help you answer some questions about your family, than by looking in the records!

Libraries have special collections with genealogy or rare books. Not all libraries have the same materials, and you may have to go to a particular one to gain access to what you need to see. They are happy to have you do this, but you have to follow their rules for access. Be prepared with your specific questions and requests. Make friends with your local librarian. Ask for help discovering the collections you need and gaining access to them.

Questions answered may lead to more questions. Hooray! They get you on the track of the really interesting stuff. Go to your library or courthouse or church with your list of questions. On the way to finding those details, you will stumble across whole stories. Talk with the people there. Look in old newspapers, follow the lead of what someone thinks your grandfather did once, whether it was write a book or shoot a bear. The story may still exist in some form in his home town. If you can't go in person, phone the town clerk and ask who to talk to about this. When you ask this sort of questions, you may or may not get answers. Don't get offended by a brush-off; people are busy with daily business. Leave your name and number and question; ask for a time to call again.

Newspapers keep a "morgue" of old issues. Small town newspapers are more likely to be kept in the paper form; major papers such as the New York Times are available on microfilm. Your local librarian can help you with access. Newspaper research is easier if you have a pretty close idea of the time period when something happened that you want to know about. Weddings, births, graduations, and even parties were frequently written up in the newspapers of small towns and cities in the 19th and 20th centuries. Newsworthy events might be followed through several issues. If your research subject belonged to any organizations or held a public office, he or she might show up if you research the activities of that office or organization. Church officials, and business leaders were newsworthy in those days. Artists, teachers, writers, and other local creative types might be listed as giving classes or lectures. Look in the calendars and reviews. Browse in the papers from the right time period. At the very least, you will get some local flavor and color that will be useful in your story.

In a small town there may still be a local gathering place; a pub, a hardware store, a drug store, the post office or general store. Older people remember. Don't think they aren't busy, but some may be interested in talking with you. They may remember things you are interested in. Clubs and meetings can provide introductions to people, too. Be up front about what you want, but not pushy. Some people are very close-mouthed and protective of others; they may be wary of talking to you—a stranger. When they find out whose child you are and how that relates to them, you are family and they are more likely to talk.

You will collect a lot of data. Some of it will be useful; some will demand further research to clarify it; some will raise questions you can't answer. Reading old letters for example, it's hard to tell which bits of information represent the way the world is or was for people in general and which bits are idiosyncratic. Both types of information are valuable. You have to keep looking and eventually decide how to take the information, how to use it. You will build a case for a particular point of view. Sometimes you have to rely on your instincts and your own world view to guide you. Your job is to sort all this information out and combine it into a whole that makes sense to you. Sometimes you do this by showing contrasts if you find different opinions about things. Sometimes it is helpful to say who said exactly what, quote items, to show the viewpoint and its variations rather than trying to combine in a way that homogenizes things.

Practical information on copyrights

You as the author or artist own all of the rights to a work until you sell it. When you sell it, you transfer some or all of these rights to somebody else. The term "rights" generally refers to your prerogative to publish the writing or a copy or an image of it. The buyer can for instance sell a book or a piece of art again, but if it is sold as an intellectual property, it may be covered by copyright or other permissions.

While copyrights can be a very complicated issue and an emotional one, most of what you need to know with regard to everyday usage and memoir writing falls under common sense and common decency. Today with the "new" (1978) law many people are confused. Actually, the problem is less a matter of the law itself, than the rapidly proliferating new means of transferring information and the short half-life of information in today's world. I will consider here some of the pragmatic, not the moral aspects of the issue. You wouldn't steal an apple, but you might not realize that intellectual properties are protected. Think about it; the livelihood of the writer is dependent on many people buying copies of their books and paying for them. Most writers do not make a lot of money from their books; in fact, most published works do not earn their advances, and self-publishers often feel lucky if they get back their expenses. Why do people write books!

Whether you are copying something or concerned about protecting your own rights, it is possible to take an attitude of reasonable and fair use to the matter. Then behave as a mature human being and take care of business. A good question to use as a standard or criterion is: What can I do when I need information to be fair to the writer? And, what would I expect when I publish something? If you take care of other people's rights, it will be easier to understand and protect your own.

Making copies on a copier

When you are copying something for your own use, make sure that you use the copy appropriately. Don't sell it; you don't have the right to sell a copy of something you copied.

Don't make a lot of copies to avoid paying for a book that is readily available. Who do you want to support, the copier companies or the writer? Consider whether it would be cheaper to buy the book. It often is not only cheaper but a lot less trouble, besides giving you a better looking copy.

If the material is out of print and/or difficult to get, copying parts for personal use is common practice though questionable from a legal point of view.

Using information in your writing:

What you have copied must be there for a good reason, and you must never pass someone else's intellectual work off as your own. It is plagiarism to skip along through a document picking up a bit here and there and presenting the train of thought or a long series of quotes with filler between them as your own work. Many students do not understand that. It is very simple: you may not copy the logical train of a work and pass it off as your own work. On the other hand, you might present the same quotations interspersed with your arguments to prove or refute the reasoning and add in your own deductions or interpretations. That is classic academic work. It meets the criteria that you have a reason for the quotations and have added something of your own to the body of knowledge.

You may not copy large portions of a work without permission. It is generally accepted practice that a sentence or paragraph may be quoted in a book or an article as well as in any a research paper or academic document without express permission of the author. You, of course, give a full citation showing who said it and where you copied it from. It is becoming the practice today to request permission to quote for publication any quotation longer than a couple of lines. Such permissions should be forthcoming since they contribute to the marketing potential of the quoted work.

You must label whatever you copied as to the source. This includes websites. In the case of materials found on the Internet, you should give the website address and the date and time you found it as well as the name of the website and author of the material. Check a stylebook for more specific rules before publishing your materials. If you can't find the information you need in a printed source, try the web for updates.

It must be underscored at this point that ideas per se can not be copyrighted. Ideas arise simultaneously in many places. Different writers will do different things with them. Only the actual product is protected by copyright law, not the idea, not the general story line.

Go to www.copyright.gov for more information on copyrights. You will find most general information covered; consult a specialist for specific questions. You will find a bit more on this subject in the chapter on Publishing. If you are not in the United States or are thinking of publishing outside the US, search on "copyright" and the country involved.

> **PRACTICAL SUGGESTIONS FOR RESEARCHERS**
>
> - *If you copy quotations for your own use, always write down where you got them so you can go back for permission to use them.*
> - *Make sure that you quote correctly if you quote something. Do not go by your memory on this. Check it word for word.*
> - *File a photocopy of quotations you plan to use with the proper attribution data on them in your personal files.*
> - *If you use information you found on the Internet, you must give the source with the date that you got it and path if possible. In other words, copy the url and make a note of the date and time and the website name, as well as the title and the author of the article.*
> - *Once something becomes a cliché it is often impossible to determine who said it first. Say where you got it, where you first heard it. Or write something new; don't worry about it.*

Interviewing Skills

Successful writers are people who have learned to interview others well. Different interviewing skills are needed for different types of writing. Journalism students and journalists learn how and when to be confrontational in interviewing. They also learn how to listen for specific key words and phrases and how to get the story the editor wants—which may or may not be the "real" story. Really good feature writers learn to listen to people in a way that makes them feel safe to share themselves.

Successful talk show hosts know how to make a guest squirm. This sort of thing gets a laugh from the audience. Guests endure the treatment for the sake of the publicity; successful guests learn to give as good as they get, and the show can be very funny. This is all performance. A press conference is largely a performance, a staged interview where the celebrity controls access and information, all the while giving the appearance of openness and accessibility. From Roosevelt forward the most successful of our Presidents have known or learned how to control the media. Since the advent of the televised press conference, one way of accomplishing this has been by allowing certain illustrious journalists with known viewpoints to parade their theories as questions. The journalists get points for their expertise, other people take a cue from them, and the President has the opportunity to communicate power and dominance. The more frightening the crisis, the more authoritative the performance.

Quite reasonably, many people have an aversion to being interviewed; and most people lack the skills to do it well. Interviewing need not be a traumatic experience. There are certain listening and questioning skills that will help you get good results in tracking down the family stories.

Listening Skills

Start by paying attention to what people are really saying. Hold your questions. Don't even try to think of a question or comment; just pay close attention to the speaker. To do this you must give up competition. "What? I'm not competing; just talking." Well, if you are thinking of another thing to say, you are in there swinging. Don't worry, we all do it. It's cultural—maybe even a basic human characteristic. Men and women do it in different ways, but we all compete for attention. We like to be right, have the best story, or the biggest problem. If you can give it up enough to truly listen to others, you will automatically become someone that people talk to.

Learn to reproduce the sense of what someone is saying and you will gain their trust. Seek feedback to be sure you are getting the sense of the conversation. Say back to someone, "I think you said…" or "I heard… Is that how it was?"

Exercise: Listening

Pair off in your group and try this. One person in each pair will be the Speaker; the other the Listener. Use about a minute for each Speaker and a minute to process that. The whole exercise can be done in five minutes, or you can do it several times with different kinds of topics. You can pick a topic from your interests or use one of these:

- My first day of school
- Something embarrassing
- A frightening event that happened to me
- What I really want out of life
- If I could live my life over, what I would do differently
- Why I am pleased with my situation
- What I would change about life in the world today

Directions: Speaker should speak about the topic for up to one minute. Listener should listen quietly and carefully to what the Speaker says. Listener will then restate what was said and wait for the Speaker to agree or correct any misimpression. See how well you do.

- If you are the Listener, keep your attention on their story and their ideas. Don't take notes; look at the Speaker. If any ideas come up in your mind, let them go on by; just listen. Be aware of what is being said and of the Speaker's facial expressions and hand gestures. Listen as if you are interested in what they are saying. Listen as if you have to take a test on this later and it's your only chance to get the information. Listen until they finish; don't interrupt. Then see if you can reproduce what has been said. Say something like, "If I understand you correctly, you are saying…" to introduce your feedback.

- The Speaker may add or correct a misimpression. Again the Listener must listen intently and restate the idea. This is important as the dynamic of competition can easily pop up again over what was said. Speaker should note that the Listener is not required to reproduce the exact words, but to have an understanding of the meaning. It is the Speaker's responsibility to convey the meaning.

- When the Speaker listens to the paraphrase and agrees that it carries the sense of what he has said, a complete communication has occurred—one where something has been said and the same thing received.

- Exchange roles and try it the other way.

Listening for stories

A tiny voice-activated recorder is useful in interviewing family. Today you can buy digital ones that don't even have to be transcribed but can be uploaded directly to your computer.

Get together with the person you want to interview. If you know them; ask for a visit. If you don't know them, ask someone to introduce you. Explain what you are doing in a way that will get them interested in helping you with the project. Let them talk with you about their opinions for awhile but steer the conversation towards the stories you want to record. Ask questions. For myself, I find it helpful to write what I remember of the story down and then ask about my notes.

The older people in my life are natural teachers; they want me to understand things the way they see them. When questions are asked that elicit the "Inner Teacher," they thoroughly enjoy explaining. For my own stories, it has been an eye-opener to me to answer my children's questions. I thought they knew all that stuff!

Older people tend to be brighter in the morning hours. Actually, we all are at our best when well-rested, even if we don't think we are morning people. But for people of eighty or ninety whose energy is limited, this may be important. Take them to breakfast, drop by for morning coffee; catch your interview subject before he or she is tired from whatever work he does each day. If that's not possible, be satisfied to visit often and ask a few questions at a time.

If there is a known storyteller in your family, catch him at a family gathering and tape the tales as they fall, or call up and get together. Tell him about the project you are working on. Get him talking about family. These people are usually glad to help you with your project. However, if they are true yarn spinners, they may be reluctant to have their fun stories recorded as the truth (they are not exactly and they may not be willing to say that.) They may not realize that you know that really good stories are based on truth but improved for the sake of story. Ask how he learned to be such a great story teller. Tell him you just love the stories.

It may be useful to approach him for help in telling a story you remember. Tell him the story and ask for help making it into a great story. You'll get a conversation going. This may turn out to be a different but more useful conversation than catching his stories on tape. However, you will have opened a deeper vein of relationship out of it, and you can come back to the stories and storytelling whenever you are ready.

When someone says no, listen to their objections or concerns; don't argue, just accept. Practice your listening skills. Show that you understand, really get all their concerns. Don't give up, but let it go, empathize and ask again. If they have a concern about what you are going to do with the stories, address it. Explain your plan. Thank them for their help. You really need it; let them know you really appreciate it. Don't argue, and don't give up. Just keep listening. Lots of times people say no automatically, then they talk themselves into doing whatever you wanted in the first place. If it has to be their idea, so be it. Just show up at the time they indicate and get started.

"Tell us the story about..." To get someone started, you can suggest ideas from things you remember, ask questions about people, or ask them about their life. Beg a little. "You remember, you used to tell us about the time..." Usually, it works best to start at the periphery with facts or well honed stories and work into the background, which is where the deeper stuff is. Listen and follow up as we did in the listening section.

Experiment with the practice of listening in your life. Share your results with others in your group. Practice, practice, and don't be too surprised if you don't do as well as you think you will. Remember "practice" means doing something in an ongoing way. Practice will lead to improvement in this area. Remember, you have to give up already knowing in order to hear what people are saying to you.

There are various levels of listening that you can practice. Most immediately available are the words and ideas, then any connotations or references that the speaker is making by his word choice or way of expressing the ideas. This is often called the background. Learn to listen for the deeper meanings that people give things. How do they feel about the matter? Is there some hesitation, some sadness, excitement, joy? Listen in an open way to get a sense of their feelings. When they pause you can ask a follow-up question that probes the meaning the speaker is giving it.

Interviewing the People in Your Life for Their Stories and Yours

Astute interviewers follow up on nuances of feeling conveyed by words or gestures. They find their most powerful story material back there behind the facts. Of course, it is important to ask permission to use material that is given and to respect your subject's confidences.

Interviewing family

Can anybody do it? Yes. Yes!

If you are a great listener, you may have no difficulty eliciting stories from almost anybody. You get them going and they love to talk to you. On the other hand, maybe you are not much of a talker or not a person people talk to. Maybe you've read Barbara Walters[56] or studied interviewing in school or learned to interview on the job, but it doesn't work with the people you love most. What is different? Interviewing loved ones is not the same as interviewing other people. It would seem easier because you and the person already have a talking relationship and they already know what you want to know. For some people it is easier.

Sometimes, however, being in a close relationship seems to make interviewing harder. Your family gives you too much information, or they don't tell you things. They think you know what they know. Or, they already know you won't agree with them, so they don't tell you. Sometimes important (missing) facts are assumed in the telling, and feelings are glossed over so that you actually miss them. This is particularly likely if you are younger but old enough for the other person not to realize that you wouldn't have known what they know or you wouldn't remember it the same way.

There are three implicit assumptions family members may make that work against you in finding out the family stories. One is that you already know whatever they know—everyone knows that! The second is that you see it the same way that they do. People generally assume that other people in the family already know whatever there is to know and have the same perspective on it that they do. The third, and most difficult assumption to deal with is that they should not say anything to you (or that you should not write down the stories) out of loyalty to the family—in other words, there is a cover-up. In any case, family members are not likely to be aware of the assumptions they are making. They may not think of their opposition as a "cover up." Certainly, our family doesn't have anything to hide; we just don't talk about Uncle Harry. He did drink a little, but hey, who doesn't? Whatever your family is like, you can learn skills that improve your results.

A Story of my mother

Before my mother died, I asked her to write some reminiscences. She was enthusiastic about the project and wanted to send them to a favorite magazine that carried such items. I went to her house with a tape recorder. She talked and I took notes. I came away frustrated, feeling that she hadn't told me a story, only a recollection. She wasn't at her best; she wasn't going to show up as the interesting, loving person she was. Her story was about something that happened that was important to her, but the completed version lacked any hook for someone else—you had to be there to appreciate it. You had to know what her tall funny older brother was like and what Newark was like in 1919 to appreciate the story. The struggle was lacking; she said nothing about her mother's arthritis and what it was like to be the five-year old child of a crippled woman who lived at the top of a long flight of stairs. Even when I asked about it and she answered, there wasn't much that she had to say about it. For her the situation was normal; it was how it was.

I came to understand it by realizing that it's like a situation that used to come up for me when my children were small. They were very active twins. People would sometimes ask how managing twins was different from taking care of one baby. I had no idea. I don't know what it is like to have one baby because I only had twins. Twins was what was "normal" for me. I could tell you that twenty-month twins wear 4 mittens, 2 hats, 4 shoes, 4 socks, 2 snowsuits, multiple shirts, pants, underwear, etc.–which can easily add up to 30 pieces of clothing they would rather take off than wear–and they can do it faster than you can find the diaper bag!

For my mother, her recollection was like an old photo, well planned but not much in it. The story actually lay in the background. It was bursting to come out, but not visible at all. At the time, I let it go. I didn't even transcribe the tapes we made. I put the notes aside somewhere—I'll find them—and I went on with my life, trying to be more available to her as she might need me, trying hard to visit and find things to talk about with a woman who was usually too tired to say anything.

In the years since her death I have often thought of this, and I didn't know until recently what the problem was: I didn't know how to interview her effectively. As a writer and editor, it's very hard for me to confess this. However, this is the way I see it: If I can learn to do this, you can.

Interviewing effectiveness

If you are getting answers to your questions, but not getting as deep as you would like, ask some questions that result in an expression where the person says something about the kind of person he sees himself as. Follow that question up with, "Tell me a story about a time when you were..." The following example may make this clearer:

> Interviewee: I was very successful in business. Unlucky in love, but successful in business, you know.
>
> Interviewer: ...Why would you say that is?
>
> Interviewee: I'm very lucky. Yes, lucky and smart.
>
> Interviewer: Tell me a story about a time when you were lucky and smart.

Alternate forms of the first sentence are things like: What would have you say that? Is there something about you that would make you say that? Can you remember a time when you were extremely lucky and smart? What was it like?

You can ask for an example in a myriad ways, but the request, "tell me a story" is very specific. People are likely to answer with a story, or at least, more information than otherwise. They may sit and think a while. Learn to be patient and wait. If nothing happens in half a minute, ask what they are thinking. (It's very hard to sit in attentive silence for fifteen seconds; this takes practice. Don't keep looking at your watch. Just sit and be with the person until they say something.)

Besides listening well and deeply, the most important skill in interviewing is learning to follow up in a way that elicits the responses you need. Once people trust you, they want to give you what you want. You must lead them gently, without forcing the issue, into the territory you want to hear about. Besides patience and genuine interest, it takes practice to interview well. Learning to do it enriches your life as well as the lives of those around you.

Interviewing practice

In your group pair off and practice interviewing each other. Use the following scenario: Each person think of an event you have participated in or caused. This should be something that you care about. Perhaps you have done something recently that is important to you, something related to work or volunteer efforts or an organization you belong to. Perhaps you have given a party, held a meeting, or had people over to dinner. It doesn't have to be anything major, but it should involve some efforts on your part that you can talk about. Maybe you make pots or cook well. Think of something that might be in a newspaper or magazine if you were a well-known individual. Or make something up. Write down the event and the organization name on a slip of paper. The organization can be your family, but the exercise is easier if you can think of an event connected with your work or a volunteer or religious organization.

- Pair off. Exchange event information slips. Take one minute to think of some questions to ask.

- One person will interview the other, asking questions about their life, their work and about the event. Allow ten minutes for the interview. Take notes or use a recorder. Stop even if you are not really finished after fifteen minutes.

- Let the interviewers share with the group what they have learned.

- Do the exercise the other way so everyone gets to be interviewer and interviewee.

- Discussion for the whole group:
  - What questions provide the best information?
  - What types of stories could you write using this information?
  - What else do you need to know to write the story you want to write?

- Each person will write an article or story based on the interview they have completed. Take a few minutes for follow-up questions, or exchange contact information to follow up between meetings. Share these stories at the next meeting. What did you learn?

Exercise: Remember the time...

Write what you know of a tale or story or event. Think of questions you need to ask to have the facts straight. Think of who might have been involved or who might remember the story.

Find pictures (or objects). Ask your interviewee to recall events related to the pictures or objects. Don't be surprised if they don't remember at first. Tell them what you know or remember; ask if they think that is correct or what they think about it. Listen patiently while they sort it out. Page through an album of pictures slowly having an easy conversation about this one and that one. When there is a strong reaction to one item, ask them to tell you what they remember. Run your recorder. You may want to leave the album with the person and get back together with them in a reasonably short time to look at it again. You will be surprised how much they will come up with in the interim. It takes time for recollections to surface if they haven't been accessed in a while.

If you don't have any pictures or stories to go on, just ask them to tell you about someone they know or knew. Asking Aunt Lizzie to tell you about your father is more

> **Questions to ask:**
>
> - What was John like?
> - What did Aunt Mary do? What did Uncle Harry do?
> - Do you remember a time when they came to visit or when you went to visit them?
> - How many children did they have? What were their names?
> - Did the children work?
> - Who did you live with?
> - Who lived with them? How many people?
> - What happened?
> - What happened after that?
> - What did you do then?
> - Where were you when all this happened?
> - Tell me a story about…

likely to get her started talking about family than flat out asking her to tell you about herself. Most people just don't know where to start talking about themselves, and if they do, it won't be what you wanted to hear. However as they tell you about their family and friends, they will be telling you bits about themselves. You can follow up with questions about them directed towards what you want to know.

Run your voice recorder and take a few notes. Your notes can serve two purposes: 1) they may help you index your recordings; and 2) they should include questions you want to follow up on when the person gets to the end of the story.

Ask about people, what they were like. Everyone has an opinion. Ask what they did in life if you don't know. Interviewees assume you know things like this. Then ask about that work, and how they felt about it. Ask about who was the oldest, middle, youngest child. Ask about how many children your ancestors had, whether any died, what happened. Ask how they felt about life. Ask any questions you want to. Try to ask questions that lead into something. If you get a yes or no answer, follow up. Sometimes a "no" will lead to a different story if you will let it.

Memoir to Honor Someone

To write about someone else, it is necessary to put together information about the person and appreciation for the person. You may have a lot of material or a little, and you may have strong feelings about the person or the task. You will need all the judiciousness you can muster to present a fair and true picture. Your love will show through that effort. There are many ways to handle this project. You can write the recollection entirely in your own words, add some memorabilia or photos if you have them, package it nicely and you are finished.

You can create a memoir through an individual's writings, which can be letters, published pieces or journals; or through quotations from interviews. It depends on what and how much material you have. Probably you will want to pick and choose among the passages, using the best or most interesting chunks of material. One way to approach this project is to organize what you have; then find and add anything that is missing. Write some narrative to hold it together, and Voila! You have it.

Perhaps you want to present the memoir through an individual's writings by interspersing the person's own work into a running commentary which holds it together. You probably have a sense of what the person's life was like, so you can spot the missing pieces. However, you aren't too sure what to put where. Or, you may have little or no writing from the individual you want to honor, but you have newspaper articles, awards, notes and letters about him. Maybe you have photos and cards, etc. Whatever is going to hold it together, you are going to have to write.

Let's say that the individual had an active civic life or was the local mainstay of the Boy Scouts. Everything else is covered, but you don't have any writings from that part of his life. You will have to research for that information. Sit right down with your sister or best friend and make a list of people who might know something, organizations that might have letters from the individual, organizations who gave him awards or plaques for accomplishments. Approach these people and see what you can find out. You may find stories, letters, or other items. Be open to whatever comes up. Bring a recorder and a camera when you visit so that you are ready to record any kind of data you find.

Let's say you have a lot of material of different kinds. Read it. Organize it according to subjects by putting it into piles. When you have it sorted out, you can put the piles into different folders or boxes. Make a list or an outline–very top line, no detail so that you will know what you have. Label the containers. Take a step back from it mentally; in fact, take a break from the whole thing for a few days.

Sit down some time later and write an outline of what you want to communicate. This is the story you have to tell. Write it however it comes to you—bullet points, bits and pieces, lists are all acceptable "outlines." A mind map provides a non-linear outline. Some people use flow charts or other planning processes at this stage.

Start writing. As you go check your outline against your materials. Or, you may want to pick out pieces to put in your story, line them up, and then start writing. You may want to copy them to avoid spoiling the originals with marks. Anything you just don't have, you can find through research. If you can't find anything on a subject, don't get stuck there, make a note and go on. Either it will turn up later, or it's for the next book.

There are several effective strategies for weaving disjointed original material into a coherent text. The most important first step is to accumulate the material. Read and study it, then ask yourself what theme is present. Would it be possible to organize this material around some core idea or belief the individual seemed to embody? Look for ways that people perceived the person, themes running through activities, belief patterns. You are looking for an organizing principle that clarifies the meaning of this person's life. Whether you find that or not, you may be able to organize the material meaningfully around events or activities. Can you organize it into time periods? Would a series of events organize it? Once the organizing theme is found, material can easily be written to introduce or follow up each writing or example that you include. Often interviews with persons who knew the individual may be useful in placing information in context. These individuals may even be willing to add comments or stories of their own to the project.

There is more about organizing material from multiple sources in the editing chapter.

Assignments

1. Practice listening.
2. Put your research skill to work to amplify or improve any story you have already written.
3. Write what you know of a family tale or story or event. Ask the storyteller in your family to help you turn it into a good story.
4. Write what you know of a tale or story or event. Look for what is missing, what you want to know that's not in the story. Interview family members to find out what happened from their point of view. Work it into a better story.
5. Think of a list of questions you want to ask a particular person. This may include some things you know or think you know and some you aren't sure of or have no idea about. Interview them and ask your questions.
6. Write a story or article from an interview you have done, either with your group or on your own.
7. As always, add to your list of possible story topics. Visit your list when you are ready for a new idea, write something using one of your ideas.
8. Keep adding stories to your project.

Chapter 11

STORY STRUCTURE

Writing memoir, whether it is biography or remembrance, story or appreciation, is writing about people, what they are like, what they did, who they are. Most such pieces will not be stories with a plot in the way that a traditional novel or short story is. There are suitable structures for every type of story. A well structured story has a goal and gets the reader there. It rumbles along like a train on the tracks; and when you get to the end, you are satisfied. You feel that you know what happened, why and how.

The purpose of this chapter is to give you a basic introduction to story structure. The type of structure you use depends on the story you have to tell. Structure is how you present your story, what is related to what, what holds it together and makes it work. We are going to start with some basic information and simple structures and work towards some more complex approaches.

First we will take a look at fiction and non-fiction in relation to memoir; and we will briefly consider various story structures. Then we will take another look at the formulas which work well for a memoir.

All stories have certain essential elements. and all stories follow a pattern of raising and resolving questions in the reader's mind. I call this a story ladder. As the reader moves through the story, she forms hypotheses and questions about what happened and why.

In fiction structure is plot. Novelists make a distinction between plot-driven and character-driven plots, meaning that plot or characters are the more important force in the story. Memoir is generally character-driven, even if it is fictional. Fiction and biography have a lot in common. Understanding something about plots will help you to make your own story more compelling. If you have a story that fits the traditional story model; one with a plot, plenty of suspense, action, and a resolution, you will find additional help in fiction workshops or books on writing fiction. Please study the material on story elements and story questions anyway as it should help you to get your scenes off the ground. Even if you aren't sure that your story really has a plot and structure, or that you want to unfold it as a story, review this chapter to learn more about what kinds of story structures work. Having an understanding of the inner workings that move the reader through your writing will help you to make whatever you write interesting.

Truth or Fiction?

Memoirs may be offered as fiction or non-fiction. It depends on the writer's judgment and preference as well as on the amount of factual material available. It also depends on the writer's purpose in sharing the story. If your story lies in the past it may be necessary to invent a good many of the details as records may be quite limited.

Biographical fiction in general is intended to remain true to the underlying nature of the person and the times, but it shows the characters in imaginary situations or adds details that are common to the times in order to bring up the actions and decisions that person had to make. Sometimes writers have a great deal of information about persons and events, but the material is relatively dull and uninspiring without humanizing details and character motivations. If the writer applies fiction techniques in organizing the story and supplies believable but not verifiable details for non-crucial elements of the story, it will be more interesting to read. Truman Capote, a journalist who created a model for telling the true-life story is sometimes credited with launching the "creative non-fiction" genre, which is also called "true fiction"; however, there are many models of this kind of writing from life, including works by Thomas Wolfe. Stories with teaching value or stories of the ancestors may lend themselves to one of these categories or to historical fiction.

Creative non-fiction fills in the gaps or makes a biographical story more accessible by setting scenes instead of just reporting facts. Writers with an investigative or journalistic background will move into this area when they write a story or biography for its impact rather than for the purpose of providing data. Sometimes it is very hard to tell which your story is. You be the judge; call your story whichever category seems most appropriate to you.

Many Stories, Not So Many Structures

All stories have an underlying structure.

Plot is only one type of structure; most popular novels have plots. There are actually only a limited number of plots, only a small number of different basic patterns that any story can take.

Newspaper reports, newscasts, magazine features, profiles, scientific reports, dissertations, and various types of books have different sets of predictable structures.

Writing the Stories of Your Life

The structure is the backbone of the story, what you would have if you boiled it down to a few words and showed how different parts are related to each other. Theoretically one can draw a simple diagram of the structure of a book. And you can if you take it down to it's essence. It isn't as easy as it seems, however, because many book structures are multi-dimensional. Plots are likely to have subplots which wind through the main plot and may or may not get resolved. Non fiction writers are likely to need changing structures from chapter to chapter or to introduce complexities from various lines of reasoning.

The best model for many memoirs is the journey or the quest plot. If you think of your story as the story of a person on a journey or a quest, you can look for the obstacles to be overcome, and the meaning of it all. You can identify the places where original dialogue or comments from the person the story is about will be especially helpful. You can make sure that your reader's questions get answered.

If you are a reader, you probably have more implicit understanding of the structure of your story than you think you do. If you have a sense that this particular story should be written as a recollection or as an interview, you have an underlying sense of its structure. Some of the same exercises we have used in other places will help you to uncover the hidden understanding that you have of your story.

There are two ways to approach story structure. You can start with some elements such as characters and events and build a story, or you can start with a thread of action called a plot. A plot is often likened to an engine that runs from beginning to end carrying the reader with it. If a story has a good strong plot, it is satisfying and we say it "works." If not, it may need some sort of tune up—like an automobile engine.

If you are writing non-fiction, you can start with the person or characters involved and let the story unfold, or you can start with a plan, an interview or a point to be made. All stories have an underlying structure; the structures vary according to purpose and the writer's preferences.

Story Elements

All stories have certain essential elements. A common exercise in writing workshops is to give the students a few elements; for example, a character, a job or vocation, an instrument or an event, and a motivation. Sometimes a magical or symbolic element is included in the basic four or five. The student is supposed to write a story using these elements. The imagination fills in the rest. It is surprising how easy this is to do. Different sets of elements may be used. The elements may be drawn randomly with no attempt to fit them together, and it still works. Students easily come up with interesting stories from arbitrary elements, especially when there is something mysterious or unlikely about the combination of ideas. Think how much more you can do when you know a number of the elements before you start.

There are two ways to approach story structure. You can start with some elements such as characters and events and build a story, or you can start with a thread of action called a plot.

If you are writing non-fiction, you can start with the person or characters involved and let the story unfold, or you can start with a plan, an interview or a point to be made.

All stories have certain essential elements.

There are many elements that may be important in a particular story, but only a few that you must have to get started. To begin a story you must know who it is about, what happened, and something about why, when, where and how. You don't have to know it all; you don't have to have all the answers. This chart shows the essential elements for writing a memoir or true story.

Essential Elements for Writing a True Story

"Must have" story elements	"Nice to have" story elements
A character	Another character
Character's goal (and motivation)	Second character's motivation and goal
Setting	Details of where and when
Obstacle(s) to be overcome or events—what happened	Details of the action
Outcome	How the character achieved the goal Resolution, meaning

You have to have at least one character, and preferably more, to make a story. You, the narrator, can be the one character. Interaction with another character makes a plot possible. A quest or a journey, which can have one strong character as the focal point, will be more interesting if there are other characters and conflict to be overcome.

Characters, Goals and Action

A goal is what the character wants in the real world. It will be something important enough to that character to cause something, or there won't be a story. The character's motivation is more a matter of reasons. What makes that character tick? Why would he do something like that?

It helps to know the goal and the motivation of the main character. If you don't know exactly what it was the character wanted and what made him want that, you may be able to figure it out. Let's say this is an often told family tale. There's a reason the story is retold. If you know what happened and something about the persons involved, you can figure out what motivated them. If that fails, you may be able to do some research to find out more about the characters involved. Sometimes, you just don't know; but what happened is still a good story. Write the story.

Writing the Stories of Your Life

For the story to have a plot, there has to be some action in the middle. It may be that the character is on a quest and has to go through some trials and tribulations. He may have to overcome one or several obstacles to get what he wants. This isn't as difficult to write as it sounds; you've probably told tales a hundred times about days filled with obstacles. You had to overcome something to get your car started, your children to school on time, your groceries bought, bills paid, obligations fulfilled, and your work done. We love to tell about the reasons we almost didn't make it to work on time. For a story to have lasting interest, it's needs to be more important than the daily set of near misses, but it has the same structure. The character intends something; something goes awry, some obstacle gets in the way, something else happens. The character overcomes something and triumphs. Identify the nature of the obstacles to be overcome, what they represent at a deeper level, and how the character overcame them. What did he or she have to give up to overcome these obstacles?

Something important is at stake in a story. The character wants something, wants to do something or achieve something significant; and there is a major obstacle in the way. Otherwise there is no conflict or tension in the story, nothing to be accomplished. Often the real obstacle is the daily grind of duties and expectations; unfortunately, the daily grind makes for boring writing. Find the event where the character took definitive action. What did he risk or loose to go after what he wanted? Leaving home, succeeding on your own, establishing relationships, coming back from defeat, are the stuff of myth, the same things that the heroes of sagas and tales do. We love stories where the human spirit triumphs over obstacles and circumstances. Show the fight in your story through a representative event.

Setting is important. Time and place help to give your story context. They increase the meaningfulness of the story by grounding it in a particular place and time, which may imply certain social meanings as well as provide physical impediments or facilitators to the story. We talked more about this in an earlier chapter. If you have a general idea of the location, you may be able to research the story for more specific details by asking someone or finding other sources.

In writing a true story as a saga, it is almost imperative that you know how the character achieved his goal. You don't have to know everything that happened or who everyone was that was involved, but you will need a pretty good idea of the main obstacles to be overcome and the means of doing that. You have to know something about the action, even if you have to fill in the details.

The action may turn on a specific conversation. Perhaps you don't know the exact exchange of words, but you know who was there and what the result was. That will work, you can fill in likely details. Maybe the action is just going to class every day and working at night, but there is an important result—education. Perhaps within that context, there is a specific event that stands out. Pick an significant story or detail to represent the action. It should be something that made a difference, shows the character's motivation, or brought about a change. Find a story or vignette that illustrates the character's motivation.

If you are writing a story which you remember personally, you may be able to fill in everyday details from habitual patterns. If your mother always walked to work you might put that in. If you often had oatmeal for breakfast but you don't remember what you had on that significant day, say you had oatmeal. Specific details make a story more real. They are not untruths, but likely stories. If it is a story you have heard often and valuable details are lacking, interview the person for more back story information.

As always, if you don't have all this material at your fingertips but you have an idea, start writing. You probably know more than you think you do. You can use the techniques we have learned for finding stories, doing research and interviewing people. You can brainstorm lists on anything from people to plot points. Don't reject any details. Keep them in a story notebook so that you can draw on them as you work.

Story Ladder

Not all stories have plots, but all stories follow a pattern of raising and resolving questions in the reader's mind. As the reader moves through the story, she forms hypotheses and questions about what happened and why. I call this a story ladder, and I visualize a ladder of questions and answers, questions and answers. The reader climbs the ladder.

All stories follow a pattern of raising and resolving questions in the reader's mind.

Your reader opens the book, begins to read, and his or her brain goes to work. The brain's job is to make sense of what the reader is reading. Simple, isn't it? How the brain does this is to wonder about meaning and to form hypotheses. What do the words on the page mean? The reader forms a question. The first one might be: Is this the main character? Followed by: What is this person like? Is this typical behavior? How is this person going to get what he wants? What happens next?

In a particular passage the questions that form will be specific: Is Joe going to get the gold? What was Mary doing there? Who was the stranger? Hypotheses, like, 'The butler is the one who did it"; or "John was the father of the child," form as different strands of information are added to the story. The reader may not even be conscious of these thoughts. They come and go in the short term memory.

The plot is the main thread of action. It forms a path for the story to follow. There may or may not be subplots; subplots take the reader down alternate paths. If a large number of characters are involved, it is likely there is at least one subplot. Every plot or subplot is a path from a motivation to a goal. It runs from desire through various obstacles and crises to the objective.

If you think of your story as a series of questions raised and answered, you will be able to see the questions as a sort of ladder for the reader to climb in pursuit of the characters. The characters follow their own paths, the reader makes up questions and finds the answers. Every story is a mystery for the reader until he gets to the end. Don't make it too difficult. Anticipate the reader's questions and answer some of them, a few at a time, building towards the big answers at the end. Your reader always wants to know what happened and what happened next.

A scene answers one question and raises another until the reader is satisfied. In writing it is important to answer the questions that the reader will form as you go along. If you put in a bit of action that doesn't seem connected to anything, the reader will wonder why it is there. He will be distracted to the structure rather than satisfied with the story. In a well written piece, the structure functions like a smooth, level path. The reader never looks at it, but glides smoothly along it. The structure is invisible, or transparent. The reader's attention is on the story.

Your job is to raise a few questions and answer them—but not all at once. The reader should have the main question at the beginning; this one is not really answered until the end. Along the way many small questions are raised and answered. It's like taking the path to the creek or deciding to walk the Appalachian Trail. Maybe you want to take a trip to Europe or Africa. At first all you know is that's where you want to go. You do a little research and make a plan—what day, what time, whether to fly or take a boat, how to get the beginning point, what to take with you. Then you start out in the right direction. You follow an itinerary or a roadmap. Along the way you encounter various obstacles and events. Maybe you get there in a few hours, or perhaps it takes a lifetime. At each step of the journey, there are questions to be resolved, what road to take at a crossroads, whether to rest or push ahead, what to eat, who to visit. The action is driven by the question, "What will happen next?" The resolution is the result of whether you reach your goal or not and how you feel about it.

Exercise:

You could use a short story or first-person novel, but I suggest you start with a scene from a true fiction or creative non-fiction book by a well-known writer. Use something you haven't read before. The questions will come more easily if you don't know what is coming.

Group version:

- Pair up. One person reads and the other listens. Then reverse roles and do it again.

- First, one person reads and the other writes down questions and hypotheses. The reader will have to read slowly and deliberately. If necessary, pause after a paragraph so your listener can catch up.

- Listener: Jot your ideas down quickly. Don't cross anything out. New ideas will form on top of old ones. Try to catch as many as you can. Don't backtrack; there are no right or wrong questions, only new ideas.

- Do the exercise again with your own writing.

Individually:

- If you possibly can, recruit someone to do this with you. They read out loud, and you write down the questions you hear in your mind. Or use an audio tape of a book.

- Using a story that you like (not your own), go through it attentively. Read with your mind alert to its own process as well as paying attention to the story. You may want to read aloud. Write down the questions and hypotheses that form in your mind.

- Later when you have processed this, you can do the exercise again with your own work or find someone who will do the exercise with you.

Process

- What did you notice? Are there a lot of questions or only a few?

- What type of questions form? Hint: Who? Where? When? What? What happened? Why? How? Are there more of one sort or another?

- What kind of questions form early on? Next? And toward the end of a story? Are they different in any way from each other?

- Do questions give way to hypotheses? Or do they form in about the same proportion through out? Notice where in the story questions give way to hypotheses—if they do.

- Notice when questions are answered. Is a new question formed? What type of questions are formed as others are answered?

- How do the questions form a ladder or path? Do they carry you through the story? Are you satisfied with the answers?

- Do this with several stories from well known or favorite writers. Is the number of questions you have different? What percentage of your questions ever get answered?

- If you haven't already done it, number the paragraphs of the piece you are reading. Now go through the story again and put a number beside each question to show where the question or hypothesis occurred and another to show where the answer occurred.

Writing the Stories of Your Life

> Write yes or no beside an hypothesis to indicate whether it was answered.
>
> Read an entire biography or a novel that you haven't read before. Notice when questions occur to you and when the answers come. You may find that a question recurs down the road and has a different answer as the plot turns. Notice whether and when you pay more attention to details versus overarching issues.
>
> Notice as you read whether some writers seem to raise more questions than others and how they answer the questions. Which pattern seems more interesting to you? Which do you prefer?

Story Formula

In a very early chapter, you used the basic memoir story formula and wrote a simple story to share who you are.

This is actually a more involved version of the story writing formula we have already discussed. Answer the questions on the left, and you have the story part on the right. As you craft your story,

Secret Formula for Writing the Stories of Your Life

Question	Story result
Who was I at the time?	Background or Back Story
What did I want?	Goal, Motivation
Who else was involved? Who were they?	Secondary Characters
What did they want?	Goal, Motivation
What difficulty, obstacle or conflict is present?	Crisis, Objective of Story
What happened first?	Action—Beginning of Story
Where and when did all of this happen?	Setting
What was the result of that?	Transition to the Middle
Who did what about that?	Action—Middle of Story
What did that action cause?	Action—Middle of Story
What else happened?	Action—Middle of Story
What was the outcome?	Climax, Beginning of the End
Who am I as the result of this?	Sequel or Explanation

The answers to who, what, when, where and how questions are the ingredients of all stories. Sometimes we are interested in why, particularly why in its how forms. How come? How did it happen? How much? We want to know how something came about, how it turned out, what was a character's motivation, etc. in order to understand the story.

In stories from life, it is important to consider who, what, when, where, and how, carefully. You may not have all the answers. Sometimes you may want to say why something happened, or at least what you learned from it, and sometimes not. Or, you may need to say that you don't know. That's OK; you may have a perfectly good story without all the answers. A very short piece does not need complete answers to everything in the story. The more information you can remember or fill in for yourself the more story potential you have. Make lists, play around with ideas. Collect these things in your notebook. Get started. You can do research, find pictures, add to it later.

Shaping a Story

Find a story you have written or use the one you just did. Where does the story actually begin? Did something happen that made a difference in the characters' lives? Was anything irreversibly changed? If it didn't, you have a vignette instead of a story. Contrary to raging popular opinion, there is nothing wrong with a vignette. Some very poignant pieces are not really stories. The purpose here is to have you distinguish a story from other narratives. Traditional stories have a plot; that is they move forward along an action line that moves to a climax which may be unexpected, but is inevitable somehow, and which is the point of the story. Other types of stories–vignettes, character pieces, and other narratives–have other types of story ladders.

A general strategy for shaping a story is to present the crisis or story problem in the first paragraph in some dramatic way. Introduce characters; then fill in some of the background. Depending on how long the form is (book length or short piece), action and background may alternate for a while. As the story builds to its climax, the pace picks up: action, action, action. Then comes the climax, the most important happening in a book, the point where the middle turns into ending and the ending begins. Generally, there are only a few pages, or words in a short piece, after the climax, just enough for the writer to wrap up any incomplete subplots and get the characters offstage gracefully.

This will work for a three-hundred word piece or for a book. Even a short recollection written for a retirement dinner "roast" can begin with a tiny vignette of the character in action. Who he is, is encapsulated in that vignette. Then tell a story and finish off with an appreciation for the person.

Third person version

This version of the secret formula is particularly good for a story that turns on the transformation of a person. Use it for any story that depends on a change that happens within a character.

Third Person Story Formula
(for stories about someone's transformation)

Question	Story result
What was this person like?	Necessary Back Story
What did he want? Why?	Goal, Motivation
What happened?	Action
What exactly caused the shift inside the person or in the person's state?	Climactic action
What decision did the person make about himself or life?	Transformation
What is this person like now?	Result

Of course you must have a setting and probably some other characters. There may be a lot of action or a little. Probably there is back story material, how it all started, how you were involved.

Transformation is a pretty big concept, especially if you think in terms of sudden or miraculous change such that a person is completely different. You may argue that a true transformation may not happen in real life. People may change state in some way, such as becoming married or divorced or educated or imprisoned without truly being transformed. My unabridged dictionary discusses both sudden and gradual, incremental change under the entry for transformation. The core idea is that the person or thing that is changed appears to be different and is in some way different in use or behavior. Transformation is not automatically a positive change, although we tend to use it that way. In each and every one of the state changes listed above, a person changes in a way that he or she can not go back from; for example, a person who has raised children can not go back to a person who is not a parent.

If the person did not actually change or we don't know if he did, but his status in life changed, the story is said to be external. It follows much the same path, with more emphasis on "real world" events and less on internal knowledge. This is the path many fiction works take. The truly rich stories, the teaching stories, the ones we can't forget but tell or watch over and over, partake of the hero's path.

The hero or heroine of the story is the person who is transformed. A much more extensive treatment of this idea is central to Joseph Campbell's ideas about the basic myth of the hero. Useful books on that subject are Campbell's *Hero with a Thousand Faces*[57], and Vogler's *The Writer's Journey*.[58] Also see Carol Pearson's books *The Hero*

Within and *Awakening the Heroes Within*[59] for an extensive treatment of a variety of archetypes with somewhat different paths.

Assignments

1. Write a story using one of the formulas above. First answer each of the questions; then work your answers into a story or narrative piece. What did you learn?

2. Write another story using the other version of the secret formula. First answer each of the questions; then work your answers into a story or narrative piece. What did you learn?

3. Read with an eye to understanding the journey of the hero. You will find material on many websites since this has become a popular topic. How will this help you in your writing?

4. Read and watch for the questions and answers that form in your mind.

5. Try writing a story as a series of questions to be answered. Then write the answers. Work it into an interesting story.

6. As always, add to your list of possible story topics. Visit your list when you are ready for a new idea, write something using one of your ideas.

7. Share a story you have written with someone else by reading it aloud or exchanging papers, letters, or emails.

Chapter 12

HOW DO THEY SPEAK?
Dialogue, Dialect

Dialogue that works brings a feeling of freshness into your story. Remembered words are significant words. In a recollection or a memoir these priceless words are your legacy.

A little bit of well placed dialogue can carry your story to a powerful new level and make it feel real to the reader. Dialogue can move the story nicely, enhance characterization immeasurably, and bring realism to your story. Dialogue or speech between people in a story can carry important information on several levels. Many important true stories lead up to a single word or sentence that someone said. What people say is important.

People talk. It's one thing that sets us aside from the rest of creation. We love to talk, and we do a lot of it. But what do we say? We make a lot of sounds, a lot of grunts, groans, shrieks, chortles, laughs, and other noises. We make sounds that we call words and organize these into languages. And here is what makes it special: We think it all means something. We think when we talk that we have communicated meaning to some other person. And, usually, we have.

Fiction writers use a lot of effort trying to capture the sound of their characters' language. Linguists have sneaked around for whole days with hidden tape recorders gathering the sounds of a region. They get a whole lot of *hello, how are you, thank you very much,* and other ritual noises. What have they learned? People talk a lot just to make noise, just to connect; they tell each other about their bowels and their illnesses and their dogs. They scratch and they stretch and they grunt and tell the same jokes over and over. That's not the dialogue to put in your story—unless it happens to be

I recommend that you use dialogue sparingly in memoir writing.

significant. If you write all that stuff down, it's just stuff. Your story will be bo-o-o-oring, and no self respecting adult will want to read it, let alone a teenager! Teenagers, in case you don't know, are certified experts in determining what's boring. Just ask one!

On the other hand, students, who have read in a writing book that dialogue should move the story along and should contain information that the characters have or need, sometimes fill their dialogue with facts until it reads like an overstuffed calzone. Also boring.

The good news is this skill can be learned.

Dialogue is not as difficult as it seems. Having said everything that might discourage you from using dialogue, I'm going to tell you how to write good dialogue, and when to use it. Just like this discussion so far, it's going to seem paradoxical. Here's what you need to do: Focus on the reader; write conversation that sounds natural while carrying information relevant to the story and contributing to the plot or story line. Make all of that seem real. Mama mia! How do I do that?

Dialogue Is Not Ordinary Speech

If you have a natural storytelling style (which may be the result of long years of practice), it will seem that you are just writing down what the people in your story say. If you don't have this (yet), make it your aim. Your goal is to write dialogue that seems to be just exactly what the characters would say. If you study well-written dialogue carefully, however, you find these things:

- Dialogue reads like an excerpt from a conversation, not a conversation.
- Dialogue carries important information, but usually not many facts.
- Dialogue always moves the story along in one way or another.

Dialogue is not filler, and it is not conversation. It's a *written shorthand* that records information shared between the characters in a story. It stands for the conversation it represents, but it isn't the conversation. It should sound like ordinary conversation, but, it is not. Dialogue is a special kind of conversation. It moves your story along; that means it is important, it makes a difference in keeping the story moving and on track to the end. In a memoir you will not have great amounts of dialogue. You probably don't remember exactly what was said in every conversation you ever had—and that would be boring if you did! You can however say what you said, what the other person said, and what it meant to you wherever it is important to the story. It makes it seem more real. It makes you and your other characters seem alive.

One way to approach dialogue is to think of it as an excerpt from a conversation. You will not report every *"hello"* and everything each person says; you will include important agreements, ideas, commands, and memorable words. You will report the words that occur at a crucial point in the story. They may be ordinary sounding, but they are quoted because they make a difference.

Dialogue carries important information. The information conveyed may be contained in the content of the words. If you take notes on a lot of facts and then try to work them into dialogue, it sounds wooden. Except in the classroom, people don't usually convey statistics and data orally to one another nowadays. They might mention one fact that they want to discuss or give directions about. *"It's only forty degrees outside; wear your jacket!"* or *"John said to meet him at ten o'clock."* The rest of either of those statements is probably ritualistic, like, *"OK."* You can leave the part that people will assume out of written dialogue. On the other hand, if the other party to the dialogue pitches a fit about the jacket or can't meet John at ten and you are setting up a scene that makes that communication important, you might include an additional line or two. If the whole thing is unimportant to the story, leave it out.

People tell what happened to a person. They speak their feelings about some important event (or sometimes fail to speak), or they provide a call to action. *"My father invited me into the business"* is an important event. Reporting it a little closer to the story, we have: *"I want you to come into business with me: you've finished college. I'll help you get set up..."* This dialogue is memorable; my father remembered it for about seventy years and mentioned it the other day. This little conversation represents a call to action and a turning point in a young man's life. He also reported how he said no. *"I've studied engineering. I don't want to be an accountant; I want to be an engineer."* And he found a job in Syracuse, many miles from home.

The information carried by the dialogue may be factual. *"The truth about your father is that he was never here,"* Aunt Hattie said. *"Your mother hardly saw him for years."*

It may be structural, as in: *"Let's go!" she said and got into the car. I knew if I didn't hop in I'd miss the most important event of the year.* When I say structural, I mean that the comment signifies a "turn" of the plot, in this case an important event about to happen. If the boy hadn't hopped into that car, where would he have wound up? Those two words are stronger dialogue writing than a long verbal description of where they are going and what is about to happen. Character is present, and purpose, in two words. The writer can cover the rest of story of the event in narrative.

The information may be an exchange between two or more characters that contains an agreement, a plan, or some important transaction. *"I'll be on the ten o'clock train to Bonn."*

Sometimes the exact words a person said are important. They may even be the point of the story. If the exact words are not available, a suggestion of what the main character would likely have said may be used instead of dialogue. *I'm sure Grandpa said "yup"; that's how he talked.*

Sometimes there are no words and the story needs them. In this example, *They shook hands. That's all the agreement they every had,* the words are made present by being absent. The agreement is signified by a handshake and all that such an action means.

I'll never forget that night when my father said to me, "Son, take care of your mother and sister. I'm counting on you." There is a directive in these words which guided a young man's life. More powerful than the content, is the emotional impact of the command. The words themselves may have been spoken only once or they may have been a ritual spoken at every leave taking, but this time they were memorable. What makes them memorable? There is an unspoken commitment in this passing of the baton, something which could set a pattern for a man's life. The reader is ready for the story after that short quote.

For significant turns of the story, pair the character's words with action as in the *"let's go!"* example above. This moves your plot along. It brings the reader closer to the action. Notice that in this example it is the pairing of simple words with decision and action that makes them meaningful. If they weren't paired with a plot turn in this way, they would be meaningless ritual words. The writer could have simply said, *We got in the car and drove to...* Narrative would cover the change of place.

Quotes have more power than narrative, but you don't need them everywhere. They are more powerful when you use a quotation to emphasize a point. *John told me that Susie and Jim were divorcing* is not as powerful as what John actually said, but it is a way to say what needs to be said. *"He's filed for divorce,"* has more power than the same information in narrative. Note that a rather ordinary quotation has more power than a summary. Judge for yourself when you should use a quotation versus narrative depending upon the importance of the comment to the story.

Dialogue helps to move the story, make it more real, and carry information more effectively. Some students worry about whether the person said exactly what they remember them saying. Write it the way you remember it. If you know what a person probably said, use it as dialogue at an important turning point, summarize otherwise. Write words that you can hear your character saying. If have the feeling that's what he said, write it that way. Whose recollection is it anyway? You are writing what you remember. This story is in your voice. The person you remember said what you think they said.

First, listen!

Listen for the sound and feel of character.

Before you try to write dialogue, listen to people talk. Listen for the rhythm and pace of speech. Spoken language is different from our proper written English—the kind you use in essays and business letters. Listen, and write down the things people say to get the flow of their use of language. Listen for favorite words or colloquial phrases.

Listen for the way they form their sentences. Do the verbs tend to wander out to the end? Do they finish their sentences or leave a lot to the imagination?

Notice the amount of ritual material; the words that are almost meaningless. Sentences like: *"Hello; how are you?" "Fine; how are you today?"* etc. express cultural rituals. They serve to structure and give status to our relationships, meeting, parting, setting the tone. In life, one can tell a lot from how a familiar person says "hello." On the page, it's just "hello." The writer has to use something to say what it means. "Hello" can be warm or sad or sarcastic. So if you have to explain a bit of dialogue in a memoir, just use the explanation and avoid the quotation. (This rule of thumb like many others, is meant to be broken occasionally.)

Listen to people. Do they use slang or jargon from a particular field (such as medicine, engineering, or psychology)? Do they favor regional words, or have a peculiar way of pronouncing a favorite word? I remember Pat, a well-liked government official, who always said "pacific" when he meant "specific"; otherwise, there were no quirks to his speech. His grammar was impeccable; his arguments cogent. He was a brilliant administrator.

Listen for the quirks. They make your characters real. A friend named Peggy always said "cabbage on to [something]" meaning to pick up something or to grasp an idea. The phrase also carried the idea that one should hold tightly or keep whatever it was. I think it was a local or family quirk; I've never heard anybody who didn't know her say it. Though it doesn't mean exactly the same thing, the phrase has the same feel as "cotton to" meaning to be attracted to someone or something. "Cotton to" can also mean to like or understand something or to be close to a person. Words such as these carry a special feeling of culture with them. They convey place, time, ethnic heritage, class, and personality. Find them. What they say is what makes your people as special on the page as they are in life.

Listen for specific personal idiosyncrasies. Actually, most people that you write about will not speak in a noticeably unusual way. They will sound normal to you. You will not need to call attention to their pronunciation; but they will have some favorite word or way of saying something that will make them more interesting on the page. If you hear such a phrase, get it down just the way it is said. Other people who know or knew your subject may be helpful. Make notes as you find these treasures.

Don't overuse the quirks. Regional words are wonderful. Put these idiomatic expressions in your story. Write down what Aunt Hattie would have said, not what you would say now. But don't belabor the story by trying to spell it in dialect. A few words or idioms here and there in your story will give a flavor of the life you are chronicling or the person you are quoting better than a lot of exact, but long dialogue.

Don't spell out long passages of dialect; use the flow and style of language and idioms to convey character.

Exercise: Listen for Character

Try listening to one person for a while. Write down what they say from time to time over several days. Is the person's word choice pedantic or snobbish or uneducated? Do they use short choppy sentences or long flowing ones? Do they use particular expressions to convey familiar ideas? You may have heard them all your life, but they are important expressions of character.

You can use a voice recorder. Then write or type out the material so you can examine it. Read it out loud when you are by yourself. See if you can write a sentence that will sound like that person said it.

How much do they talk? What gestures do they use? Is it the pronunciation, the pace and rhythm of the speech, or the word order that is unusual or individual? If you can identify the particular variation, you can reproduce it more easily.

Second, Write for the reader!

Focus on the reader. Dialogue must happen between the characters, but it is written for the reader. It helps the reader to know the people in the story, to feel included, to hear them as well as see them.

Dialogue must carry information necessary to the story. You are actually turning the wheels of the plot engine, moving your story along, when people say things to each other. You are letting the reader know what happened next. Use dialogue when important information can be passed between characters more naturally and more efficiently in their words than yours. Show, don't tell. Unless the person is a professorial type, don't let your character lecture—and maybe not even then!

Stories from life are likely to be stories with more telling than showing; that is, they are told in the storyteller voice about something that happened in the past. If your story is long, bits of dialogue will help to break up narrative passages and make it more interesting. There are natural places in your writing where somebody is likely to say something. If this is a point where something is decided, something changes, some one is changed, or an important life event has happened, this is a turning point in your story or plot. It's also a good place to consider using dialogue.

Write dialogue to communicate with the reader.

Select a story that you think might benefit from the addition of dialogue. Write what your characters say to one another. Write it all down, completely. Who said what to whom in each place that you plan to use it in your story. Write it all out. Use a separate paragraph each time the speaker changes.

Look at the dialogue a sentence or paragraph at a time. Does this piece provide important information? Remember that significant content is not all there is to dialogue. Valuable information about feelings, decisions, etc. may be conveyed along with a character's words.

Writing the Stories of Your Life

Does it move the story along? Eliminate ritual words that don't contribute to moving the action along.

How does it sound? Does it sound like the individuals you are portraying?

Third, Make your story work

You are writing to tell a story. In most cases you yourself were present for the event, so you are telling the story in your own voice. Tell it as it happened and you don't need much dialogue, only those exact quotes on which a story turns.

Tell it like you remember it.

On the first draft, write what you remember including all that the people in your story said. Ignore that little editor's voice that spreads doubt and gloom from its perch in the back of your mind. Or maybe you don't have that particular voice—you are blessed with the skills of a natural storyteller. Craft your dialogue so that the meaning of the story is true.

The first rule in story telling is: Tell it like you remember it.

The second rule in story telling is: Keep the intent; correct the quote if you have to. Accuracy of intent is more important than exactness of words.

The second rule also applies to all the cases where people said something, but you no longer remember exactly what they said. You think you remember what they said; however, when you sit down to write you find that you remember they said something but you are not sure exactly how they put it. Write what you think they said. It's your story.

On the second draft, craft your dialogue so that the story works well technically. Read what you have written aloud. Is it interesting? Leave it alone. Is it boring? If it's boring, eighty percent of the time you should take it out. Twenty percent of the time you sharpen it up. To tell whether dialogue is boring and should come out or be replaced, ask yourself these questions:

Is a particular person making a point or is this general information? Check to see whether you need it at all. If it is general information, put it into the narrative. If it is particular information that person, and possibly only that person, had when the story happened, put the words in his or her mouth.

Is it ritual; that is something said the same way most of the time? Is it also unremarkable? Write, Johnny introduced us to Susanne Smith and Roger Jones; don't write half a page of ritual introductions. Does the story need it? If, however, Susanne started a fight in the middle of the introductions or Roger dashed off without saying anything, you might give space to the event, and you might put in a scrap of dialogue.

Does this quote contain information the listener already knows? "Well, you know, Fred, that we went to the movies..." is a boring bit of dialogue—even if your character really does talk that way. Phrases like, you know, as I said before, as I wrote you, usually indicate facts that the other character already knows. "Fred, while we were at the movies last week, Helen wrecked the car," actually says something. This seems tricky; but the trick is to catch a powerful phrase or two out of the middle of the speech for use as dialogue, and generally report the meaning with a character who talks like this. You could do it like this: "You know, that night we went to the movies," he seemed embarrassed. "Helen wrecked the car."

Does it lead to a dead end? Unless you are trying to show that every conversation you ever had with this person led to a dead end (and I don't know why you would want to do that!) take this kind of dialogue out or write new dialogue that moo-oo-ooves your story along towards its climax or completion.

In most instances, yes answers to the above questions indicate sections of dialogue that are a waste of time and effort. Take them out or shorten them dramatically. If the information needed has not been communicated and needs to be in the story, put the facts the reader needs in narrative form. Use dialogue where it is important who said something, where you want to dwell on a scene, and at a plot turning point.

Occasionally, however, a bit of overstuffed dialogue really should be two bits, and one of them should come sooner in the story. This is particularly true if one or your characters is using the word "had" and in, "Well, you know, Fred, you had heard from us..." If a letter was written to Fred earlier or a phone conversation contained an important bit of information, back up in the story until you find the right spot and write in a line or two with the necessary information. Storytellers make sure that the set up is complete so that when you get towards the end, the dialogue moves the story quickly to the punch line.

Sometimes you need to split up a long stretch of dialogue so that it is interspersed with action. Some writers write the dialogue first; for them the story lies in what people said. If you are one of these writers, reread your dialogue and make sure you have included the physical action and the setting. Probably a long stretch of dialogue is missing some of this information and can be broken up with things that are happening, "He picked up a book." or "She stood up and looked out over the blooming garden, azaleas, roses, irises—all at the same time..." Your reader needs to see and smell as well as to hear what happened.

Is anyone listening?

Notice the ways people communicate without saying anything.

Writers think everyone talks, but some people actually speak infrequently. Here is an example of a character who is a person who doesn't talk much.

Writing the Stories of Your Life

> *Of course, Aunt Bee wouldn't say anything, but she was thinking angry thoughts about Henry's coming. We could tell from the way she snatched the laundry up. She gave it an extra snap before she hung it on the line and slapped it to be sure it was just right.*

Can you hear the sounds of communication in that passage even though the character doesn't speak? When such a person speaks, do people listen differently?

Do all your characters have the same amount to say? How do people listen to someone who talks incessantly versus someone who seldom speaks? I am not suggesting that you fill your story with chatter to develop contrast!

Quick exercise:

Start a list in your notebook of all the actions or signals you see people use instead of words. The list can include actions that occur with words but could stand on their own such as a salute or doffing a cap. Add to this list from time to time.

Improving Your Dialogue

Write a wee bit of dialogue that contains a crucial thought and put it in the right place—and you've got it! Sounds simple, but the following discussion should help to make it easier to do. This discussion will be especially helpful if you have already written a story with some extensive dialogue.

Mark out dialogue that doesn't contribute to the action, show the character's feelings or intentions, or that doesn't provide important information.

Is it clear from the context who is speaking to whom?

This might seem like a silly question, but I have read student stories where the context suggests that two people, say Johnny and Suzi, are talking but the dialogue references Roger and Mary. Make sure your dialogue is in the right place and the names are clear to the reader. If Johnny and Roger are the same person, make sure we know it right up front; better yet, pick one name and use it throughout the story.

Did you start a new paragraph for each speaker? Always start a new paragraph when you change speakers.

Is it clear who said what to whom? It's OK to use the verb "said." I recommend it, in fact.

"Said" is just a tag to go with the name. Once in a while someone will shriek or yell; but most of the time characters just say things. Use "asked" and "replied" with caution. These words trip up the eye and have the reader pay attention to the process instead of the content. A question mark is usually enough to let the reader know a question was asked; occasionally you may need to emphasize the point. The reader's eye goes right over the word "said" and takes in the necessary information without a ripple, which is what you want; so that your reader is paying attention to the story, not to the writing.

Are the speakers' mindsets obvious from their own words or from the context? Do not spend a lot of time thinking up other verbs or adverbs to describe how whatever was said was said. You want your reader to pay attention to the dialogue itself. Pack your dialogue with strong verbs and precise nouns.

Don't try to convey feeling tone by adding adverbs to every "said." That's just noise. The feeling should be present in the words the character says. You want to make it sound like real conversation, however; so don't grab your thesaurus just yet. Instead of *"I'm home." Johnny said, sarcastically,* you can write: *"Surprise! I'm home."* If you also add, *His sarcastic tone made me look up,* you have a reaction from the narrator that further defines the situation.

Context refers to actions going on in the scene. *"Get in!" She wrenched open the car door and I hopped in.* In this version of our little story, the actions are clearly context for the dialogue. There is no need to say who said those words.

How does your dialogue contribute to your story?

Are characters' feelings evident? Dialogue differs from real conversation. You can provide dialogue that uses a sensory word instead of the more typical everyday word and still stay true to your commitment to accuracy. You can have your character say, *"I'm blue."* or *"I'm very sad."* or *"I'm truly happy."* instead of grunting or shrieking as they might have in conversation.

Is your dialogue overstuffed? Take out all the excess baggage we talked about a earlier in this chapter. Leave any dialogue that moves the action along. If it is a place in the story where two characters would naturally be expected to have a conversation, have them say something that makes a difference.

Do you have too much dialogue all together? Spread your dialogue out like bunches of grapes with narrative between them like a vine. Cut it into the action. Remember that dialogue slows down action. Find the natural hand-off points to balance talking with doing to achieve the pace that you want.

Is your dialogue interesting? Do you have all the ingredients of "interesting" present? Does it make a point, show character or feelings? Is there new information in the dialogue, or could you skip it and not miss a thing? If dialogue is essential to the story, it will be interesting.

Does your dialogue contain information that contributes to the story? Does it move the plot along? Does it emphasize a decision point or a turning point in your story? Do your characters give each other important and non-obvious information?

Dialogue, conflict and sound

Great dialogue is more memorable than narrative, oddly enough – since we often think we can't remember exactly what people say. It often conveys the emotional subtext, or the feelings much better than all the telling in the world. It takes the reader right to the heart of the matter; characters can't hide how they feel when they start to talk. Of if they do, that tells the reader something.

Dialogue is extremely appropriate for setting up the conflict and for resolving the conflict in a story. Conflict is a special term used to describe whatever confrontation, issue, question, concern, event, etc, exists between the main characters. Is there a disagreement? Did something happen that caused a rift or a problem between them? Is there a conflict of interest? Whatever happened that caused there to be a story probably had a different effect on each of them. They feel different about it and they have different ideas about how to resolve it. Having them say something at these crucial points will clarify a lot about what is going on and may be the best way to actually resolve your story.

Conflict also occurs to any obstacles between the protagonist and his goal. These can be internal or external. Something has to happen to make a story interesting. If the conflict is largely internal the protagonist must wrestle with it like Jacob with the angel.

One final question: How does it sound? Would that character say something like that? Take out anything that doesn't sound like someone would ever say it, or rewrite it so it works. This gets tricky because dialogue is not actual conversation. You have to know what information, feeling or idea needs to be conveyed from one character to the other, and find a way to do it at the same time that you make it sound like a real person is talking. Small bits are easier to work with at first. Listen in your mind for the way that person talked; write that down.

It's a good idea to read dialogue aloud. Read your whole story to someone and find out how the dialogue works. How does it sound? How do they feel about it? Do they get a sense of the characters from the dialogue?

To said or not to said?

That is the question.

Today dialogue is written without tags as much as possible. You have to tag the first line with the name of the character who is speaking. You don't have to write "Sally said" to do this, but you have to be sure that the reader knows who is speaking. Next the reader needs to know who else is in the conversation. Then you can go back and forth from one to the other without any tags for up to seven "lines"—short pieces of dialogue.

If there are long blocks of dialogue, it is best to tag the transitions. If another speaker is brought in, use tags. Three or four people can be present in a conversation, but the reader can not tell who is talking without tags.

Any place the dialogue might be confusing, put in a "Susan said." You can use "asked" or something else if it's truly necessary; but if the sentence is a question or the concept is obvious, use "said." Said is virtually invisible to the reader; it's like a tracking device that helps you keep your place. The reader only notices it when he needs it.

The only time an adverb or another verb should hit the page instead of "said" is when something actually happens in the middle of the dialogue to change the tone of the dialogue. Then you, the writer, have to tell us how a character reacted that was unexpected and what the effect was on the story.

Different people do sound different. We will talk more about this in the next section. If you are writing from life, you will want to try to capture the flavor of the way a particular person talks, but you can generally limit your use of dialect to a few words in the right places.

Dialect and Foreign Languages

Discussion of dialogue always brings up the question of writing dialect. When I speak of writing dialect, I am referring to the practice popular a few years ago of spelling the words with apostrophes and markings to suggest the speech pattern of the individual. My answer to this question is available in one word: Don't.

Don't write your entire book in dialect. Don't write sentence after sentence spelled in some odd or phonetic way. Even if you are trained to do this, save it for technical pieces. It may have been popular to write dialogue in the nineteenth century, but this is the twenty-first. It is very hard to read dialect visually. It's difficult to read aloud. It distracts the reader from the story to the mechanics of reading; therefore, it slows the story down. Your whole story is likely to be lost in the reader's effort while trying to read it. I have an example in my collection—a lovely book in Appalachian speech. I have no recollection of the story although I clearly remember struggling to prepare to read it aloud.

People who want to write in dialect often delight in the sound of it. They love language and accents. They really want to share the way their parents or neighbors sounded. They love the musical cadence of Appalachian speech or the twang of New England, the sound of the Southwest or the voice of the immigrant from any of the world's many "other" places. For a girl who grew up a "damn Yankee" in North Carolina, there was no pleasure any greater than riding a bus in Pittsburgh or Toronto as a young woman, listening to the flow of languages around me, some of them languages I had never heard and couldn't identify! I love listening to accents and have recorded a lot of speech samples, but I don't write a story in dialect. There are better solutions for writing down the sound of a charming character.

English spoken on the American continent is full of extraordinary words and phrases and sounds brought by the multi-hued speakers of many languages who have made this place their home. The sounds of Gaelic, Spanish, German, Russian, Yiddish, Chinese and Swahili (to name only a few) embellish American English. They give us terms which carry the scent of childhood foods and the nuance of experiences. These are our memories, our rainbow heritage. These memories may be sad or wonderful, but they are human memories. On the written page, they are best conveyed by the use of standard English with a flavor of the special cadence or expressions used by the individual. Put in a favorite word or expression as you would use a rare spice in cooking—with love.

There are also many speakers for whom English is not their first language. And the special flavor they contribute to the American language should not be ignored; for example, novelist Amy Tan, in all of her stories, gives you the feeling of Chinese speech, but she never puts in a Chinese letter. If your parents or grandparents were immigrants, it is likely there are many family stories about things they said or didn't understand and what happened. You can convey the sensibility and insight of that language in your writing and still make it easy for the reader to follow.

Speak in your own voice; spell in standard English.

Ways to suggest dialect

As we have seen, there are many dialects, not just Southern drawls and Black English. If you put in a bit of the flavor of a person's speech, make sure you do it in a way that is appropriate and relevant to the story.

Use standard spelling, with an occasional special word or phrase. Vary the word order if the speaker does. Mention a language habit that actually caused confusion in conversations with the person. There are many family stories that could be told on this premise.

Usually a single mention of an accent or preference, *"She gave it the French pronunciation"* or *"Her French was faultless and she always spoke it with Dad."* gives life to your character. Go ahead and write the material the normal way—no dialogue. No need to spell the French words. If Dad always said "au revoir" have him say "au revoir" once or twice. Don't extend the ritual aspect of the conversation just to get to that word, however. You can also say that he always said that.

If you learned Polish from your grandmother at the same time that your parents taught you English with a definite Brooklyn sound, say so. If you spoke one language at home and another at school, it has to have made a difference in your worldview. Write about it. If you did not learn your family's first language, write about how you feel about that.

Write your reaction or your difficulty in following a speaker's intent, as in this example. *My first day in New Orleans I asked a man for directions... I could not figure out what he meant! I just had to shrug and smile, but I hated doing that...* That way the language issue is addressed without any insult to the individual portrayed.

Describe how the character speaks and then write the dialogue in standard English, mentioning the language; e.g., *She gave it the Italian pronunciation...* Say something about how the way this person talks affects his character or the story, or you as the narrator. *As long as I knew him, Jesus never stopped rolling his r's in the Spanish way. It gave him a certain charm with the ladies.* Or, *Ian spoke slowly, deliberately, with a guttural sound for the 'h' which confused me at first...* Tell how they felt about it and how you felt about it. There are some good family stories there.

Listen to the character in your mind. What does he or she do besides drop consonants or mispronounce words? Do they at the sentence end the verbs put? Do the adjectives wind up always after the nouns? Are the adverbs out of place? Is different the pace of their words and the timing or shape of sentences? Whatever the difference, you can indicate it by arranging your sentence the way they would.

Do they have difficulty with the verb tenses in English? What do they say where you would say something else? Do they throw in a Yiddish word now and then? Do they have a favorite expression? These are some language characteristics you can easily work into your dialogue which give a sense of the character without putting yourself or the reader through the struggle of writing and reading dialect.

Pick a favorite word or expression that the person uses and include it in the dialogue. "God's eyes!" she would say. It was her favorite expression when upset... If the person is a colorful speaker, sprinkle your writing with her particular ways of saying things. Note that the verb I used is "sprinkle"—not saturate. If the character has a mantra, don't use it too often. If they seem to come up with just the right word, use it—don't explain it even if it is unusual; but if they use non-English or idiosyncratic words, make sure that your reader gets the sense of the meaning without having to find a dictionary in the right language. You can accomplish this with a quick translation right in the sentence, or a comment on the meaning.

Sometimes you want to really give the reader a sense of how the character sounds, of what it is like to listen to that particular person. You can do it without writing a word of dialogue or dialect as in this example: *My grandmother spoke with a bullet-like Midwestern accent. She never repeated things and never asked you twice to stay to dinner, so that Southern people often thought she was angry when she wasn't. We kids were embarrassed, but the doctor's secretary was terrified of her...*

Local dialects

It may be that you speak in a particular accent or regional dialect yourself. It may sound normal to you. Write that way when you write about your family. If you are writing something your parents said, it is likely that you talk like them or at least like one or the other of them. It will be harder for you to hear that something is nonstandard but easier for you to write what they would have said. For purposes of memoir writing, don't be too concerned about whether your own English is standard. Write the way you usually do or the way the character you are writing about would speak. A recollection has its own voice—your voice or the voice of the character—and that is the way it should be written.

Story: When I Was a Child

This story was written by one of my students as a classroom exercise. He didn't edit it because of the class time factor. I want you to read it not only for what he says, but for how the whole story sounds. Read it aloud if possible.

When I Was a Child

By Jim E. Lewis

I grew up in the rugged isolated Appalachian Mountains of Western North Carolina where a form of English was spoken that was a holdover from the time of Shakespeare's England. Speech was slow and drawn out by local citizens that felt no compulsion to speak rapidly or eloquently. Words were used that they had heard their ancestors use for several generations. Television had not come to their homes and they had only the speech patterns of their parents and grandparents to learn from and imitate.

As a child my ears were trained to hear and my mind to use words and phrases like the following examples:

Ary. ANY. I aint got ary dime to my name.

Fur piece. LONG DISTANCE. Hit's a fur piece over to Bob's house.

Heifer. Derogatory term for a WOMAN. That old woman shore is a heifer.

Kiver. COVER. It was so cold last night I had to add extra kiver to the bed.

Nary. NONE. Ain't nary one of them boys worth a lick.

Sop. GRAVY. Hand me the sop.

Backer. TOBACCO. Give me a chew of your backer.

Widder-woman. WIDOW. That old widder-woman has been feeling poorly of late.

Tar arn. TIRE IRON. Hand me that tar arn so I can change this tar.

Hankerin. DESIRE. I'm hankering for a piece of that good old pie.

Fustest. FIRST. Who got there fustest?

Whup. WHIP. Who whupped my children?

Druthers. CHOICE. If I had my druthers I'd stayed home.

After graduating from the local high school and then attending a distant college I was in for a cultural shock and some hard times from other college students and college professors. It seemed to my fellow students and college professors that I was speaking a foreign language. They insisted that I adapt to the more modern version of the English language. My professors kept telling me to change the words and phrases I was using in my oral speech and written reports to reflect current trends and styles of expression. My words and expressions made perfect sense to me but had little meaning to them because they did not have the same language background that I had come from.

I was able to change my speech patterns as a result of several things. They were:

1. *Constant criticism from professors and fellow students about my choice of words and phrases.*

2. *Learning to use the dictionary for looking up words and their meanings in modern English.*

3. *Discovering how and when to use synonyms and homonyms.*

4. *Thinking critically how to say what I had learned as a child in the newer version of the English language through experience.*

I feel like I was able to change my speech patterns with a great deal of success because for thirty-two years I was able to communicate with class rooms of students and they understood what I was saying to them. Today, it seems funny to me that scholars are now spending time researching and learning what I grew up with and accepted as everyday language patterns.

Besides the words themselves, other instructive points emerge from studying the examples in this story. The sound and pace of the example sentences are as colorful as each word he selects to distinguish. How the sentence is set is more important than the spelling. If you have any familiarity with Appalachian speech, you can hear the rhythm and sound without the apostrophes and other markings of written dialect. Even if you don't, Jim's easy colloquial spellings shape the sound for you.

Notice the doubling of concepts: "Speech was slow and drawn out," "to learn from and imitate," "current trends and styles of expression..." There are many such doubled phrases in use in formal English, but their use in daily speech is disappearing. Expressions such as "to have and to hold," "terms and conditions," or "will and testament" are fundamentally redundant. To double ideas creatively is not a habit that is encouraged today, but a holdover that comes from an English language pattern with a cultural heritage going back a thousand years to a time when England began to come to terms with its multicultural heritage. Usually one word has a Germanic heritage and the other comes from a Latin based language, generally French.

Feel the rhythm of the speech. Jim says, "As a child my ears were trained to hear and my mind to use words..." and to me this sounds like Old Testament poetry. Jim has carefully eradicated such habits from much of his formal speech and writing. He stands with a quiet presence and speaks very carefully to the class; he never hurries but chooses his words. In this discussion of his efforts to overcome the disadvantage of his Appalachian speech patterns in modern America, the beauty of his native speech comes through more than in any other of his stories.

Foreign words

If you put in a non-English word or phrase, you can put it in italics and, using commas if needed, immediately translate it right there in the sentence. You can find someone to help you with the words you actually need to translate. If the idiom has come into general use and you think your audience will understand it, don't bother to translate it. Many Yiddish words are now in everyday use in America; the same is true for Spanish words and others. As we become ever more connected by electronic communications, some of these words enter the language. At the same time pocket dialects and regional accents will melt away.

A Harrowing Welcome to Mexico

by Terry Donnelly

I felt the reverse thrust of the 757's jet engines seconds after the American Airline's Chief Stewardess announced that we had begun our descent into the Mexico City Airport. We would be landing in a few minutes. I leaned over my wife and looked out of the window at the yellowish-orange polluted clouds which were ever present every time I flew into this smoggy city. I swear I could smell the metallic odor that goes with the smog. The sort of smell you could taste. I smelled it every time and tasted it every time. Today I was childishly angry at the smog blocking Ann's view of the largest city in the world, a city that exited me like no other I had ever been in. I wanted every thing to be perfect here, especially for my wife who had made a significant sacrifice in agreeing to come.

It was Saturday, the 9th of September 1989, and as the plane taxied toward the gate the stewardess announced, "On behalf of the crew, thank you for flying American Airlines and welcome to Mexico". I remember how poignant the statement seemed to Ann and myself as we would be living here for the next two years. My Company had asked me to go to Mexico on a special project, and with Ann's approval I had taken the assignment. We had lived in England, Canada and the US but had never lived in a country where the predominant language was not English. This would be a challenge. We were both quite apprehensive as we deplaned.

We had left Greensboro, NC. at 7:00 AM that morning, changed planes in Dallas and had landed on time at 1:00 PM in Mexico. "That's a good omen," I said to Ann; and I got a look which warned me to tread lightly.

Once off the plane, we set off through the crowds to the baggage claim and immigration areas, being jostled on the way by people like ourselves, not really sure if we were going in the right direction but committed to it anyway. The Mexican officers at the desks were big and surly as usual but at least they did speak English and we cleared immigration with no problem. However we ran into our first hitch when we got a red light at the baggage check. This meant we had to go to a special area and have every bag opened and inspected. It took us about an hour for just this but eventually we were released to go and the rest of the paperwork was approved.

I said to Ann, "There, that wasn't too bad was it?" and she nodded her head.

I was watching Ann carefully and was concerned that she was a little fragile. She had just left her job at Baptist Hospital the day before, said goodbye to her three sons the day before and had left all of her friends behind her. She could not work in Mexico, and so would have to make a new life for herself in Mexico City while I was at work. She was really being challenged; it was a brave move. Several days before we left I had found her in tears and she said, " I must be crazy going to a country where donkeys still pull carts around the City, no one obeys traffic lights, or stop signs, all the noise and smells, the abject poverty, and what is worse is I can't speak a damn word of the language."

Anyway, we had now arrived in Mexico City, the flights had been perfect and except for the baggage check everything had gone well. Our next destination was National Car Rental which we found quite easily. I breathed a sigh of relief and said "There, wasn't too bad was it?"

Little did I know what was facing us.

"Una problema, Señor" I was told when I asked for our car at the National counter. "No hay un coche, Señor." "There is no car," in English.

This from the chief attendant who typified Mexican supervisors, macho and condescending; and I could imagine he would disappear at the first sign of trouble.

"But I have the documents," I said, placing them on the desk, "which should ensure we have a car."

The attendant was starting to get embarrassed as other customers were at the counter, listening to the discourse. "And," Ann said indignantly, "they are getting cars; we want ours."

There was silence, women do not make demands on Mexican males especially in Mexico City.

Ignoring Ann he turned to me, "Un momento, por favor, Señor." and he called his assistant over. They spoke in rapid Spanish which I could not keep up with. The assistant, young and eager, then spoke to me in broken English assuring me that we would have a car in a short while. He scampered away. Approximately one hour later he returned with a car, and all smiles, he said, "Your car, Señor." Little did I realize that this would come back to haunt us in the very near future.

Ann was furious, still not over being snubbed. We were loading the car, when she said, "The gas gauge is on empty," which, in turn, I pointed out to the attendant. At this, we got out of the car and he drove off to get gas. Half an hour later he returned with the tank half full, all smiles.

We climbed into the car again and Ann looked for a map of Mexico City in the glove compartment. "There is no map," she said with frustration in her voice. As we did not know the directions to our new apartment it was essential we have a map. Ann called the assistant over, and again he hurried away and eventually came back with an Avis map of the City.

We were both very frustrated now and could not get away from the Airport fast enough. It had taken us nearly three hours to get out of the Airport since landing, and all we wanted now was to get to the apartment. Ann said, "Thank God!" when I finally pulled away from the curb.

With Ann reading the Avis map and myself a very tentative driver, we moved out into the flow of traffic in the largest city in the world. Even on this Saturday the pollution from the cars, trucks, sewers and busses was stifling, and the noise overwhelming. I was excited and stimulated by the whole environment. We somehow found the apartment and, success, my wife loved it. It was the elevator door opening directly into the marble tiled living room that impressed.

We were met by the company lawyer Señor Reyes and his wife, Juanita, who gave us the tour of the complex. It was impressive. On clear days, we were told, we would be able to see the two renowned snow capped volcanoes, Popocatepetl and Pico de Orizaba, from our bedroom windows. However, with the City shrouded in smog most of the time they were not to be seen too often. Ann whispered, "I hope they don't erupt while we are here."

Señor Reyes, true to his profession and nationality, fastidiously went over the details. He also, however, did mention that the refrigerator was not working, the drier was broken, and the TV would be fixed to accept English speaking programs from the U.S.A.; and he assured us that everything would be taken care of as soon as possible—that is another story.

Señora Reyes, dressed to make an impression, took to Ann and talked non-stop in broken English with Ann nodding her head every few minutes. Days afterwards Ann told me, "I had no idea what she was saying. I just thought I would learn these things later."

A week before we left Winston-Salem we had packed some furniture, bed linen, clothes, etc.; and Atlas Van lines had picked them up to transport to our apartment in Mexico. Unfortunately I had mistranslated some information and Ann did not pack any crockery, plates etc. When she opened the cupboards in the apartment, just like with old Mother Hubbard, the cupboards were bare. "There is no crockery" she said. She was not pleased. "You told me not to pack any crockery, I didn't and now we don't have any," she said with a tremor in her voice. I quickly reassured her by saying we were going to the local supermarket to get food and we could easily pick up low-cost quality Mexican products. Señor Reyes sided with me, thus assuring that the male came out on top, as is the Mexican way.

However, I was starting to wilt under the pressure.

Sr. & Sra. Reyes left. We unpacked, and with directions from them and the Avis map we headed for Gigante, the supermarket, to purchase our wares. From our avenida we pulled out onto the Periferico which is a ring road around the City, a road I would get to know like the back of my hand in the next few months. I was getting more confident with my driving and was about five minutes from the apartment when I heard the wail of a police siren and through the rear view mirror I saw a motor cycle policeman indicating I should pull over. I was filled with dread. The Mexicans at work had told me to avoid the police at all costs, especially the Federales as they are corrupt and dangerous; and here I was the first day in Mexico being faced with meeting one.

I pulled over and, more than a little scared, I got out of the car. He was a big man with a big stomach and a gun on each hip. I was terrified. I couldn't tell if he was a Federal or not, anyway it was immaterial at this point. A small crowd started to form and the policeman started to shout at me in Spanish. I tried to reply in English but he drowned me out. The small amount of Spanish I knew was to no avail; he kept on shouting. Prior to now our problems had been laughable but this was deadly serious.

A small man suddenly stepped out of the crowd and said to me, in broken English, ten words I will never forget, "Give him fifty dollars, Señor, and he will go away."

The crowd was growing, and I knew I had to do something. "What did I do wrong?" I asked the little man.

"Nothing, Señor, he just wants money," and he quickly slid away and disappeared into the crowd.

I put my head into the rental car and said to Ann, "I am going to give him fifty dollars." Ann was already very shaken and said immediately, "No! That's bribery, you will get into trouble."

"Look, we don't know anyone in Mexico., It's Saturday, there will be no one at the office. I don't even know how to get in touch with the American Embassy; I have to do it." With that I took the money from my wallet and gave it to him.

He took it, said nothing, got onto his bike and rode off. The crowd, disappointed, soon evaporated, and Ann and I sat and tried to relax at the side of the road. Ann was really shaken and was in tears. "Coming here was a mistake," she said. I didn't argue, it would have been pointless.

As we drove off I felt myself trembling, a new sensation--thanks to Mexico City. I had never had a ticket before in my life, and here I was bribing a Mexican policeman. We later found out that the car National had 'found' for us had a registration plate which was out of date.

In a few minutes we got to the supermarket, which had an underground parking lot. It was very modern but not well lit. We parked, Ann got out of the car; and, still shaken, I got out after her, slammed the door shut with the keys still in the ignition and the engine still running! We were locked out.

I was now really upset, but yet another bystander came to our assistance. He said his name was Raul, and he took me into the store and, made a phone call. Within minutes a friend of his appeared and within seconds had unlocked the door for us. I gave them twenty dollars each; and they were very grateful and left in a hurry. To this day we often wondered if their business was getting into other peoples cars illegally.

Ann was a wreck and so was I. We did our shopping and found the store to be very efficient and friendly. It had everything we needed, which helped to buoy Ann's spirits considerably. As we were leaving the store this delightful atmosphere prompted her to say, "Maybe it won't be so bad after all." The smell of the freshly baked breads and pastry will always be one of the delights of shopping in Mexico.

Driving back to the apartment I said to Ann, "We have been in Mexico less that twelve hours and I have spent ninety dollars paying people off. I should have asked for a raise when I took this assignment!" We carefully drove back to the apartment and when we got inside it already felt like home.

Ann's journal for the day reads: Finally got back to the apartment, Terry had soup, bread and delicious cake for supper and I had two large scotches. WHAT A DAY!

Footnote: At 6.00 o'clock the next morning we were awoken by a very loud blast of a bugle. I had picked an apartment with a military hospital and army base on the opposite side of the street; and so we lived with reveille every single day until we left that fine country two years later.

With this example, Terry has given you the sense of his experience. You can feel his distress and smell the local air. He has put in a few words of dialogue where it helps the story, and a few Spanish words. He has used these words well, particularly where they heighten the experience of language difficulty.

Terry is from the town of Rugby in Northern England although he has worked around the world. Do you get a flavor of English speech in his writing? We have edited the story a bit from the first draft, but we have left it in his voice with his way of saying things. Beware of too much editing from too many people—it can homogenize something delightful into something ordinary.

Less is usually more in writing dialogue. Get as close to the sound of your character as you can. Write the way they speak; say what they say. Use a light touch so that you keep your story in balance. Pay attention to the pace. Words in odd orders slow the reader down, as do foreign phrases and excess commas. A place where you want the reader to pause and reflect on the character is the place to comment on the language issue or put a bit of dialogue with dialect or a non-English word. If you want the reader to move quickly to heighten the tension, streamline your dialogue and use short action oriented sentences.

Dialogue that works brings a feeling of freshness into your story. Remembered words are significant words. In a recollection or a memoir these priceless words are your legacy.

Assignments

1. Select a story you have already written, go over it and either add, remove, or correct your dialogue. Keep the purposes of dialogue and your goals for this story in mind as you work.

2. Write any necessary dialogue into the story you are currently writing from your life. Get clear about what you intend to accomplish by adding dialogue to your story and place your dialogue so that what you add contributes to the story.

3. Add words or phrases that are not dialogue but suggest a character's way of speaking to one of your stories. How is the characterization improved—or is it improved—in your story?

4. Find a short story that seems to lack dialogue. Rewrite the story using dialogue. Is it shorter or longer? How does your dialogue improve the story? (You can use another author's writing for purposes of this exercise; you can not, of course, publish the story if it is not yours.)

5. Usually you can find plenty of dialogue that could be improved in category fiction, the short, numbered paperback novels. Go through some of them and pick a chapter, or find any story, that would be helped by better dialogue. Write dialogue that moves the story and deepens it.

6. Keep adding stories to your project.

7. As always, add to your list of possible story topics. Visit your list when you are ready for a new idea, write something using one of your ideas.

Chapter 13

SPIT 'N POLISH—Editing

I started out by suggesting that it is not the best strategy for most people to embark on writing an entire autobiography. The best way to write your life story is to write your stories. The ones you aren't sure you want to share are the best ones to write, along with the funny ones, the crazy ones, the poignant stories. Rewriting is part of the process, not a dirty little secret. We all do it, and sometimes we need help. We can't see what we are doing for being too close the work. Share your work with your writing buddy. Help each other with the polishing process.

If you are writing a family memoir or history, this might be the time to get some of the rest of the crew involved. Maybe Aunt Mabel was an English teacher, one of the kids is good with computers, and somebody else has art skills and could do your layout. Get them involved in your project. Share yourself and the workload. You'll be glad you did.

Example

The following is the raw first draft of the beginning of this chapter. It's almost unreadable with its jumble of thoughts and errors, but it is fresh and full of ideas. I'm going to edit it into material for this chapter.

> *Polishing your work involves a totally separate set of skill from writing. Here you will apply the knowledge you have of writing technique to groom your writing just like a 4hsutden farmer handler trainer grooms a horse, calf, animal Gardener a garden 'Homeowner a house for a showing. You will trim and prune and pull uot the burrs from the tail. You will find the perfect word or phrase, fill in a sparse place, pull weeds somewhere else; trade one kind of flower for another. And when you are finished, your prose will sparkele and shine. It will*

be rich and deep with the smell of woods and horse manure, the light scent of roses with a touch of moonlight. You will find prized orchids and improve on the shape of bushes. When you are finished it will be truly a work of art a thing of your own making. What you have made. A thing of beauty a joy to behold. A joy to you and your loved ones. You may need help with this enterprise. It is all right to ask for it. You may need to clarify your thingking, to go back and imagine or remember and do some rewriting. Most of all you will need to learn the art of judicious pruning. 2 skills learn to ask questions of yourself: what happened? What else happened? What's missing? What does the reader need to know? What am I taking for granted (that the reader might not know)? How much is left out? What do I need that's not here? What do I not need that's here? 3 step editing process, more steps—maybe a table—levels...

Here's the beginning!

You have written from your heart; edit from your logical mind.

Polishing your work involves a totally separate set of skills from writing. Here you will apply the knowledge you have of writing technique to groom your writing just like a 4H student grooms a calf for show, or a gardener puts his yard in order for the spring. Just as the gardener trims and prunes and pulls out weeds, you shape your work. You find the perfect word or phrase, fill in a sparse place, pull weeds somewhere else; trade one kind of flower for another. And when you have finished, your prose will sparkle. It will be rich and deep with the smell of woods and horse manure, or the light scent of roses with a touch of moonlight.

As a gardener finds prized roses and opens a space for them to grow, you seek out those precious magic phrases, remove the deadwood and display a work of art. A book of your own making! It is a joy to you and your loved ones.

Most of all, you will need to learn the art of judicious pruning. You may need help with this enterprise. It is all right to ask for it. You may need to clarify your thinking, to go back and imagine or remember and do some rewriting. Find someone to serve as your reader.

A skill that you must learn is to ask questions of your work. As your reader is guided through your story by questions, you can shape your work by asking important questions. Let's take a few of these questions and discuss them.

What is my purpose? You have written from the heart; edit from your logical mind to create a clear path from premise to goal. If you want to write an action story, you write one way. To persuade people of something, you write another way; to report you use another style; to appreciate, something else. What you are trying to accomplish will guide what you keep or add and what you throw out.

Here are a few other questions you can use to help you sort things out according to your purpose.

- What are the strengths of this paragraph or section?
- What's missing?
- What does the reader need to know?
- What am I taking for granted that the reader might not know? What do I need that's not here?

Is there something missing? Your reader wasn't there. He may not know that Grandma's place had a hundred stairs from the front door to the bottom of the hill and falling down them would kill a person. He doesn't know that Rex was not a boxer but a tiny dachshund who thought he owned the palace. He doesn't know how the springhouse smelled or where the goldfish hid when the sun was hot. You have to tell him. He can relate. He knows how it was at his house or in his imagination. Give him a chance to fully experience your story. Explain what you mean and tell him how it felt and sounded and smelled. He can relate to your experience from his own, but you have to show the way. So go through your writing with the question: What have I left out? Or what is missing? Or what don't they know? Add in the feelings and the details. Make notes in the margin until you are ready to rework the piece.

When you have assembled the content you need, it's time to shape it into the type of piece you want to write. Every kind of writing has a standard pattern. You can learn more about these patterns from observation or a journalism book, or a book on plots. Questions you can use to help you shape your work include: Where does this story really begin? How can I best present it? Shape and structure must fit with the purpose you have in mind. Edit to be sure that you have given lots of space to the important parts. Get tough with yourself about all those irrelevant words and ideas. If they distract from your purpose, take them out. You can use them somewhere else.

When all of that has been accomplished, review for tone and pace of the work and sensory detail. Make your work the best it can be. Then run your spell checker again. Have someone else read for word usage and punctuation. You can't do that yourself; you won't find your own mistakes. You are finished.

Three Phase Editing Plan

My approach to editing is to work from large matters to small ones. There is not much point in checking the spelling and punctuation until you are sure you are going to use those words. Editing is a process; here is how I work through the process.

First I take an overall look at the content. Do I have everything? What do I need to add? What type of piece did I want to write? Have I done that? I work with the order of presentation and structural matters. Correcting structural defects will show you what content is missing. In the second phase I make sure the piece starts in the right place, take out unnecessary repetitions, clarify sentences and paragraphs to say what I really

Three phases of editing:
1) Content and Structure,
2) Clarity and Focus,
3) Details

want to say. The second phase is sometimes called copy editing. Finally I do details including punctuation and spelling.

Doing third phase editing makes no sense until you have all the words you want in the order you want them on the page. It wastes your time and energy to worry about spelling and other details early in the process. Unfortunately, many of us learned to do that first. No wonder we never write much! Before I quit, I run the spell checker one last time.

Phase 1: Content and structure

What type of piece do you have—story, article, interview, essay? And what do you want it to become? If you find from your first writing that this piece needs a different approach, look at other possible structures. Perhaps you have an article that needs to be a novel or a recollection. If it is a story, what kind of story is it? Novel or short story? Recollection, eyewitness account? Journal or diary? There are really two considerations; deciding the length and picking the genre or approach. Decide whether the material supports the approach you have in mind. If not, what type of story would better serve your purposes? Try things; sketch out your ideas. Settle on a way to present your information. Settle on the type and length—in a general way—for your piece.

What is the best structure or order of presentation for this piece within the genre? Where is the best place to begin? End? What is necessary to get to the ending? What kind of plot or what article type works for this story? Should it be an interview or profile? Choose a beginning point and a viewpoint. Arrange scenes or segments. Cut, write, and rewrite as necessary to complete the piece. Rewrite at this point can be a rough draft or "just the bones."

Now ask yourself, Have I said everything I want to say? Do I need to do some research, test some ideas? Interview people, do what you need to do to have everything together. Add anything that is missing.

Review the ending; is it strong? Is everything in the piece contributing to the finish? If not, backtrack from the ending to the beginning step by step. You will see what is missing. Compare your ending to your beginning. Some articles and stories demand a circular approach; the story winds back to its origins in the end, or echoes the purpose stated at the beginning as it winds up. Make sure everything you need to support the ending is somewhere in the beginning or the middle. Along the way, if there is information that is required by the story structure, make a note to add it.

Is there any redundancy? It is one thing to recall events or look at them from different perspectives; it is another to repeat large chunks of material. Make sure you cull accidental repetitions. Are there any unnecessary sidetracks or detours in the middle? That "out take" or lecture you love on the origins of algebra may not add to the purpose of the piece. Delete unnecessary material to focus the piece. Save it for a book talk or a book signing, or write an article on it.

Does the story begin where it needs to? Is the protagonist introduced first, or soon enough? Is it clear who the narrator is and who other characters are? Is any foreshadowing taken care of? Is the setting clear including time, place and social setting? If there are problems or missing pieces, make notes of them.

Phase 2: Clarity and focus

Whereas in Phase 1, we looked at the project as a whole, in Phase 2, we get a little closer in and start redoing portions of the text. You may notice that Phase 1 merges into Phase 2. Like the beginning, middle and end of a story, the three phases blend smoothly into each other; the focus is different, however. If you will keep in mind that you are doing the big things first—adjusting the core or bones of your story; the middle size tasks– developing your story through rewriting—next; and save the small details for last; you will save yourself a good deal of time and frustration.

The purposes of Phase 2 editing are: first, to complete the portions needed for the flow of the story; and second, to polish the story by pruning the small branches so the flowers show up better. In Phase 1, we made notes about missing segments; in Phase 2 we write or rewrite to fill them in. In Phase 1, we cut out whole scenes; in Phase 2 we focus on paragraphs. Cut out excess foliage, pick the perfect word, and the flowers will shine.

Pay attention to the questions your reader or your writing buddy asks. These are the things that are missing or unclear. Answer those questions at the appropriate place in your writing. Focused the work by clarifying cause and effect.

If there are problems with the beginning, work on them to improve it. You may want to open your story in a different place; try it. Does the beginning of your story serve to introduce the main characters, set up the problem, set the scene, etc.?

Write the ending or rewrite it, if needed. Study each scene or section. Within the segment, what is missing? Add missing material to clarify the story. Write or rewrite other portions of the work that you made notes about. Rewrite sections that have been moved or just need help.

How are your paragraphs? Do your paragraphs make sense—is the structure right at this level? Do you need any headings or subheads to make your work more accessible? Make sure your sentences say what you mean because you have chosen the right words and put them together correctly. If you need help, this is the point where a good editor or a kind friend who was an English major may be helpful.

Begin to cull paragraphs, sentences, or chunks that don't contribute to the writing.

Does your beginning now lead seamlessly into the middle? Is the middle interesting? Is the ending satisfying? Is any foreshadowing taken care of? Is the content, which was present before or added, now fully expressed? Are other structural matters working now?

As I write this, I know that some of you need to hear: Write more detail and feelings into your story! Others need to hear: Take out repetitious paragraphs, untangle complex or circular thoughts, cut the piece down as a diamond is faceted or a shrub is pruned; and it will sparkle! Some of us need to do both: write up to flesh out the thoughts, then trim to make it shine. If you are that type of writer (like me) you might think of writing up, or fleshing it out, as part of Phase 2; and trimming words as moving into Phase 3. It is very like gardening, there are different ways to do it. I trust that you can see where you are in this. Remember to move from large issues to details. You will find your own best process.

Phase 3: Detail

Now it is time to get down to paragraphs, sentences, punctuation and details. You will be surprised how much better your writing is for a little polishing.

First, take out extra words, unnecessary words, and words that distract from what you are saying. You will find that as you do this, you will bring yourself and your reader closer to the subject. If you wrote, *I was trying to think of what to say to her—she was my sister-in-law...* you might now have, *I thought about my sister-in-law; what could I say to her?* Is the second version better, brighter, closer to the subject? Is that what you want in this passage?

Eschew laundry lists. Take out unnecessary lists. Pick one word that says precisely what you mean; limit yourself to two or three representative items in places where you want to show how sumptuous was the feast or how delightful the amenities. If you want to list all the people who came to a party, use a sidebar or put them in an appendix. Only name the people you have something to say about.

Work your way through a segment spotting any dull words that could be brightened up. Pick words that sparkle. Make sure your words say what you want them to. Don't rely on a thesaurus to supply you with synonyms and leave it at that. Most synonyms are only effective substitutes where their meanings overlap. Look up any words you are not sure of in a good dictionary; use the right word!

Address your punctuation issues next; then go over your spelling. Don't believe everything your grammar checker says—they are generally terrible and wrong as often as they are right. Spell checkers are pretty good these days; however, the most sophisticated spell checker will not catch certain types of errors. Look for words that are misplaced, correct forms of words, and homonyms, especially those that are spelled differently but sound the same; e.g., their, they're, there. Run your spell checker a second time after you finish editing to make sure you have caught everything. Then read it, or even better, have that kind friend read it and mark the details. There will probably be some; you can't see your own mistakes at this point. Don't be embarrassed to ask. You can read hers sometime.

A Word about Rewriting

Writing is a process—in case I haven't said that before! You can't do it all on the first pass. Writers struggle to finish a work in three of four drafts, then get sent back to edit several more times after they submit a piece. And not all because something is wrong; more because the work improves if you let it stand a while. It's like fine wine; it improves if you leave it alone for a while. It gets better as you read it with new eyes and work on a particular thing each time you go through it.

Becoming a great writer is a process of rewriting to improve your work in one way or another. What you need is a little talent, a story to tell, and a lot of willingness to learn. Then you practice; that is, you write and write and write. You edit your work and you share it with others. You can edit yourself to success!

Tricks of the trade

Thank God for computers! They make this phase of the project much easier.

Save your original—however you wrote it—until you are finished and have completely polished your story. Sometimes it is useful to go back to the beginning to catch the nuances of what you wanted to accomplish.

Whenever you make a major reorganization or try out a different viewpoint, make a new file for that version of your story. It helps if you number the versions as well as add descriptive notes such as "Karl VP" for "Karl's viewpoint," or "Beg Act" for "Beginning with the Action," or whatever will tell you what your purpose in that rewrite was. "REV" for "revised" or "ED" for "Edit, "F" for "Final"" can be useful; but one REV can turn into 2 or 3 or more if you tend to tinker with things. I number them using "0" (zero) for the Original and "REV1," 2, 3, etc. after that. For example, a file might be labeled FIC TECH START HERE or CH10 BME REV4 or BACK CVR BRAINSTORM. Do what works for you.

Back up your computer files regularly somewhere off your machine. Disks, CD's, online storage are among the options. Crashes can happen any time to anyone.

If you write by hand or type in the time honored tradition, carry everything to a copy shop occasionally and shoot yourself some photocopies for safe-keeping. You have put a lot of yourself into your work; don't loose it needlessly.

Copies are also useful in the rewriting process. You can use them to cut and paste changes, to try different arrangements, to have someone help you edit for style, or make corrections.

Putting Together a Memoir from Different Sources

Suppose you have Aunt Hattie's letters and some letters from your mother, and you have your recollections. The letters are interesting, but not complete. One approach is to organize the letters as a correspondence and fill in details and information. You write some narrative that goes between the letters. Aunt Hattie is Viewpoint 1; Mom is Viewpoint 2; You are the anonymous editor or writer of the narrative, which you write in the omniscient viewpoint. Or, you can write in your own voice—first person, using narrator or omniscient narrator viewpoint—and tell what you remember.

If there are different people who are interested in the tales, get them to help. Maybe you have letters or memorabilia that your sister knows more about than you. You are the family historian, but you were not yet born when this happened, but there are people around who remember. Maybe someone in the family has a particular perspective on the events. Perhaps your older sister tells an entirely different story of one particular event that you have written about, and your brother was there for most of what happened but he was much younger. What if each of you wrote what there was for you to say, and you put in Aunt Hattie's letter also?

Somebody has to be the editor and decide how to fit it all together—that might be you. Your first task is to collect all the material. Have it come to you electronically if you can. This is what computers are good for. But also have a paper copy of each piece.

If there are a lot of different authors with one story each, the traditional anthology style with a title and by line for each chapter will work well. Even if you have two or three pieces from some authors, you can organize this material so that each piece is a separate chapter. Associate the ones that are about the same event. You can write introductory or connecting material if you want to. With this format, poems, photographs and memorabilia that can be copied or photographed can go in between the chapters. You will need to write "cut lines" or captions for the photographs. Be sure you give credit to the photographers as well as the authors.

You could have several stories from each of a few authors. You have some choices, you could relate the stories one after the other in some internally logical way; you can arrange them in topical or chronological order. Another solution is to group all the stories from one person, and then from the next, and so on. You as editor or compiler write some introductory material, add in pictures, etc. and you have it.

Integrating different types of material from assorted sources

A client of mine put together an extensive memoir based on tapes that her father had dictated in answer to an interviewer's questions. He was an extremely well-known and popular individual in their area. She then asked several people to contribute recollections of this man. If you decide to do something like this, I suggest that you do the interviews yourself to get the stories. Get a voice recorder and have people tell you the stories they remember about the individual who is the subject of the memoir. People generally talk more freely than they write, and it is sometimes hard to collect the stories. Make it as easy for people to contribute as you can.

Working the sections together is difficult if you try to do it all in a seamless layout. However, you can easily interweave sections of text from different sources by using different styles and plenty of headings in your layout. A professional can do this for you, or you can do it yourself if you follow these directions. This is a happy situation where the easiest thing for you to do is also the best thing for the reader.

The following process is much easier and goes faster with two people who have a good relationship. A friend or a sister might be a good choice. It helps if you understand each other's thinking and work well together. Find a place where you won't be distracted for a considerable amount of time, or where you can leave the work in piles until you can finish the sorting.

Let's say you have a pile of old letters or a set of tapes from the person who is the subject of the memoir, you have some stories you have written about the person. You have a few pictures and memorabilia. Let's also say that the letters relate to some of the stories. I'm assuming you have everything on paper at this point. Clip pages together or put segments in folders so they won't get mixed up with other items.

- First put each pile (letters, tapes, stories, photos, etc.) in some order. This is mainly to make it easy to find and handle items. You might put each group of items into chronological order, but it isn't required. The important thing is to get all the letters from one person into one pile, all the stories from one person together in another pile, all the letters or stories from someone else together, etc. so that you have a small number of piles according to author, and everything in each pile is from one source. You might have a miscellaneous pile for single items.

- Take the largest pile or the most important pile of stories or letters (but not the miscellaneous pile) and lay them out on a big table or on the floor in chronological order or in the order you think might work.

- Take the next pile of stories or letters and relate items to the sections already on the table.

- At this point you may discover that there is not an exact correspondence based on events, but you might be able to relate segments by years or decades, or by such concepts as childhood, graduation, military years, home life, career, retirement, etc. Or you may have material that is topical in some other way. Make some labels with a big marker on full sheets of scrap paper. Lay these out and start associating items with the labels.

- You might decide that the tapes from the subject individual or the letters from one person should be the driving force. Make your labels based on the topic of each one. Spread those out and relate other things to them.

- Deal out the piles until you have looked at everything and associated it with something.

- Now (if you haven't already done it) look at the miscellaneous pile. Do these things fit between the cracks? Can they be associated somewhere? Do you need them in your memoir? Set aside the things that really shouldn't be there, find a way to fit the others in. Are they special cases? You may have to resign yourself to a couple of very, very short chapters. That's perfectly acceptable.

- Once you come to terms with what goes with what, then put the piles themselves into a working order. You may be OK with your chronological order, or you may see something better from going over the materials. Try different arrangements, until you are satisfied with the flow of material.

- Write or find the missing pieces. You will find that once you have created an order, you know what is missing. Perhaps you know exactly where it is; more likely, you will have to ask for help. Get your team involved. Find the missing letter or have someone write some notes about what was in it. Interview someone who remembers the story. Ask others to write about a particular topic from their points of view.

- Write introductory or explanatory information.

- Associate the pictures and memorabilia items where they should go. You may want to copy a particular old letter or newspaper article and include it as an illustration. Make some test copies. In the case of old letters, you may want to have all of them typed for easier reading of the text and only use one or two as illustrations.

- Now design a heading for the letters and a different one for each of the other types of contribution. If there are several parties contributing, you will probably want to use their names in the header for their materials. Start new sections on separate pages or leave a certain amount of space between the end of one segment and the header for the next.

- Another way to show different sources of material is to use different typefonts for each, or use the standard font for one source and put the other in italics. Keeping dates and locations with items also helps to identify sources so that the reader easily follows the change of "voice" associated with the source.

Adding relevant memorabilia can help or hinder a published memoir. Generally, it's helpful to see a few photos or drawings, a letter in longhand, a list or some other note from the time of the story. A diary page is a nice touch. Have someone with some knowledge of design and printing work with you to sift through the memorabilia to find the right items to use. A few powerful images will convey your story more convincingly than a lot of foggy old photos, especially if you are publishing the book. Use only the best and most relevant photos in the finished memoir.

Assignments

What you will do with this section depends a lot on the type of project you have taken on. Begin to apply what we have covered in the way that works best for you.

1. Begin to polish your stories.

2. Keep adding to your stories by checking your list and writing new ones. Spend some time on new writing and some on editing this week.

3. Further your personal memoir project by improving your stories.

4. Consider how best to organize your stories.

5. Organize a group of relatives or friends to work on a family history or other group project.

Chapter 14

FICTION TECHNIQUES TO ENRICH YOUR WRITING

When you have structured your story or narrative to your satisfaction, it's time to pay attention to details.

Most of us have to rewrite to find the best way to present our stories. Your writing is more interesting when you engage the reader's senses so that the experience of place and people is fuller. Using the exact word that says precisely what you want to say gives your writing clarity and energy. Fine-tuning your word choices provides the right tone, and controlling the pace of telling helps you to create the effect you want the reader to get.

Details often convey the nuances of meaning which can carry emotions. Emotions are often missing in our first writing, perhaps because in real life we seldom state them in words. We are more likely to convey our feelings with smiles, nonverbal gestures, flowers, gifts, lawsuits, fights, and other emotional gestures. Emotions are a function of the body; our feelings are a result of the brain's ability to decode the complex coding of the endocrine system. Beyond that we decode again at a higher level to make sense of our feelings. As we are complex, we have developed a complex language for emotions. Learning to use it is one of the challenges writers face. For memoir writing emotions are particularly important. There would be no value to writing only about the ordinary happenings of life – and let's face it, most of the happenings we have to write about also happen to other people – if we did not express our selves, our feelings, our beliefs and values through this medium.

Three main sections in this chapter, each with its own exercises, provide the briefest introduction to fiction techniques which will help you to make your writing fresh and moving. "Show, Don't Tell" rounds up a theme that flows through our work in distinguishing story and presenting a story. The next section is called "Using Strong Language." Hint: It's not about swearing, but about choosing the precise word. "Sensory Detail" presents some ways to become aware of all five senses and the words that carry sensory data.

Show, Don't Tell.

A lot has been written on the subject of "show, don't tell," enough to deaden the senses, kill off creativity, and suffocate the beginning writer! The idea seems much more mysterious than it is.

This is what it is about: Readers want not only to be able to see what happened, but to feel the feelings, to be scared or tense with anticipation, to feel joy and sorrow and love. If you are thrilled, the reader wants to feel the thrill, experience it. Your reader wants to come away with a sense of knowing what happened that is like being there.

Well, how in the world would you do that? You "show, don't tell."

How do you do that? Depends.

Many of us write a rather generic report, a list of facts and figures, instead of a story. We say we had breakfast, took the car to be repaired, picked up the kids, almost had a wreck, and it was a good day. Can you see what is missing?

Actually, a lot is missing. Two important things that are missing are story and emotion. Take a look at one of those events. Did something happen that made a difference? There's a story there. Was there something that moved or touched you? Write that into a vignette. Maybe when you took the car to be repaired you ran into your long lost love, or when you went to pick up the kids you couldn't find them. What about the wreck? How would you feel if one of those things happened?

You can tell your reader why you felt a certain way, or you can create an emotional response in the reader by drawing them into the story. Which is better? Sometimes one, sometimes the other. If you don't want to spend a lot of time on something that is incidental to the story, it's OK to tell your reader how you felt and why.

If you want your reader to be drawn into the story, to anticipate the drama, and to feel the feelings along with you, show, don't tell. Write in such a way that the reader experiences the story along with the characters. Get close to what's happening and have the reader as present as possible. This means use action to carry the story. Use less explanation and use it in the right places. Unfold the events, don't summarize them.

And don't bother with the obvious. If the story lies in finding your long lost love, there is no real value in the rest of the list of activities. They are just activities, not story. The key to rewriting is to pull out passages that list happenings, gloss over details and generalize. Change them to put the reader in the driver's seat with the character. Get close. Instead of:

> *After dinner at the diner I thought I had better get some gas. I drove into the service station and I saw a woman there; I only caught a glimpse of her. I didn't know who it was but I wondered if it was Susan. I left the car in front of the bay that was empty...*

Write:

> *As I turned into Max's service station, I caught a glimpse of a familiar profile. Could it be her? No, of course not, I told myself for the millionth time. Those days are over; she left town years ago. I parked the car and strolled into the shop office, trying to act normal...*

What happened next? The scene is set, there is a tantalizing hint of back story; the reader wants to know what happened. In the second version I have chosen only the actions that move the story and I have paired feelings with those emotions.

Your story evokes an emotional response in the reader that is directly comparable to the energy you put into it through the words you choose.

> *My father is interested in trains and mechanical and electrical things; he can wax ecstatic on the subject of algebra, knows a lot about computers and is a good listener.*

Edited version:

> *My father is fascinated by trains and things mechanical and electrical; he can wax ecstatic on the subject of algebra, actually saw the first computers, and can listen me into changing my mind! How he does this...*

This version is a little better because the words are brighter and more precise.

If I wrote the story of Dad's experiences with the computers of the 1940s, in his words as he experienced it, the story would be even more interesting. If I took you through it just as it happened, computer buffs might find it fascinating.

Using Strong Language

Speaking directly to the point, using precise words usually improves the quality of writing.

In a short piece there is little room for developing character and creating background. Character has to shine through well chosen words. The setting must be described very briefly, and only enough to give the feeling of the place and the people in it. This means that the writer of a short piece gets to do everything a novelist can spread out over many thousand words in a small fraction of that space. He just has to do it quicker. Good news! Quicker is usually better.

Language Precision

I hope you love words, love the sound and the feel and the variety of them. Choosing the right word can give your writing real power. Use the correct word, the one that gets your meaning across clearly. The perfect word brings an "ah ha" of understanding to the reader. It doesn't have to be a twenty-dollar word. If a ten-cent one is a perfect fit, use it. A simple word is more likely to be understood by everyone. Spend time with your dictionary; a thesaurus is helpful, but it is only a cross-referenced list of synonyms. It is no more powerful than your full understanding of the word meaning. Look up a new word before you use it.

Imagine a set of hoops something like the Olympic Games symbol. Each one stands for a different word, in the case of our example. Each of these hoops has a certain amount of space inside; that's where the word meaning lives. If two hoops next to each other don't overlap, they mean different things–even if they sound the same or look alike. If they do overlap, they mean something similar even if they appear to be different at first glance. The hoops can overlap a lot or a little, but they never quite line up perfectly. There is almost always a little difference between the meaning, or the implication, or the proper use, of a pair of synonyms.

Exercise: Words and Concepts

- Draw a set of circles or shapes on piece of paper. Have them be at least a couple inches across so you can write on them.
- Start with the words, memoir, autobiography, and biography.
- Look each word up in a good dictionary; copy the meanings of one word on each shape. If there are a large number of meanings, be sure you collect the definition which relates to writing for each word, even if you don't actually copy all of the others.
- Cut out your paper shapes.
- Play with the shapes to show how much the various word meanings overlap. The space that doesn't overlap is the space of difference.

Writing the Stories of Your Life 185

>   Hint: some of your shapes may need to be larger or smaller than others, cut them down to fit.

> ❧ Now add recollection, remembrance, and reminiscence, journal to the first list to make it more interesting.

You can or pick a group of related words starting with any word that interests you from your thesaurus. Story, journal, diary, tale, folk tale, and fairy tale might be an interesting group.

Using the word which means exactly what you mean to say provides efficiency; you don't have to fumble around with a whole string of adjectives or adverbs trying to convert a weak noun or verb into something strong. Using precise language imparts both power and beauty to your writing. The novelist Ernest Hemingway was a master of short sentences and everyday words. His works can be read easily, and they have depth because of the precise use of words.

Action words—verbs—are usually stronger than adverbs; the right noun is stronger than a string of adjective. As you begin to polish your work, watch for ways to bring core meanings to the fore by choosing powerful language.

Seeing and hearing as a writer

>   Two things a writer must learn to do:

> ❧ Learn to see as a writer

> ❧ Learn to read as a writer

The second is actually easier to learn than the first. The second can be learned from a linear process; the first is something to be grasped as an "ah-ha!" and then to be deepened by looking for the experience in other places. Seeing as a writer is related to understanding the structure of human interactions, the "what leads to what" and how to capture those relationships. To a certain degree, you will learn to read as a writer over time as you write. You will listen for words and pay more attention to their meanings.

A useful exercise for learning to read like a writer is to read your work in a monotone so that you learn to hear the words and depend on the meanings of the words rather than the context. In written work the words must carry the meaning. This reading is about as interesting as reading the phone book. Expression is something the reader brings to the reading experience. If you have been thinking of "readings" you have attended with writers reading their poetry and stories, caressing each word, letting it fall from their lips like dewdrops of grace, that is not the kind of reading we are talking about. You already know how to do that. You will automatically read your own writing with your own sound and rhythm, and it will sound right to you. What we want to accomplish here is to have you hear your own words, just the words, ma'am.

The easiest way to learn this according to Sol Stein[60] is to have a friend read your material to you. The catch is you must find someone who really can't read, the worst reader you know, someone who calls the words clearly but with no apparent comprehension. Have this person read your story aloud. Listen, and learn that the words on the printed page must carry the meaning by themselves. Excellent writing is based in two word skills: clarity and precision. You must choose the word that carries the precise idea you have clearly to your reader. Then and only then is there the opportunity for communication to occur.

Does your writing lack the color provided by words that generate emotion? One way to make information interesting and, incidentally, communicate information more clearly, is to use words that convey the exact meaning and emotional tone that you want to communicate. Pick your words carefully; your words carry your meaning.

Get in the habit of using a dictionary. Buy yourself a good one. It doesn't have to be the latest edition although that is preferable, but get an unabridged. Look up words to get the fullness of their meanings. Especially if you have the thesaurus habit, look up words to get the nuances and differences between words that lie in the same ball park. Using the right word makes all the difference.

Sensory Detail

Readers want to experience the feeling of the place, whether it is warm with love or stinking with fear. They want to smell the fragrance of the blooms, be scared silly by the ghost when it finally does appear, hear the soughing of the wind in the pines, stagger around with sea-legs, and really be able to touch the roughness of linen. They want to use all of their senses, they want to be able to "see" the story.

A picture is worth a thousand words, and a passage laden with sensory detail will engage a reader's feelings and imagination.

There are two essential strategies, a short term and a long term approach, that you can use to enrich your writing with sensory detail. One, a brainstorming exercise, will specifically make a difference in whatever you write any time you use it. It is presented as the warm up and writing exercise. The other, a more general strategy, is to let yourself become aware of sensory detail, feed your Inner Writer, and allow yourself to become a more interesting writer over time through letting yourself say whatever you want to in your drafts. It's easy; let your subconscious do the work. There are a number of exercises provided with the discussion of sensory detail; you can go as far as you want to with this subject.

Warm up and writing practice

Remember the "My Friend Susan" exercise we did earlier? We will use the same idea for a warm up today. Write the name of a person at the top of a page in your notebook. Have this be a person you want to write about today. She or he should be a central character in your story or recollection.

- Begin each line by writing "My friend [name]..." is or has... Make a list of details about the person. Concentrate on getting sensory experiences of the person. Use feeling words as much as possible. (If your thoughts are really hot, you don't have to show them to anyone!) Persevere. Let yourself put down whatever is there for you.

- Now, write as much as you can about that person. Write for five minutes in continuous writing as we have before.

- When you feel that you are warmed up, move right into your story. Keep up the pace.

Enrich your writing with sensory details

People, places and things all have qualities. You may be able to count them but your reader wants to get the sense of them. It may be less important that exactly one hundred and twelve people were present than that the little church was packed with "people sitting close together" the women's hats were touching. Enhance your writing with sensory detail; detail that lets the reader get the feeling, not just the facts. When you write, you do more than make a picture for the reader. A picture may be worth a thousand words, but it's still just a picture. You can't smell it, taste it or hear it, and your reader wants all of that. She wants to feel the silky smoothness of the velveteen rabbit and the thrill of being scared to death by an unexpected touch.

Qualities may be just words on a page, but we experience them with all of our senses when we read, not just our eyes. OK, we perceive them as if we had experienced them with all our senses. The brain makes this interpretation whether we read the page visually or hear the words read aloud. The imagination goes to town. We salivate to the sumptuous aroma of a feast and wrinkle our noses at the stench of rotting flesh in the moat of a ruined castle. Qualities may be out there in the person, place, or thing, but our senses tell us how we feel about them. Later on, we may be unsure whether we read or dreamed or imagined a story that is very real to us.

Much of the pleasure for the reader comes from the sensory data in a chapter. Not everything has to be beautiful. Some stories are about terrible things. We want to feel frightened or angry as well as happy or sexy. A passage has no sense of reality without sensory data. We process all of it as though we experience it with our senses.

Read a page or two of any really rich piece of narrative. Whether it is fiction or non-fiction it will have a number of words that give you something sensory. Everyday words are all it takes to create sensory images, good old four letter words with Anglo-Saxon roots. The more abstract your words are, the less sensory they are likely to be.

Facts and figures are the food of the thinker perhaps, but the reader of a story wants to feel something as well. Even if you are writing technological science fiction or an action novel where verbiage is eliminated, the plot is packed and fast paced, and nobody seems to have any feelings; you must use words that titillate the senses or your reader will depart. Men (especially) pride themselves on being tough and strong and hard-nosed, etc., but even those ideas carry some sensory information. Hardness, strength, and endurance are sensory characteristics. In the thriller or the fantasy, feelings are built up under the surface as characters charge down one blind alley after another and experience yet another narrow escape. The reader is charged up with his own feelings about the events.

Je ne sais quoi—that certain something

Many, many words, especially common words, carry sensory data, if not in their actual denotative meanings, in the connotative meanings associated with them. Je ne sais quoi implies mystery, the "I don't know how to say it" experience. What is it about a woman that attracts a man? That which attracts, sexual or otherwise, is often not available to logic, but something that appeals to the senses. Sexual tension is built more by the sensory quality of words than by the clinical depiction of the act. It is not an accident that the message of love is carried by the scent of flowers, the velvet of rose petals, the taste of chocolate or the caress of a soft summer breeze.

Conveying sensory data is important and it is not that difficult. A lot of change for the better comes from just becoming aware of the issue. I suggest that you do a couple things that will improve your writing generally and especially enliven and enrich your stories.

Read a lot and notice the words that catch your imagination. Are they sensory words? Notice especially words that carry information triggers.

Coach yourself to use simple words in your writing. Earthy, everyday, one-syllable words are laden with associations and emotions. Abstractions may crystallize thinking but they distance the reader from feelings. When you pick longer words, use words that carry some sort of image or sound; words such as the word "crystallize," which I used in the last sentence instead of "harden," as I first wrote it.

Tuck this idea in the back of your mind somewhere that all your writing will be rich with sensory detail:

Writing the Stories of Your Life

> *My writing is rich in sensory detail
> and interesting to my readers.*

Over time, your Inner Writer will provide you with more choices of words that are rich in taste and smell and sound to go along with your visual description. You can decide how to use them.

Assignments

1. Write a short piece (no more than 500 words) using only one-syllable words. It can be on any topic, contain dialogue or not. If a word ending turns a word into two syllables, you can use it if you have to.

2. Try writing in the present tense only.

3. Read! Read, and be aware of the words that convey smells to your nostrils, colors to your eyes, sounds to your ears—sensory details to your mind. Make notes of particularly piquant words and poignant phrases.

4. Go out into the world with all your senses humming. Notice things that you don't usually pay attention to. This is a great thing to do with your lover, or a friend, or even your children—depending on the mood! Notice butterflies and birds and grass and rocks and buildings. Find sensory words to express your feelings.

5. Create something–just for fun–that requires at least three senses to appreciate it. Then write about it. Hint: food projects can fill this assignment, but there are many other possibilities.

6. Look back at your story ideas list; pick something with lots of potential for feeling. Write a story or recollection.

7. Keep adding stories to your project.

8. Check over previously written stories to enhance the sensory experience.

9. The other assignments for this section have charts associated with them; therefore, I have put each on a separate page. Please go to the next page for additional assignments.

Sensory Detail Chart

Walk around with this chart for twenty minutes. Write down sensory details that you perceive in this chart. You might write tree in the first column. Look carefully at the tree; write down its different parts (use the first column). For each part write down the colors you see, the shape, the texture under Sensory Details. Touch it; how does it feel to you? How does it smell? What sounds do you hear? Write all of this on the chart; then write down any feelings the specific sensory details bring up. They don't have to make sense. Let yourself explore your feelings and make notes.

Find words that particularly represent your sense of the people, places and things you examined. Use your thesaurus or dictionary to help you. Add those words to the last column of the table.

Person/Place/Thing	Sensory Detail	Your Feelings	Feeling Word

Sensory Words Chart

Select a page or two of a novel, story, or any narrative that you like. List all the words you notice that have sensory meaning or connotations. Look up any that you are not sure of in a good dictionary. Do one passage that has a lot of feeling and another that is very business-like. How are they the same or different?

Reference: Author, Title, Location, Page		
Word	**Meaning**	**Feeling**

If you want to get more from this exercise, select the same number of words (approximately) from several different narratives or several authors. Make a note of your feelings about each passage before you count the sensory detail words. Repeat the process above and compare your lists.

Comparison of Sensory Detail Words Chart

For a slightly different take on sensory detail, select several passages from novels, short stories, or any narrative writing and create a chart. Try to get works of similar quality. Use about a page from each and note the reference in your chart, so you can find it again if you want to. Note the type of work (genre), the number of words in the passage, the number of sensory words including words with sensory allusions or connotations. Figure the percentages by dividing the number of sensory words by the word count in each case.

Reference: Author, Title, Reference Including Page	Genre	Word Count (#)	Sensory Words (#)	Detail/ Words (%)

You can compare these percentages directly. Group the passages from the same genre, and just looking at the numbers will show you where there are differences between genres. When you have as many as thirty passages of each type, a simple statistical analysis may be run to verify the differences.

Differences between authors in the same genre may also be very great. You can use this general strategy for a number of other useful comparisons.

Chapter 15

THEME—What Is It All About?

My intention in this chapter is to help you take a look at the core statement of your memoir. I have suggested that you write a number of pieces, perhaps simply a collection of stories, but possibly arranged around some "theme" or organizing principle. Now we will look at them again and see what the underlying message is. This will be helpful in pulling your work together and finishing it. Notice that we are now talking about "theme" at a different level; for example, suppose the organizing principle was holidays and you have written stories of experiences or traditions in your family. Along the way you might have discovered that you are really writing about the way that the women in your life band together and interact, or the way the family members help each other. At a deeper level your theme might be love or community. Your life story and your life is about these messages.

A broad literature has been written about theme in fiction and essay. It seems to be a favorite topic of literary minds. You may be in one of several places on this. It may be unimportant to you. Theme is vastly overrated; you are only interested in story. Any theme that shows up or doesn't show up is OK with you. You may feel that theme is not so important as it is cracked up to be, but interesting. You may believe that knowing your theme is important if you want to make a difference in the world. You may think that theme is what it's all about, the most important aspect of writing a story. Wherever you are with this matter is perfectly OK; it will be helpful for you to know where you are as it will affect your choices regarding what you do to polish your work, and what you do with it afterwards.

Don't try to figure out what your theme is, just write your stories and you will see it.

Identifying Theme

Theme is meaning. Human beings can make meaning out of anything, and we do. That's what we are all about. It's part of our learning style and our success as a species. It gets away from us sometimes and leaves us trying to pick up the pieces. Different people see things differently. You may or may not see your theme the way someone else sees it. All you can do is shrug, "So you see it that way?"

There are several levels of the concept "theme" ranging from a statement of the meaning of the story, or the main character's viewpoint, to a life philosophy. The word "theme" may also be used to describe the line of reasoning that the author explores in an essay.

To make this even murkier, theme in a particular story is whatever worldview is being presented. For example, one might say that a particular story is about finding true love or transformation or the idea that the world always stays the same. At the story level Dickens's A Tale of Two Cities is about self-sacrifice as is de Maupassant's Gifts of the Magi. The theme in Kafka's Metamorphosis is that we are helpless without others.

Questions for finding your theme:

- *What feeling am I left with?*
- *What does the story provide?*
- *What am I left thinking about when I get to the end?*
- *What underlying value is important here?*

Sometimes authors seem to demonstrate a particular theme; but it is difficult to tell whether they believe the viewpoint and are trying to put it across or they are simply writing as if something were true to explore it; in other words, the theme may be limited to a particular piece or it may be an ongoing worldview. The word is used both ways: we have "theme" in the sense of a continuity of interests and "theme" in the sense of an underlying hum of meaning within a particular piece of writing.

Theme is easier to identify in some stories than in others. One way to look for the theme is to ask questions like: What am I left with? What does the story provide? What am I left thinking about when I get to the end?

Exercise: Identifying theme in stories

English teachers spend a good bit of time on "theme" as an aspect of composition—or they did when I was in school. It was never very clear to me and most of my compatriots what theme was all about—but we were young then and our quest for meaning had a different character. We knew what was wrong with the world and how to save it! We didn't know that such thinking could become a life theme.

Theme in the literary sense tends to show up after the fact. It's there when you look back at it—meat for literary criticism for the next two hundred years—but not too

Writing the Stories of Your Life

important when you are busy inventing your life or eagerly telling your story. That is why I have saved this section until you have several pieces of writing available to review.

- Select a story that you have read before. Read it again. You are already familiar with the plot, the dialogue, etc. Look this time for what the author is saying about life. What is the author's basic premise? What does the author care about? What core value is he expressing?

- Ask the questions: What am I left with? What does the story provide? What am I left thinking about when I get to the end?

- What values does the author demonstrate?

- Is there something else that tells you anything about the author's beliefs in the story?

- Make a judgment of the author's theme. Write your summary of the author's theme in your notebook along with a quote or two to support your judgment.

- Make a chart for one author. Put the author's name at the top; then use the following headings for three columns: Title, Quote, Theme. Read several stories by this author. Fill in the chart provided at the end of the chapter or make your own.

- Is there any consistency to the author's theme? If not, you haven't yet gotten to the deepest level. You have probably found the theme of the story, but not the life theme. Some people, however, have a complex of themes and opinions. They are hard to categorize.

- Re-read the works and see if you can get further insight; or find other works by the author for further insight and validation of your perception. Include their autobiography if it is available.

- Repeat this exercise for other authors. What have you learned?

Life Themes

A life theme derives from one's personal set of beliefs or underlying philosophy. "Rebellion seems to be a theme with her;" or "Everything he writes carries a deep sense of spiritual commitment," express the idea. Theme may or may not be articulated; it may just be there as a selection factor which only shows up in the type of tales one tells. It is likely to be so much a part of you that you don't see it.

It is often easier to see the theme in someone else's work than your own. Yours is usually transparent to you. I see it, but you see right through it. It has taken me fifty

The book [of memories] is not about who I am but about what has happened to me in my life… If you want to know who I am, then read my novels.[61]
—*Andrew M. Greeley*

years to see mine. I am about creating a space where people are self-expressed and creative, where new ideas, and new models show up. My best work is an expression of that theme. I know a couple of people whose life theme seems to be adventure. They are happiest when trekking through parts unknown or taking on new challenges. Many (not all) artists are dedicated to beauty. You may be about peace on earth, protecting the environment, being the best you can be, or you may hold a space for love, vitality, health, opportunity, or any other possibility you can think of.

If I boil my theme down to one word, it is probably love, but it could be family or self-expression. My early life was pretty heavy on independence. My parents' favorite story about my first words has me stamping my tiny foot, curls bouncing, clouds hovering, insisting "I do by self!" You can't always boil your theme down to one word, but you will find a sentence or two that embodies it if you try. Themes may change in expression as you grow, but your life theme hums along underneath it all.

There's no requirement that you know what your theme is. Write your stories and don't worry about it. But if you just can't stand it and you want to know, here are some exercises.

What's your life theme?

Listen for yourself. What do you say about yourself to others? Listen for "I'm the kind of person who..." Such ideas as "I'm the kind of person who tells the truth, who loves beautiful things, who enjoys good friends, food, and fun, who loves adventure..." may carry your theme along with them. You may find that you have several ways of saying it with a similar underlying meaning. After you find these ideas, see if any of them relate to some underlying concept or intention. That will be your theme.

Some time you will hear yourself say something like, "That's the story of my life, always arguing..." Or "Always a bridesmaid..." or "Here we go again..." That's your theme at the level of your self talk, the things you are always concerned about, always worried about, never quite resolved. It's sometimes called the "negative ground of being," or your "sentence."

You may need to listen intentionally as you talk with people. It may take days or weeks to begin to hear yourself. Persevere; it will be worth it. Write in your journal about what you hear. Discuss your findings in your group or with your writing buddy.

After you have mastered this approach—hearing what you say about yourself—listen to yourself again. What lights you up? What are you passionate about? Listen to yourself as you talk to different people over a period of time. What will you just not shut up about? An important one in my life is family: family loyalty, being there for my family; nurturing and helping others. "I'm not much of a caretaker, but I'm fiercely loyal," is one expression of it. Another is, "I love my kids, and if you wind me up I will talk about them for hours." Family matters to me; too bad it took me decades to figure that out!

Writing the Stories of Your Life

Notebook Exercise: Who are you?

- Complete the sentence stem: "I'm a person who…" as many times as you can in ten minutes. Move fast. Don't sit and think; just write. Do you have a page or two of items? Look for your theme among those items.

Oral Version

- You can do this one orally in pairs, too. The listener should say "thank you" after every expression from the one who is working. Go for about five minutes each way and then discuss it. Make notes for yourself.

- Discuss what you have learned about yourself with your writing buddy. Share with your group.

- Write about it.

Your theme should be stated as something ideal. It will be something you think is important, possibly much bigger than you think you are. You don't have to perfectly embody this idea, but you do express it in your life to the best of your ability.

Our most creative writing carries a subtext of who we are, deeply and indelibly. This is the writer's voice. It appears whether you want it to or not. It is simply there when you tell the truth about your life and yourself. It is the things we say when we say, "I am a person who…"

Group exercise: Interview for theme

Sometimes another person can tell what lights you up more easily than you can. Talk with your writing buddy about this. She will be able to see the change in your eyes or your voice when you are expressing something that has heart for you. That is where your theme lies. Your theme literally lights you up.

- Pair up with another person. Interview each other about your interests, your personality, what is important to you. What matters to you as a person? What you are looking for will show up in questions about the person's dreams and wishes for the future. This exercise may take some time.

- Interviewers: watch and listen for hot buttons. What is the person really ready to go on and on about, or really proud of? What topic really puts a light in the eyes?

- Interviewees: Let the other person know when you hit a topic that's important to you.

- When you have identified something that both people agree is a hot button, dig into it, mine it for the best sense you can get of what's important about that topic. That's where you will find the person's theme.

- Interviewees: Work with it awhile to get the exact wording for yourself—then check back with the other person. Have them watch your face as you talk about this theme. They will be able to tell if it is a core theme. Interviewers: A life theme is present if talking about it lights the person's face up.

Exercise: Turning Points

Many of us have more than one theme, or seem to. Usually if you stay with this, you will find that there is an underlying consistency to it that pulls it into one idea and can be expressed in a word or a short sentence.

Here is another exercise that you can do in your notebook, which may help you uncover your life theme through actions and choices you have made.

- Draw a line down the middle of a page. Make a list of important things you have done on one side.

- Beside each make a note about why you did it or what was important about it. Nobody has to see this but you.

- Is there any consistency? Do you see some core beliefs emerging?

- Keep going at this over a period of time. Write about various events that come up. What emerges from those writings?

Take time to mull over the why questions and figure out what you learned from these events. Then look at what you brought to the table. What did you contribute that was unique in the situation? What might not have been there without you? Was it a consideration of the effects of the event on families, or some knowledge, or leadership or love? What did you bring? Fun? Joy? Action? A spirit of adventure?

Life is an adventure!
—Ann Charles

If you are in a writing group, you may want to have everyone in the group do Assignment No. 6 at the end of this chapter. Share your findings. Bring the essays to the next group meeting and read them aloud. After reading all of the essays, discuss your various viewpoints on the matter.

Alternatively, have everyone do Assignment No. 5 and share your findings at the next meeting. Rewrite one story each and read a selection of your rewritten stories at your next meeting.

Literary Themes

Look for the underlying themes in literature and persuasive writing.

Freud's theme was that the core energy is sexual and it drives everything one does. His expression of this theme was shaped by the narrow Victorian world in which he lived.

Jung's theme was that the inner symbolic life drives us, and this is a group as well as an individual matter. There is a mystical connection between and among all persons at the core of being.

The mythologists, eg. Campbell, Pearson, Pinkola-Estes are intrigued by the idea that stories express our theme and drive our lives.

Mists of Avalon and some other books by Marion Zimmer-Bradley are driven by the exploration of the inner being as the story plays out in life—the relationship of inner and outer story and the feminine side of things. How does the intuition operate? How do human beings operate when they allow intuition to guide them?

In *Mirrors of the Self; Archetypal Images That Shape Your Life*,[62] editor Christine Downing presents a fascinating group of writings by writers on this subject. Carol Pearson, another Jungian, has written extensively on the archetypes that shape our lives.[63] I have found these books very useful, both in writing and in life.

What animates your writing at this deeper level? It may be hard to talk about, but this is the writer's work: to bring to the surface that which is hidden and to present it so that it is understood by the inner being or even the soul level of the reader.

Theme in Memoir Writing—Pulling your stories together

Theme is that underlying issue that your story is about, the central focus, or the heart of the matter. Theme is closely related to your motivation for presenting a story; it is your view on the meaning of the story. It is the answer to the why questions. Theme may be a statement you consciously wish to make to demonstrate some understanding you have, or it may be nothing more (nor less) than the underlying communication of your world-view through your work.

Bringing your book together

Now that you have explored your theme or themes at different levels, can you see how it can be useful to you in organizing our writings? Perhaps you started right out with a plan to write stories based on a particular interest. An organizing principle like "places I have dragged my family to" or "old-time objects we no longer use" or "one story for each grandchild" or "family recipes and holidays" has served you to get the stories written. If you want to pull your stories together into a book, this is a good time to review your organizing principle for it's relationship to your life theme.

What does your writing provide?

Is there an interest or a core belief which has been a theme in your life? Perhaps you believe that families should stick together and help each other. Do you also collect recipes, love food, cook for family holidays? Cooking with the kids, holidays, or recipes may serve as themes around which you organize your stories. The deeper theme might be family loyalty.

Does your story have a theme as a result of one crucial incident or set of experiences? How does that relate to your deeper life theme? Did you handle this experience in a certain way because of your beliefs or values? What did you learn about yourself and about life as a result of this experience?

Many true adventures, stories of plane crashes, polar expeditions, solo flights and voyages, wars and other shocking or terrifying events or situations have done well on the market. The theme of such a book will be the writer's net feeling or learning about the situation; e.g. a book about war experiences may be the heroics of certain people with no comment on the underlying issue of war per se, or it could be the greatest antiwar book ever written. Different themes.

Theme in a body of work is the expression of a belief about life that permeates the whole thing. It is a personal philosophy. Read a piece of your own work. What does your writing provide? What do you have to give? What life theme do you bring to the table? Themes are like different notes; get a group of them together and you have music.

Review your stories. If you read several of your stories, is there a consistent theme? You may want to use that theme to help you work your stories into a whole. Are you saying what you want to say with your work? Is there a good title that derives from the theme?

Ask yourself what you are saying if you boil it all down to one sentence. Try that in fact, boil your story down to one long sentence. Don't worry about grammar; write the guts of the story quickly into one sentence. If it's a page long, cut it in half. Then cut it down again. Cut it again until you have less than fifty words. What belief about life, or fundamental point of view, is expressed in this short statement of the story?

One final caveat, there is no requirement that there be a theme. And, it may be easier for others to see it than for you. Don't worry about it if you don't see it. It's there. Ask someone close to you what they see as the theme in your life. Share your stories with them.

Assignments

1. Find a story that you have read before, possibly one that you have used for other exercises. This time read for the theme. In your notebook write out the theme of the story. Also copy a line or two, or reference passages where the author indicates or develops the theme. See if you can follow the development of the theme through the story. How well does it work?

2. Do the above exercise for several stories of one type; compare the stories.

3. Go beyond the exercise above using several stories of one type and several of another category; compare the types. Is theme more or less evident in one type of story than another?

4. Write a short essay on the subject of Theme in True-Life Stories; include your findings from these exercises. If you use stories from one particular magazine or anthology, limit your discussion to that specific type of stories (Your findings may or may not apply to all true-life stories). If you use printed sources, be sure you reference them correctly.

5. Do the same assignment given in No. 1 using your own stories. Is what you are saying what you want to say with your stories? How do you feel about this? Are there other themes or stories you want to tell?

6. Write an essay that expresses the fundamental ideas you have to share with other people, the ones that turn up again and again in the stories you tell.

7. Go over the stories you have written as part of your memoir project. If you don't have one, look for an organizing principle and/or theme in the stories you have written which will help to pull your stories together into a volume.

8. Take these ideas and exercises to your journal and continue to work with them over time.

Themes in Literature, Chart

Author		
Title	**Quote**	**Theme**

Chapter 16

AND THEY RODE OFF INTO THE SUNSET
– Drawing Your Work to a Close

By now you have written a number of stories; you have grappled with the technique of writing. Congratulate yourself on your efforts and persistence. You are almost there. We have studied character, emphasized action and feeling in short pieces, We have written stories and short pieces or scenes and chapters and tried various approaches to individual pieces. We have looked for our themes and enriched our work with details. In short, we have developed a rich process for working with stories. Now we want to apply this approach to the whole body of work.

My intentions for this chapter are to point you in the direction of what you need to complete a book-length memoir. This chapter will help you shape up and complete your story with a final look at the flow, movement, or structure. I will add a few other story techniques which may be of value as you draw your work to a close. Whether you intend to publish your work or share it with your family and friends, you will want to put it into the best shape you can. We have covered structure for a particular story in a previous chapter. This chapter is focused on arranging the whole book to get the best effect.

No matter how short or long a piece is or what type of story you are writing, it has a beginning and an end. Everything in between is the middle. Presenting your story well involves deciding where you have the strongest opening, what should come next and where it should end. The order, or structure, you give your story contributes to the type of tension that the reader builds up going through it. The right order can transform a story from dull to exciting; it can build suspense, create surprise, joy, or satisfaction in the reader, or give you a better way to make your point.

Finding the Right Structure

A memoir can be written in almost any story format you can imagine. What distinguishes a memoir is the particular perspective on a true story, the perspective of memory. A memoir, short or long, acknowledges or recounts a person's existence—yours or someone else's. The discussion of structures for memoir could fill an entire book.

All story forms are appropriate to the memoir. Probably the least likely way that you will write your story is as a traditional novel with a well developed plot; however, it can be done. Any one of the two dozen or more plot varieties might be used; however, a looser approach to plot such as a literary or creative approach usually works better. A collection of stories is my favorite approach for most memoirs. It is the easiest way to do it, allows you to add significant portions as you finish them, makes for good reading and is easy to share by reading aloud short segments or stories. A number of nonfiction forms can also work well; not only the forms usually used for biography, but many others, depending on the life lived and the material one has to work with.

Top down

Sometimes the best order is backwards, where the writer tells the punch line, or outcome first and fills in the details. News reports traditionally use this structure. It's called the "top down" structure and is visualized as a triangle. It is written so that the most important question is answered up front, followed by the next and the next in order of importance, until the full journalistic set of questions (who, what, where, when, how) is answered. The inside story about that structure is that by going from most important to least important answers in the days before computers, the editor could quickly trim material from the end of any story and still make his deadline. Today news stories are still tightly written but don't automatically follow that pattern. The media sound bite has evolved from this approach.

Top down, or a variation on it, works well in longer works when there is some mystery to solve or the background of the story is complex and the reader won't be able to follow it–or possibly won't be motivated to follow it–until he knows something about what happened or the outcome. Classical mystery stories begin with finding the body and unraveling the events leading up to the death.

A variation, the police procedural, opens with the law enforcement organization trying to solve the crime and proceeds through the process of bringing the perpetrator to justice. The crime appears to be the beginning, but as the story unfolds it can also be the culmination of the story. This would be a circular structure.

If your story is complex, multiple viewpoints may be necessary. Whether it is a short piece or the whole book, a complex will be best told from the point in the action where it is clear what happened. Start on solid ground. Move that into the next phase where there is a natural pause, then bring in the important threads that led up to the main event. Exploring the paths taken by various people to get to the point of their convergence—a point of high tension or conflict—is one of the things that makes retrospective writing interesting. There is time to look back and see what led to what. Then spend time on the outcome and results. Bring everything to a conclusion and end. This is not as complex as it seems. Reread your draft stories and you will see whether your story fits this model.

As memoir writers we can learn from the top down pattern that putting the end in the beginning is one effective option for some stories. Getting the details up front of who, where and what can set your story strongly on its path. The rest of the story is about what happened, how and why. For the memoir writer, musing on how and why is important. People like to read these stories; they want to know your perspective on the events or they wouldn't be reading your story. Give them the full treatment—your knowledge, your thoughts and your feelings. Put in the details.

Plots, quests and journeys

Let's suppose you wrote your whole story or group of stories starting at the beginning in time and working through to the end, and furthermore, you think this is a good structure for your story. Your book would have a chronological order. This is a traditional structure for memoir, biography and autobiography. It's a good way to tell what happened clearly in a whole life–your life, your journey.

The journey approach works well for any linear story, that is to say, an event or sequence of events that builds clearly, one step following another along a path. Whether winding or straightforward, the path is linear. Boy meets girl, they fall in love; there are obstacles to overcome, they overcome them; they get married and live happily ever after. There is room for complications, even an extra path that leads back to the main path; but the difficulties don't bloom into a maze of circularities and ambiguities. This is the basic path of a traditional novel. Any category of fiction that tends to have a single plot line will include stories of the quest or the journey. A romance novel is the story of a marriage in the making. This is also a good path to follow for the story of a career. There may have been sideways leaps and discontinuities, but the story involves one person's career and life, not several.

Any story which follows the movements of an individual through time is something like an old time saga, the story of a hero such as Siegfried, Finn or Ulysses that tells the tales of their exploits wrapped between the magical birth and tragic death of great hero. Mankind has loved these stories for thousands of years. In the middle you have all the space in the world to tell what happened. You can make up a new tale for each freezing night of the year and tell it around the fire. The tale of each of these events can stand on its own, except for the tales of birth and death. The birth and the death are not caused by the hero; and, oddly, they are ordinary, unless they are somehow enhanced by prophecy, madness, a shadowed past, or wizardry. They are dependent on the rest of the story for their importance.

A fairy tale (which is a teaching tale) about the birth of a prince or princess always begins with a prophecy. From the story of King Arthur, to Snow White or Brunhilde, and all of the heroes above, there is a terrible prophecy associated with their birth. This prophecy foreshadows the events of the hero's life, it foretells the nature of the obstacles to be overcome. It, in effect, defines the quest. The modern equivalent might be the expectations of parents and society. Were you born with a silver spoon? Or invisible? Ralph Ellison begins his story with "I am an invisible man."[64]

Here are a few first lines which foreshadow something:

> *"Everyone had always said that John would be a preacher when he grew up, just like his father."*
> —Go Tell It to the Mountain; by James Baldwin.

> *"'He is very ugly,' said his mother."*
> —Great Lion of God; by Taylor Caldwell.

> *"In my younger and more vulnerable years my father gave me some advice that I've been turning over in my mind ever since."*
> —The Great Gatsby; by F. Scott Fitzgerald.

> *"In the week before their departure to Arrakis, when all the final scurrying about had reached a nearly unbearable frenzy, an old crone came to visit the mother of the boy, Paul."*
> Author: Herbert, Frank Title: Dune

What did you have to overcome in your life?

A quest is an adventure in which the hero seeks something. Winning the princess from the tower, finding the secret of the grail, exploring a new frontier, setting out to find hidden treasure, and many other purposes can be the stated goal of the quest. There is in all of these stories, however, a hidden goal. An inner quest exists which must also be satisfied in order for the hero to return to the world with the needed object or the new knowledge. These two things are the external and internal motivations for a quest.

Thinking of your life as a quest, what have you sought? What have you found, perhaps instead of what you sought? What have you accomplished? How have your accomplishments moved you on to other things? Are there a number of tales to be told? It is possible that your life has involved a particular quest, one thing sought above all others, one achievement which involved many triumphs and a few defeats along the way. You have had help from others, you have found the object, and you have completed that journey. It could be the story of a scientific quest such as the story of Marie Curie who studied radium with her husband Pierre, or the quest for a vaccine, a cure, or the understanding of a disease, or a historical quest. It could be an adventure such as Thor Hyerdahl's Kon Tiki or Ra[65] stories.

Novels with a quest plot require a solid ending where obstacles have been overcome and everything is resolved. Popular autobiographical accounts or adventures must show that something big has been achieved, some obstacles have been overcome. Climbing Mt. Everest can be told on the external level; however, if you read these accounts, you find that the internal motivation which is present makes all the difference. Why would anyone practice and train for a marathon or a bike race or a climb? What do other people really want to know? How they did it, yes; and how come? What actually made it happen? Why would anyone get up day after day at four in the morning to run ten miles? These questions are about internal motivation. We want to know what makes people do what they do, why they do it, and how.

Perhaps you have not climbed Mt. Everest or traveled to exotic places, but you have made a difference for people in your town or through your work. Quest stories tend to depend as much on internal as external motivation. The hero or heroine goes in search of something in life, and it often turns out that the important results are a lesson learned or a change in the person. The personal growth is as important as the discovery of a new technology. The nature of the journey itself is of interest to others.

Maybe you are on the journey, but you haven't found the grail yet. Your life story may not have a clear ending; you are still alive, after all. You want to share what you have. Perhaps you are writing about something that happened in your life and there isn't a recognizable plot with a lot of action and an exciting climax. Don't give up. Most of the recollections people write are like this, and other people like to read them. You are writing about the journey. Your writing will be more interesting if you allow yourself to explore your motivation and your achievements from both the internal and external levels.

Taken together, your entries in a diary, your journal, or the log of your discoveries, and the exploration of its meaning can be of value beyond price to those who come after you.

What has the journey been like? Now that you look back on your life so far, is there an underlying continuity? If you wrote about that in the chapter on Theme, you might use that material to set up your beginning and your ending. In between, place your adventures, however large or small, particularly the things that seem most relevant to your theme. These will be the stories of events that directed you from one place to another on the journey—the turning points—and the stories that explore what it means or might mean. They are vignettes, pieces of the journey, snapshots taken along the way. Write about what you thought and what you learned, people you knew and what happened. Write about flowers and trees and birds and dogs. This memoir weaves and flows among the hills and valleys of life; it takes time to smell the flowers and consider the ways. The purpose is to take a look at something, see how it fits together perhaps, and see what treasures it holds.

Collections

A good strategy for writing autobiography is to write a collection of pieces; I have emphasized this approach. Depending on what type of materials you have, you might now have an anthology of stories you have written, a coffee table book with photographs and a bit of information, or a scrapbook with lots of photos and mementos and a number of short catchy recollections to go along with the other colorful material.

Your could arrange your stories into a memoir like Isaac Asimov's *I. Asimov*, which we talked about earlier. Like him, you could take your individual short pieces and arrange them chronologically or according to contents. His are numbered and each has a short title that tells you candidly what it is about, a person, a place, or an event. It works very well. You could break the whole group into years by grouping them in a meaningful way using years, or time periods in your life, such as school days, travels, and your career path; another grouping might be childhood, single years, marriage, children, empty nest. You can use your career, the places you have lived, ideas that interest you, hobbies, cooking, etc. to organize your memoir. You might place a distinctive page in front of each group of stories. They don't have to be chronological if they are grouped around a theme, but you may want to add a date or year or some reference to each story to help the reader find you on your path.

Besides arranging your memoir chronologically, you can tell your story through various other strategies. You might chose certain interests and devote a section to each. Suppose you have been successful in a business career and you have also been a photographer or a writer as well. Maybe you have been a minister and a missionary and a musician. Or a singer and a banker; a screenwriter and a physical therapist. Or a painter and an undercover cop. Ah, the day job! Perhaps you have not clearly changed careers, but have run two or three interests side by side. You have the perfect life for a thematic arrangement. Devote a section of the book to stories about each life path. Where they come together, articulate your path to fit your life. Make your book work for you.

Assemble the stories you have, shape them up, and arrange them in the order that unfolds the story to the best advantage. If necessary, fill in with short bits of narrative to explain or create transition. You may not need much; a heading with the date or location is often enough. Today many stories shift point of view or time and space with no transition. In a book with multiple narrators use the narrators' names as headers when you shift viewpoints. Chapter heads, section titles or specific space arrangements and other layout techniques can also be used to make the shift in time or viewpoint clear, depending upon the type of story you have.

Beginnings Middles Ends

This section addresses the matter of revising your story, now a book, to present it in a more dynamic way. Whatever order you decide to use in presenting your story is good. It's your choice. One way will likely work better for that particular story than all the others. You can try several approaches, or you may already know exactly how you want to do it.

Read your story or collection through from beginning to end. Identify the back story or background, the beginning, the middle, and the end of the story itself. Mark the sections with different colored markers in the margins or circle the paragraphs. On the computer highlight blocks of text with different colors, use a table, or put page breaks between sections and print them out so you can shuffle them together in different ways. Check the help section of your word processor if you don't know how to do one of those things. Underline important turning points in your story; use a different color.

That is the question: Do you start in the beginning, the middle, or the end?

Is anything missing? Is everything in the story or stories that you need to have it make sense to someone who never met you or the story's protagonist? What important event is missing? If so, all you have to do now is decide on the best order of presentation for the story or stories.

First, identify your ending. Your ending is your story's goal. When you know where you are going it is easier to get there. Next look for the best place to begin. Everything else goes in the middle. In the middle you should be particularly concerned with the flow and pace of the story. You want to draw your reader along from an event which sets up a story question to another action or event and story question to the answers at the end. At the end you resolve everything.

This reasoning applies to whole books of stories as well as to individual stories. Note, you may have a lot of stories and not have a beginning or an ending written. (Hooray! You have the middle!) Put your stories in order; look to see if there is a good story that you haven't written yet that would serve either of these purposes. Your story to open your book or story doesn't have to be something from your childhood. It can be something typical of your life theme or a story that sets up the story problem or quest. If you still don't have a beginning, or lack an ending, think about your theme and write a simple narrative frame for your stories.

Evaluate the Flow of your Story

The flow of your story is its path from beginning to end. It is also the sense that the story is moving along, happening, getting somewhere. Pace is a related concept. It refers to the rate of movement of the story. You want the pace to be quicker in the exciting parts and slower in a dreamy romantic space, for example.

This section is mostly questions. Read through the questions until an idea occurs to you that seems to be the right way to handle your story. Then try it. If it works, go on to evaluate your story in other ways using other questions. If it doesn't, try something else.

- What is the main point of your story?
- What should some one get from reading your story?

It's OK, by the way, if it is just a good story; but do think about what you want the reader to come away with and how you can facilitate that experience. Strive for a sense of immediacy, of being present, event after event or story after story in your collection.

- How do you want your reader to feel? Is the story sad, happy, funny, nostalgic? What feeling will come from reading the story? How can you rev up the feeling level?
- How can you arrange the story so that your reader will be informed, or entertained, or surprised, or whatever you want them to feel?
- Should anything be held back? What will be the effect on the reader if you hold back information?

The next few questions have to do with characters, especially the protagonist.

- Who is the main character?
- When do we meet the main character?
- Is the main character the narrator? If not, does your reader have a feel for who the narrator is?
- How much do we need to know about the main character? How much about the narrator?
- What about the other characters? Are they developed enough? Too much?

How much background, or build-up do you have? Do you need that much? Or more? You have enough back story when the outcome of the story is inevitable given the characters involved. You have too much when the story seems not to go anywhere, or gets boring before you get to what happened. Of course there are other factors also which predict the success of your story, but this rule will help you estimate back story.

- How much back story do you have? Where is it? Where should it be?
- How much explanation do you have? How much action? Is there a good balance between scene and sequel (action and explanation)?

Writing the Stories of Your Life

- Does the story move from action to more action to explanation? If not, how does it flow now? How should it flow?

Your answers to the above questions will guide you in deciding on the overall pattern for your story, and evaluating the flow of the action. You should evaluate how to build the middle, and where to end it as well as where to start.

The next few questions will help you decide where to open your story.

- Would it be best to start this story at the chronological beginning? How many scenes do you need?

- Can you tell this story better by starting with some action? Or, is the build-up necessary to the punch-line?

Actions often lead to other actions. Back story can be dusted in lightly here and there once you have set up the action line. Back story is a natural part of the resolution phase of a scene.

- If this story were fiction, where would it start?

- Can you start at the end? What will be the effect of starting this story at it's conclusion?

- What is the most interesting thing that happened in this story? Can you start with that?

- Which order of telling this story will provide the specific impact you are looking for?

From beginnings to story openings

Whereas you started at the beginning before, you may be thinking of opening your story somewhere else. Your revised story opening is our topic now. If you are not sure, consider how the order of story relates to the main character. You probably want to introduce the main character immediately. Consider how the beginning works with the point of view you prefer for the story. Consider how complex your story is. Is the path of your story a maze of different perspectives, or does it follow the shortest line with a steady stride from beginning to end? Different styles of writing and different kinds of content will call out for different structures.

The opening of a story is the place where the story begins. While that may seem tautological, think about it. A story has a beginning in time and place. It happened somewhere, some time, and to someone. But, where does your story start? The true beginning may have occurred a long time ago in a place far away and to different people. It is what will give the story meaning in the end; it is however, the back story or prologue. Sometimes a prologue can be useful for stories with important back story.

The best opening for the story is where the event you are telling about actually starts. This thinking leads us to define the beginning of a story as the point where the action begins. That is probably the best place to open the story most of the time.

It is always a good strategy to start with some action, introduce people, move into a little back story, and follow the course of events to resolve the conflict you have set up at the beginning. We have learned to engage the reader in a short story or recollection by beginning with the action. Action engages people in your story immediately. It is not the only way to begin. There are other ways to open a book that engage your reader quickly.

In a story based on the development of a character, or how a person changed or transformed as the result of some event, more time needs to be given to the nature of the character. You may want it to be a bit of action or dialogue that reveals something of the behavior and attitude of the main character. Find something engaging, something that is not predictable, not ordinary; something that is open ended, that causes the reader to begin to wonder. It may be something that becomes a sort of symbol for the life or story.

Whatever structure you use, there are certain things your story opening must accomplish. At the very least, it must:

- Grab and hold the reader's attention
- Get the story action started
- Introduce the most important characters
- Set the scene
- Provide a bit of background

Depending on the length of your piece your beginning may be a paragraph, several pages, or even a chapter or two. Whatever the length, it must captivate the reader right away; the difference is only a matter of the number of words or pages you have available to devote to involving your reader in the intricacies of the story. The beginning must stay in an appropriate balance to the rest of the book, and it should lead the reader easily into the middle.

Your opening will both raise and answer some questions for your reader. By the time he has read the beginning, the reader needs to know where and when the action took place, who was present and something about what happened. In the first paragraph or two the reader will decide whether to read a little more, and so on for several pages. On this basis she will decide whether she wants to read the rest. The general wisdom used to be that the reader would give you twenty or thirty pages before abandoning the book. Today's reader is likely to decide about a novel in the first couple of paragraphs. Your family, your friends, and people who really want to know about your life will probably be generous readers. If you are seriously determined to publish your book to the general public, keep in mind that you must engage your reader throughout to keep their attention.

Start with some action, something unexpected or unlikely. Have your reader engaged in the plot, the discovery, the journey right away. Action grabs the reader's attention; it is usually the best place to start. Unfortunately, most of us tend to get caught up in the back story instead of the action. When we first write something, we think about all the reasons why we are writing it, why it happened, why it was important, instead of writing and developing the story.

Back Story

The early beginnings or antecedents of the story are like seeds planted a long time ago that will turn into a garden when they germinate. They are the back story, not the seedling. The beginning of the action is like the seedling. This is where a chronologically told story should begin—with the action. The plot leads from the beginning of the action to the climax and then finishes quickly in a burst of color. Most stories have an event or central happening that is the point of the story. A quick resolution comes shortly after that.

Back story for our purposes is the same as the background of the story. It's a fiction writer's term for the story that is behind the story. Visualize back story as a treasure trove of reasons and details that you, the writer, reach into from time to time to explain things to the reader. You have written the back story in your notebook in the form of lists and other exercises to tease out details. You need the back story to get going; but when it is time to revise your piece, you may need to trim the fat a bit. Back story usually shows up in a novel or a strongly written biography some time shortly after the first scene—not all at once, but in bits and pieces as needed to explain matters.

While most of the back story that is necessary will have been shared with the reader before the whole story is resolved, a better place to do it is between scenes. Necessary back story can be inserted as part of the resolution of the action, or can even have its own mini-scenes.

Most good stories are like trees; they have roots that don't show and a few that do. The "real" beginning of the story may have happened years before the action began, or in a totally different place. The writer needs to know this; the reader may or may not. Among these roots the answers to the why questions may be found, but you as the writer will control how much prowling around in the roots the reader needs to do. As writers we can easily get fascinated with the roots and forget the story. Don't get stuck in the back story and give the story short shrift.

Check your story to see where it really gets started. That's the place where you –as a reader–would actually get interested if you didn't already know the story. That's the place to begin.

What is the essence of your story? Capture the core feeling that you want the reader to be left with in a few words. Use that idea to set things up. Make sure that your words call forth an image, a sound, a feeling that intrigues the reader. He wants to be seduced and enchanted by feelings as well as wowed by the facts.

The Hook

A hook in a story is that first line that makes you want to read the whole thing because you just have to find out what happened.

The hook is a curve ball, a little mystery, something that grabs you and pulls you along and eventually draws you in. Think of a fishhook or a shepherd's crook, boat hook or any other type of hook. Used actively, it draws something toward the user. A hook in advertising is anything that grabs the reader or viewer and makes them pause. In that pause they wonder and imagine and question. A hook in a story is that first line that makes you want to read the whole thing because you just have to find out what happened. The wanting more is what makes your reader bite the hook.

There are some truly magical first lines in literature. You might take on the exercise of examining a number of your favorite books for their first lines. Or go online and find a website that lists a number of them; I found several very quickly[66]. You will find, I expect, that some first lines are wonderful and some just get things started. Aim for getting the story started well, and you will get lucky now and then with a magic phrase that says it all.

The hook must capture the reader's attention, but it can do it in a number of ways. Until inspiration strikes you, use the first paragraph to get your story going. Introduce the most important character, set the scene quickly or say something unlikely but true. You can provide a bit of background, but beware of the lure of the back story.

Let your first line set up the story problem, show a conflict or theme that is central to the story. Hold the background for a few pages. After you have introduced the main thread of the story and the main characters, start giving the reader bits of the back story as he needs them to understand the story. Think of a "first line" in the way that actors use the term "line": a single speech or a group of words or sentences that belong together–not necessarily one line, not necessarily one sentence, but a definite short segment.

While the hook should come early in the story, it doesn't have to be your very first line. It is the idea that attracts your reader into the story, entices him to turn the page, has him wanting to know more. A hook creates a question that must be answered in your reader's mind. Design your hook to interest the reader you are writing for. A children's story must have a beginning that appeals to children and plunges them quickly into the story. The same actually applies to stories for adults, but what interests them may be different. Who is your target audience? What will grab their attention?

Writing the Stories of Your Life

Besides action, you can begin with a quotation or a fact or description. It may be a poetic prose line of your own, such as Dickens's engaging lines which open The Tale of Two Cities:

> *It was the best of times, it was the worst of times, it was the age of wisdom, it was the age of foolishness, it was the epoch of belief, it was the epoch of incredulity, it was the season of Light, it was the season of Darkness, it was the spring of hope, it was the winter of despair, we had everything before us, we had nothing before us, we were all going direct to Heaven, we were all going direct the other way--in short, the period was so.*[67]

Your opening line can be thoughtful or controversial. It can be a statement that engages the reader's mind or it can sketch a scene that sets up the visual experience of your story. The trick to writing a good hook is to capture an aspect of the story that sets the tone for what follows. It may be a bit mysterious, philosophical, or seductive; it might hint of disaster about to happen. This story is told from the point of view of the deceased victim of a tragedy.

> *"My name was Salmon, like the fish; first name, Susie. I was fourteen when I was murdered on December 6, 1973." -- The Lovely Bones, by Alice Sebold.*[68]

The opening gets the reader right into the story and makes the unusual viewpoint clear. The writer follows the opening lines with a description of the character and the central action. The opening moves the reader quickly into the story.

Take a look at several of your favorite novels or biographies. Study the opening line, the opening paragraph, the first scene or chapter. What does it accomplish? What does the writer do? Look at the openings of books you have read and categorize the information in the first paragraphs. What works? What doesn't?

Exercise: Story Openings

Take a look at several of your favorite novels or biographies. Study the opening line, the opening paragraph, the first scene or chapter. What works? What doesn't?

What does the writer do to accomplish his purpose for the beginning?

What questions does the opening set up in the reader's mind? Are these questions answered satisfactorily in the book?

Make a chart similar to others you have made in your notebook or use the one at the end of this chapter. Copy the first line or so along with the reference information. Define for yourself the portion of the book that constitutes the opening. What specific goals does this author have for the opening of the book? This exercise will be easier if you work with first lines separately from story openings as a whole.

Use categories including: Action, Dialogue, Symbolic, Poetic, Background or Back Story, Introduce Characters, and so forth to indicate the author's accomplishments.

Middles

In a story, the main question to be answered in the middle is what happened? And what happened next? What happened after that? Not all memoirs have a plot, but all stories have a middle. Whatever is between the beginning and the end serves the function of carrying the core of the story. The middle may not be about what happened, but it is likely to answer a similar question. The middle is not a good place to dump a bunch of material that doesn't seem to belong anywhere else. Keep that stuff for another piece. Have everything that is in the middle serve the purpose of answering the reader's questions, raising more questions, conveying the interesting events and results, and getting to the end.

Life is a journey, not a destination.

Some of the things that you write from your life may be perfectly satisfactory without a powerful crisis and a definite resolution. You may have an interesting "travelogue" or "slice of life" piece that needs to be included. What is important here is to be sure there is something more than a just picture of "me in front of the hotel" in your stories. Take the "picture" in front of the pyramids or on the beach—in action! The most typical book-length memoir or adventure story is the story of an individual's journey, a biography written in the first person. It has a plot that is similar to the quest plot, but is not developed in the traditional manner of plotting, it is more of a journey than a quest. Writing your story as a journey allows you to focus on events and action—external motivations and causes; or, on the other hand you can focus on motivation and meaning and write less action. You can shine that literary flashlight on the emotions and feelings and personal networks involved. Creating a true quest story requires you to relate meaning and motivation with action and results, and to deal with internal motivations in relation to obstacles.

The middle of a novel is all about action; the middle of a memoir is about the journey. It will likely consist of a number of stories, vignettes, or recollections. If there isn't any important crisis – a place where something shifts and the important question is answered, where something or someone is permanently changed for better or worse as a result of action, your narrative does not have a fully developed plot.

Remember you don't have to have a plot, you are writing about your journey. You do need a story ladder, however. Look to see whether there was a turning point for you in your life, some time when everything shifted. Would you share that? Perhaps it is there, but needs to be brought out in order to show up clearly in the memoir. Perhaps there are several such important moments, times when you were at a crossroads and made an important decision or chose a new direction. Something that was a defining moment for you may have a story attached, or the change may have come about gradually so there is no "real world" story, only a something you recall as important to you personally. Write about that choice or decision. Include your feelings about it.

Your personal recollections of the journey are interesting in themselves. You may have more of an internal motivational structure where you concentrate on what you learned in your life or how you made your choices or what you believe. A story moves along on the parallel tracks of action and feeling. Tell the things you found interesting, share yourself; answer the why questions. Use plenty of details, give inside information from your experiences, tell about people you have known. Be specific. Tell the good and the bad; don't gloss over your mistakes. Your honesty will endear you to others, and may be helpful to them. Say what you learned and go on.

Endings

The ending is arguably more important than the beginning of a story. Everything in your story leads up to the ending, the climax of the story. While the beginning engages your readers, the ending satisfies (or doesn't) satisfy them. Your readers remember the ending. If they don't like it, they may not like the story; but if they aren't satisfied by the ending—whether they like it or not—they won't read any more or your stuff –which may or may not matter to you.

Endings must accomplish several things:

- Resolve all the plot lines of a story
- Result from the story
- Answer the reader's final questions and the main question
- Leave the reader with a feeling of satisfaction

An ending that feels "stuck on," or discontinuous from the story, won't be satisfying. If you don't like your ending, your reader won't like it. The ending can be sad but if it follows clearly from the events of the story as a necessary result of the story, your reader will be satisfied with it. While you answer some questions as you go along, most of those answers lead to other questions which lead back to the main plot line or story ladder. The overall goal of the protagonist is usually not reached until the end of the story.

Endings from life

Usually you will know where a story ends. There's nothing more to write; it is over. Take another look, however. Does your ending accomplish its goals? Sometimes there is something that needs to be said to really wind it up, to give the reader a full sense of the meaning and consequence or your story. Since you are still alive, your life story is not over completely; however, you have reached the end of what you have to say for now. Review your work; add whatever else rounds it out. Explore meaning. In the case of a quest which has been accomplished, write about the results and rewards of the outcome. Tell how you felt receiving the Olympic Gold medal or the keys to the city. Tell where you see your life going from here.

In writing from life, it is likely that you do know the outcome of an event and of the major action threads before you start writing. Use the ending as a place to bring together the threads of meaning in your life so far. What do you care passionately about? Write something about that and how you came to be that way, why it is important, and what you hope others will get from your story.

Assignments

There are no specific assignments for this chapter. You probably know what you still need to do to complete your project. If you don't and you read straight through this chapter, go back with your work in hand and make a plan for yourself to get it complete.

You might need to do some research on beginnings or endings. Check the ending of a number of biographies or memoirs and compare them. How do these stories end? Which ones do you like best? Why? Do the same for story openers. Which approach will work for you?

You may need to take all of your stories and lay them out on a table or the floor and see what happens when you put them in one order or another. This can be a powerful tool for finding out what is missing, what works and what doesn't. It's a great thing to do with your spouse, child, or writing buddy. See the "Spit 'n Polish" for how to use this tool.

Take a look at your goals for the project. If something is missing or incomplete, work on it to improve it. You might need some pieces you haven't written; you might need to do some research or reshape a story or two. You are almost finished; don't give up now. Find your writing buddy and go over your materials together. He may be able to see something you don't, and vice versa.

It may be time to find a coach, editor, or ghost writer. Interview the person carefully to see what they can do for you and what experience they have with this type of writing. Read some of their work; talk about your backgrounds. A good fit with your style and an understanding of where you are coming from and what kind of help you need may be more important than formal credentials. Do, however, make sure that the person is good at the things you are not so good at, whether it is structure, grammar, or making prose sparkle.

Please don't send your work off to someone who advertises in a magazine or on the Internet until you have talked with them personally and know what they can do for you. Get references and check them. Try a small project with them before you commit to the whole project.

The next chapter is about publishing. If you are thinking of making copies—even just enough for your family – please read the relevant portions of that chapter. Most memoirs will never see the National Library or Library of Congress, but your memoir is valuable to you and your family. You have worked hard on it. You have done well. Take the next step with courage and all due caution.

BEGINNINGS: The Hook

Author, Title, Citation	First lines	Type of Hook	Accomplishments

BEGINNINGS: The Opening

Author, Title	Opening section	Reader Questions

Chapter 17

TO PUBLISH OR NOT TO PUBLISH
– And How

Most stories have value to the family and individual involved, and many have some element of universal appeal. We do love stories, especially true stories. Your story is of value to someone; and you are to be congratulated for your success in completing the project! You have put a lot of effort and time into it. Pat yourself on the back. Celebrate finishing your book! You have accomplished something that a lot of people talk about and very few people actually do.

The purpose of this chapter is to provide some options for finishing up by publishing or sharing your work. You will know which strategy is consistent with your purpose.

How you publish your memoir depends on your goals for the book and your resources for doing it. Sometimes it is hard for people to see that what is important to them has little or no commercial appeal. This is the time to get really tough with yourself. You have to sell a lot of copies to make back the hours and expense of writing and publishing a book in dollars.

It may be that your interest has been primarily in finding your own past and clearing yourself to go on. It is possible you have no interest in publishing your work. Put it in a notebook and put it on the shelf. You have accomplished what you set out to do. Most likely, however, you originally set out to write something for others to read; perhaps for your family or grandchildren, a legacy of experience and wisdom. You already have a lot of time and energy invested or you wouldn't be reading this chapter. Please use this chapter to get clear about what you are doing and what you want out of your next steps.

Copyrights and Publishing

You as the author or artist own all of the rights to a work until you sell it. When you sell it, you transfer some or all of these rights to somebody else. The term "rights" generally refers to your prerogative to publish the piece or a copy or image of it. The buyer can for instance sell a book or a piece of art again, but if it is sold as an intellectual property, it may be covered by copyright or other permissions.

Put a copyright notice on your book. Include "copyright" or "copyright reserved" and your name and the date. It is a good idea to put in the location and how to reach you in case anyone wants to quote you. That's usually enough for an informally circulated book. Even if you only make a few copies, your notice lets anyone who reads it know that this is your material, and you have the right to publish it.

To fully establish copyright ownership it is necessary to register the copyright when you publish a book. You can not copyright an idea, only the exact expression of it; e.g., the author's exact words which express the idea. Derivative copyrights apply to copies of art work and to plagiarism of ideas or reasoning, where whole passages are reproduced, even if not exactly.

While the principle of giving credit where it is due is immutable; permission to quote is normally secured during the period of final preparation for publication. A traditional publisher usually handles this task; however, having them correct is the author's responsibility. It is the author's responsibility to verify permissions although publishing houses often take on the actual work. If you are self-publishing, you get to handle all of these concerns yourself.

it is best to seek permission to quote from published works, as well as

> ***Important Points about Copyrights:***
>
> The following information is intended only to get you started. Do not make assumptions based on this material; seek further information as appropriate.
>
> - You automatically own the copyright when you create the work whether it is music, art or writing.
> - Copyright stays with the artist or writer unless it is transferred. Just as the purchaser of a copy of a book does not own the copyrights, the purchaser of a photograph or art work does not automatically own the copyrights to it.
> - Registering the copyright when you publish a book has the effect of establishing copyright ownership. There are advantages to you to register your copyrights on publication of the work.
> - Since 1978, US copyright generally lasts for the period of the author or artist's life plus 50 years. There are exceptions.
> - For publications before 1978 the US copyright period depended upon registration of the rights. As a rule of thumb, if the work dates before mid-century it is probably in the public domain now. A librarian or a lawyer can help you with this.
> - Go to http://www.copyright.gov/circs/circ1.html for information on US copyrights. You will find most questions answered there. There are also forms and links to additional information.
> - For information on Canadian copyrights, see http://strategis.ic.gc.ca/sc_mrksv/cipo/cp/cp_main-e.html
> - For specific information regarding your situation, consult a lawyer who specializes in copyright issues and intellectual or entertainment properties for the country in which you plan to publish.

give attribution. Usually such permissions are not hard to get—who does not want to be quoted? But getting them may take time, and the writer must give attention to the matter before the book goes out. At the point of publication you enter a world where money is involved. Suddenly copying a photograph, a line of reasoning or a passage of writing has financial ramifications. Beware!

Publishing Options

Do you want to give a few copies to the people you love? Do you have a story that people need to hear? Are you burning with a passion to inform the world about a crisis which needs to be resolved, or do you want to share some recollections with a broad group of people? Your goals for your book should determine your approach to publishing. Resources such as time and money are a consideration, but if you know what you want to accomplish you can find a way. Let's look at goals first.

You need to answer a few questions for yourself and come out with a goal statement for your book. Completed, your goal will actually be a mission statement that includes your purpose for your book, what you hope to accomplish, and your marketing goal. Then you should do some research among the available options to decide what route to publication is best for your book. From that information you can create a plan for publishing and distributing your book. The following discussion can only provide a few examples and rough guidelines.

One handmade book

If your primary focus has been getting your stories written and you have no intention of making copies, collect the stories into a looseleaf notebook or bound scrapbook. Illustrate each story with a well-chosen photograph or two. Write some material to tell why you have done this and what you hope others will get from it, and put this in a preface. If you want to talk about what you got from doing it, add one last chapter with that note at the end. Make a table of contents, and you are complete. Put it on the shelf where you can add to it from time to time. You can have copies made if you ever decide to.

A good strategy for finishing up a single copy is to put your pages into a nice new album or scrapbook. Find a title that somehow expresses your life theme and piques a potential reader's interest. It can be funny, pithy, or detailed—your choice. Add your name and the year in which you completed the work to the title page. Make an attractive cover.

Photographs, letters, and drawings are wonderful additions to handmade books. If you have a lot of this material, you may want to arrange your stories between groups of items. Because there is a lot of interest in scrapbooks these days, you will easily find suggestions for making attractive pages and special materials on the Internet, in books and magazines, and in craft shops. There are courses in scrapbooking and specialists who will help you with it.

Publishing without becoming a publisher

Suppose that your book is a collection of personal and family stories that will be of interest to a select group of your family and friends. You expect to need no more than forty or fifty copies. Maybe you only want to print a dozen copies and give them to your two children, three grandchildren and a few friends as gifts. You want to keep your expenses down, do a nice book and be done with it. Let's say you have about 100 pages including some photos and a table with a family tree. You have a color drawing from one of your grandchildren that you want to use as the front cover. You have typed your stories into your word processor, put in some headings, page numbers, etc. One of the grandchildren is really good with the computer and has helped you pick a type style and layout design. It really looks pretty good. You might print a few extras to use later, but that's really about the extent of it.

Take it to a couple of local copy shops. Ask about their options for doing booklets. You should be able to get a color cover and a spiral binding almost anywhere. Sometimes you can have a photo placed on the front. Decide whether you want it copied on two sides of the paper or just on one; actually get a sample page or chapter copied on two sides before you decide. Some bond paper is fairly transparent, and you may want to use heavier paper. Ask what other options they have. Ask how many copies you need to make to a price break.

Take note of any special options different shops offer. Find out about any special formats they may offer. Some copy shops have special deals for "chap books." These are small books, usually poetry, but the printing style is appropriate to memoirs.

If price is a concern, visit two or three of the best copy shops in your area and get an exact cost estimate done at each. Ask what it will cost to have it copied with a color cover and a spiral binding—or the option you prefer. Make sure you compare the price for the same thing (same number of pages, one or two sided print, same paper, covers, etc.) from one place to another. It may seem expensive, but when you compare the cost for a few copies to the cost of publishing including the necessary up-front costs, you may decide that the cost per copy isn't too bad. Then bite the bullet and do it. If you don't ever expect to copy more than a few copies, or if it is strictly a one-time thing, a copy shop is often the cheapest way to go even if the cost per copy is comparable to buying a hardbound book.

What if you need 100 copies?

If you have a large family, or think that you might want to reprint the book next year, or think that your book might have some interest to others in your community or a special interest group (such as your church or the local historical society), you may want to use print on demand (POD) publishing. POD is computer driven publishing. You pay for the set up and other services up front, and books are made available as needed. Books are generally perfect bound paperbacks although there are other options. No large print run is necessary. My research shows the break even point when compared to copy shops as being around a hundred copies after you factor in the upfront cost.

Even if you have no goal to be represented in a bookstore, print on demand can provide a high quality product at a good price and give you flexibility for the future. You can add to or change the book later, or bring out a new edition. It is only a bit different from working with a copy shop, and arguably easier because POD publishers keep your book in their database. If you need one more copy, you can get it with no trouble.

POD is likely to be the route of choice for publishing enough copies for a large family reunion or a church or community event. If you have some small potential market like that, please research this new type of publishing. It will definitely be less expensive than having books manufactured the traditional way. Before you settle on a POD publisher, check into the various package deals they offer and compare the offerings to your goals. You may find that their most basic offering meets your needs.

Also check with high-end copy shops as they often have connections and deals available for short-run publishing or chap books. They may have the equipment themselves or job it out. Sometimes they can provide a small number of very beautiful books through a connection like this. Find out exactly how they handle it; and make sure you see a sample that you like before you sign on. Find out how firm the price is. Printing is notorious for price changes; get it in writing.

If any set up is involved, be sure you get a proof (often called a "galley") before the actual printing is done. Go over it carefully with someone else, preferably a good proofreader, before you sign off on the print. One person holds the proof, the other the manuscript. Read the proof aloud against the manuscript, including the punctuation. You don't want to be stuck with five hundred copies that have a wrong date or name or some other small but serious mistake in them.

If, after reading this section, you are not sure that copying is your method of choice, please work through the rest of the chapter, particularly the section on goals. There is additional information about POD in the section on self-publishing. Also study other resources, beginning perhaps with the bibliography in this book, until you have satisfied yourself that you know what is best for you.

Your Goal Statement

Get quiet with your writing materials available. Use a moment to center yourself as we have in our warm up exercises throughout the book. Ask yourself one or more of the following questions:

- What is the purpose of my book?
- What do I want to accomplish with this book?
- Why did I write this book? Really?

Write out your own personal answers to the questions above. This material is for your eyes only. You may find that one or another of the questions triggers an important response. Dig into this area thoroughly.

You may find it useful to use one of our favorite techniques for teasing ideas out of chaos: make a list. At the top of the page, place the words: "Purpose of [Title of My Book]." Brainstorm a fast bullet-point list of your purposes.

Do the same for goals. Then take a look at your motivations or reasons if you haven't already.

When you have finished your brainstorming, boil each section down to a sentence or so. Type out your goal statement and see if it really expresses your intention.

There may be more than one purpose or goal for the book. Purpose is the answer to the why questions, the ideal. I have expressed this in the preface:

> *This book is for everybody who is interested in writing from their own experience, sharing themselves. In it I share the things I have learned about writing, stories about my life and my family, stories my students have written, and the techniques of writing and editing that are most useful for writing your stories.*

My purpose is to share what I have learned, to contribute to individuals and society, to help people to write their stories so they will be able to get closer to people they love. I want to make a difference in the world, and this is something I can do. So I do. I also have writing and marketing goals and strategies for fulfilling on them.

Some of your ideas may reflect your motivations and reasons more than they reflect the purposes the book will serve. In the example, I am motivated to have a book to sell to my students and clients, other teachers, and individuals. While I have not printed all the pages of brainstorming I have done, I include statements at different levels. Some statements turn out to be motivational statements rather than goals. Ah ha! I begin to see who my audience is when I run across these motivations. If you are like me, your answers may come in a jumble; you may have to sort motivations from goals and purposes. It's a matter of levels, things you want at different levels. It may not be important for everyone; however, if you plan to publish, you need to know why you are doing it, what you hope to accomplish, and then to devise strategies for publishing and marketing.

What It Takes To Publish a Book

Do you want to take on looking for a publisher or doing it yourself? Either way requires commitment.

Finding a traditional publisher requires a great hook in your story, a thick skin, a lot of time and some marketing savvy. Work up a proposal. You can learn to do this; there are books and people who will guide you. You will probably have to find an agent at some point—likely after you find a publisher yourself and before you sign. Very few, less than one percent, of memoirs are "commercial." Unless you are a celebrity, have survived a newsworthy ordeal, or there is a murder and sex in your book, you are not likely to attract much attention at a major publishing house. You have a better chance if you have a well-known biographer working with you as "ghost" or "as told to" writer.

> **Purpose of *Writing the Stories of Your Life***
>
> - *To help people write their memoirs.*
> - *To show people how to write a story so that it is interesting.*
> - *To have a book to use in the classes and workshops I teach.*
> - *To explain the writing techniques and strategies that are useful in writing memoirs.*
> - *To help people review their lives so far and be ready to look ahead to whatever is next.*
> - *To share what I have learned about writing in a way that widens my audience and provides me with income.*

Timing is everything. Inventors and scientists will find that their biographies are unlikely to command ready money in their lifetimes. Books about sports figures and other heroes sell while they are popular. By the time you have written it, the newsworthy event and consequent interest in your subject may have passed off the information horizon.

This is hard to face, but you must be honest with yourself about your goals and your material. If you just can't tell–and this is most likely where you are—have someone you trust evaluate your material. If you are thinking of self-publishing, develop your goals, look at your costs and options. Find an editor and a marketing consultant. Find yourself a team to help you make this project a success.

The publishing world today

Traditional publishing has changed a lot in recent decades and may not be the best option for your book. To put your best foot forward, you will have to have it edited before you submit it. Very little editing is actually done in publishing houses these days. You may have to get "blurbs" or testimonials to use on the cover and seek permissions to quote or use material from other authors yourself. You must verify that all the material you have included is accurate; ultimately, you are liable for errors, not the publisher.

You should note up front that even if a traditional publisher takes your book and gives you an advance, you will have to get very involved in the marketing if you wish to sell any books. If you are not known, you may have to create your own publicity tour or hire a publicist and pay for it. Publishers may send celebrities on marketing tours, but the individual still has to make the appearances. It will take your time and energy to get your book noticed and sell a decent number of copies.

Ask yourself: How much am I willing to put into refining the book, getting it ready for publication, finding a publisher or publishing it? You will have to decide for yourself whether to find a publisher or self-publish. Either way, there is a lot for you to do. Today there are new options that lie between the traditional options of publishing with a publishing house or vanity publishing.

> **ISBN**
>
> ISBN stands for "International Standard Book Number." This number actually indicates the publisher and the specific book. Your book, down to the exact edition, gets a special number all its own. Publishers buy a block of these numbers and assign them to their titles. Bookstores, distributors, and libraries use this number to order books.

If you publish your book yourself, you will pay for the services a traditional publisher would pay for. You will be the one to seek the right marketing approach and get your book noticed. You will have to get the cover and layout designed, find your own editor and proofreader, add illustrations, get your ISBN, register your copyright, and handle printing.

There are book manufacturers who will offer you a package deal which include some of these services. You can find them on-line or in the pages of various writer's magazines. You may be able to get a recommendation from a local printer or high-end copy shop of someone they use when customers want these services.

Be aware that different printers have different equipment and different strengths. One may be good at full-color work; another does great chapbooks or manuals. Another has a variety of sizes or binding options. Ask for samples and be sure you understand what they will do for you and what you will have to do for yourself.

You really have to get tough with yourself. Even if you have led a truly exotic life, it takes something special to turn it into a "commercial" project, meaning a project that actually earns money. If you do not have writing experience, you will probably need a coach, editor, or consultant to help you with writing and polishing your book and another one to help with marketing your book. Most of us need several such people. Even if you write for a living, it is hard to find the problems in your own work. Besides learning from my students and clients, I have used the services of several editors, two of whom went carefully through the whole manuscript. I also used a professional proofreader and a graphics designer. Some of the things they have done for me I normally do for other people; some I'm not so good at.

Don't give up without reading the rest of this chapter; just be aware that there is a lot to getting your book out no matter what route you take.

The Business of Publishing

According to Publisher's Weekly approximately 8,000 billion dollars are spent on trade books per year. In the year 2000 about 1.6 billion books were sold. Of those about 50 million were biography or autobiography.[69] Book industry statistics compiled by Andrew Grabois, Senior Director Publisher Relations & Content Development for RR Bowker show a steady increase in sales of biography, the category which includes memoirs.[70] There is a market for memoirs.

Bookstores buy books on a returnable basis. Think how many sheets of paper it must take to put one copy of just one particular title in every bookstore in the country! At least half of these books are likely to be returned unsold, even with a considerable advertising and marketing expenditure. Reaching the market efficiently is the advantage that Internet bookstores have over traditional sales distribution channels. While the Internet accounted for only 6% of sales in 2000, it is the fastest growing sector of the market.[71]

Publishing is about buying and selling. The publisher buys the rights to a book, manufactures it and markets it. The idea is to make a profit. Publishing is a business with many built-in unknowable factors, so there is considerable risk in bringing out an unknown author or an untried topic. Publishers love to discover new writers and great ideas, but they must see market potential to spend the big money it takes to launch a book the traditional way. As is true of many other industries, the major publishers have consolidated themselves through buyouts and mergers into a handful of huge corporations. Like most large corporations, publishers actually generate profits on a rather small margin of success compared to the number of projects they launch.

You must know what makes your book special and be willing to call attention to it.

Economies of size have resulted in homogenization of brands (former publishing houses and imprints) and even less attention than formerly to individual writers and books. Today a writer who wants to make it out of the heap must think very carefully about the potential market for her book. Anything but the select few books by established writers and well-known celebrities will get very little marketing support from a standard publisher. You must know what makes your book special and be willing to call attention to it. Even before that, you must get the attention of a publisher and make them care about getting that particular book out to a very large number of people. Otherwise, the economics simply don't work and the book is never published. It is very disappointing to have spent a year on a book and several years trying to sell it without success.

This brings us to the first advantage of publishing your own book. You can get the book to market faster, and having done that, a hidden advantage appears. A published book with a sales track-record behind it has a better chance of catching the attention of an established publishing house.

Study the market

It's actually important to take a look at marketing before we go further into the nitty-gritty of publishing. Take the time to study the market for similar books and to figure out who will buy your book, what your best channel of distribution is; then focus your book itself to maximize its effect in that channel. This applies whether you are self-publishing or trying to find an established publisher for your book.

This Book's Audience

We covered the concept of audience first in Chapter 5, Writing Letters. Here we apply the idea again to conceptualize the broadest group of people who might be interested in your book. From that group you can decide who your potential market is. That is called your "target audience."

Examples of target audiences include all the people in a particular organization such as a church or profession, or grandparents, or people who live in a particular town or state; or train buffs, or writers. My friend Walter Turner's book *Paving Tobacco Road*[72] serves as a good example of a book that has a distinct market: people who are interested in transportation history and people interested in North Carolina.

For a memoir your first target audience is your family and friends. There may be many others. Your audience may include people who have interests or affiliations similar to yours, people who belong to the same civic or religious organizations that you do, people of a certain age or ethnic group.

If you served in Korea or Vietnam, or if your stories all have to do with a certain unusual location, or the development or demise of a particular industry, there is a definite group of people in the world beyond your family who will be interested in the stories. Certain people are interested in trains and collect books on them; other people want to know about oceans or dogs or technology or making baskets.

Take a page in your notebook to brainstorm the audience for the book. First answer these questions for yourself:

- Who am I writing this book for?
- Who else might be interested?
- Who will read this book?
- Who is my audience?
- Who will likely buy this book?

List the obvious kinds of people, then list people who might relate to a topic or area of interest that the book speaks to, like mental health, engineering, politics or parenting. Would your book be a good choice for a gift? Who would buy it, and for whom?

What is my book's story?

Answer the question: What story does my book tell? While it may be obvious that your book tells the story of your life—that is its purpose, that is what you set out to do; and you have done it—it may be that your story parallels another story. Is your story the story of the building of a railroad, the story of a scientific breakthrough, a rescue, a mission to a third-world country, or an unbelievable adventure? What story is embedded in your story? What story would not have happened if you had not been there? It may be a story that permeates the entire book, or it may be something that appears only in a limited portion of the book but colors your whole life story.

Would a corporation buy your book or support you in getting it out? How about an industry organization, a political party, or non-profit organization? If you have spent your life making a difference for mental health, civil rights, Girl Scouts, wild animals or the environment, is there an organization that would partner with you in producing the book in return for a portion of the profits? Or, do you want to donate the book to them? Make a proposal to an executive of the organization or to someone who has vision and authority in that arena. Another place to start is with someone who wants to make a difference through the organization and might sponsor your book. There are as many possible arrangements as your creativity can develop.

List any benefits from your book for your audience. Will people learn how to meditate, how to cook without electricity, how to cope with disaster? Will they be inspired, educated, moved to action, or entertained? What will people come away from your book with? Write this out briefly.

Who are my target buyers?

Consider also who will actually buy the book. The audience who buys a book may not be the same person as the target reader. Is your book directed toward children, for example? The buyer is likely to be a grandparent, teacher, or parent. Is your book the sort of book people will buy for a gift? A good book to take to the hospital? Or the beach? A book about your life as a midwife might make a good baby-shower gift, for example.

Almost any topic can have an audience, but you have to do some thinking and research to figure out who the real buyers or target audience should be and what they are likely to want. Then you do some more research to figure out what they are likely to spend and how you can reach them. Are there enough of them to warrant publishing by conventional means, or would you be better off with some limited distribution approach? There are several books and Internet sources which can help you with marketing.[73]

Brainstorm the question: Who are my buyers? Ask other people to help you get a broad idea of who would be interested in your book. Then narrow it down. Do some research to find out how many people are interested in your particular topic. You can find out how many people belong to various hobby or interest groups as well as other demographic information. A librarian or marketing consultant can help with this.

Where do my buyers buy books? How will they find out about my book? Do they like bookstores, direct mail or the Internet? How much will they spend? What kind of books are they likely to prefer? What will it cost me to reach them? Spend time with this analysis. If it doesn't all come at once, add to it as you go about getting your book ready for publication.

After you have settled on your audience, your target market and your book's story, focus the book itself a little more tightly toward the audience you have defined. Go to a bookstore and study the books on the shelf that houses the type of books you have defined as your target. You may have to look in more than one area if you are writing a memoir and you have a special interest area like sports or railroads or cooking.

Online bookstores can be very helpful for comparing books. You can easily search for authors, subjects or publishers online, but a real bookstore will let you get the feel of the quality of the actual book a publisher puts out. Study books at a bookstore so you will be looking at books that are actually in print at the present time. What is in the market now and what is in the pipeline is important. Libraries and bookstores have access to a reference source called *Books in Print*.[74] This has a section on forthcoming books which you may want to look at.

Make a page in your notebook for each book that interests you. It is OK if there are other books similar to yours; it actually simplifies your job somewhat. You don't have to prove that a book of railroad memoirs will sell, you only have to show who would be interested and how your book would meet that interest. Write down the reference information including the publisher. Make any notes that will help you remember the specific book. Try writing down its purpose or focus and a description that shows what the book accomplishes. How is your book similar or different?

Finding a publisher

If you think you might have a book that can attract a major publisher, talk with an agent or editor after you have a first draft written and polished. There is much to know about this that is beyond the scope of this book; educate yourself about the process. Get some critique from a knowledgeable person. You may find such a person locally or at a writer's conference.

You may need to find a professional ghostwriter or editor to help you complete it well and quickly. Be cautious of approaching people from advertising; make sure you understand what you will get for what you spend. Find somebody who is knowledgeable of topics that will be key ingredients in your book. Find someone who will be able to understand and write well in areas of importance to your book. Make sure they complement your skills and are easy to work with.

Create a book proposal which includes a query letter, outline, and sample of 20-50 pages of text. Indicate how many photos or illustrations you have available and whether you have appendices or indices. In your query letter you ask them to consider your book. You will send this proposal package to agents and publishers, but it is often useful to inquire first by means of a one page letter whether they are interested in taking a look at your proposal. Many publishers and agents do not handle memoirs at all. You can learn more about this from Writer's Market.[75] There are special editions of Writer's Market for particular fields like children's books; and there are other guides to various aspects of the market. Today online guides may be your best source since they can be updated quickly. If you have a paper guide, you can usually find a publisher you are interested in online and verify that they are still in business, still interested, etc. Remember to check the update information on the website, too!

Be prepared to offer your market analysis based on the research suggested above and why you think such a book as you are proposing will sell as well as other books. Bestseller lists rank only a few top-selling books. There are special lists for particular topic areas as well as general lists such as The New York Times Bestselling Books list which is published in the Sunday supplement. Your book may not relate to anything on such a list, however. Amazon.com posts a complete ranking of its titles by sales volume. You may not need so much detail, but it is good to know that it is there. Almost anything you want to know can be found out with a little sleuthing and some help from a librarian.

Another route for publishing your book is to try one or more of the small or medium sized publishing houses. You will have to do some research to find the one that is right for you. Most of them specialize in one type of book. If your book is the story of a railroad told through your involvement with it, you would look for a publisher who specializes in railroad stories. Work through the section on goals to get clarity, then make a plan for publishing and distributing your work. As with major publishers, do not send unsolicited manuscripts, and do not use a scatter-shot approach. Study their interests and learn as much as you can before you write to them. Do, however, create a short list and work from one to the next. You can send a one-page query to several at once to find out if they are interested in seeing your proposal or manuscript.

Special interest groups or organizations, clubs, churches, and even corporations publish books. If your story is intertwined with the story of a particular movement or organization, you may want to discuss the possibility of publishing it with leaders of the organization. If the organization serves a purpose for public relations or consciousness raising that is aligned with your purposes in telling your story, you may have a match. Do not discount this option. It is an excellent way to go for certain books. If the organization itself is restricted from doing something of that sort, influential individuals may see the possibilities and assist you in getting the job done at a benefit to both parties.

Small Presses and Self Publishing

You probably already know that *Celestine Prophecy, Spiritual Marketing, The Long March to Freedom*, and *The Christmas Box* were originally self-published. *Prescription for Natural Healing*, and *What Color is Your Parachute* are other examples.[76] Your best bet for a memoir may be self publishing in some form.

Over 10,000 new publishers offered books for sale in 2002.[77] More than half of the books brought out today are published by small publishers, including self publishers. That's about 80,000 new titles in English per year. Including new editions, U.S. publishers released over 150,000 books in 2002, an increase of 5.86 % over 2001. New titles from the largest trade publishers declined 5.02% although sales dollars were up, which means large houses made more money on fewer titles and small publishers got out more new books than ever.

No discussion of self-publishing could be complete without mentioning Tom and Marilyn Ross, quintessential self-publishers and experts in book promotion. Marilyn and Tom have generously encouraged many writers to use their creativity and find a way to publish and promote their own work. Their *Complete Guide to Self-Publishing*[78] has gone through several editions since its first publication. The Small Publishers Association of North America was begun under their sponsorship.[79] The Rosses are true experts in making independent publishing work as a business and a lifestyle. Pick up one or more of their many books and attend a workshop under their leadership if you can. Whatever you choose as the best level for you in publishing your work, you will benefit from their experience and advice.

Self-publishing and print on demand

In the past if you wanted to publish something you had to turn yourself into a publisher. You could either become a publisher of books for sale by buying an ISBN and setting yourself up as a business in other relevant ways, or you could "vanity" publish by having a short run of books (usually 3000-5000 copies) printed by a printer and buying them yourself. Of course you could sell them yourself, but you could also wind up with thousands of unsold books left over. Vanity publishers generally do not provide services such as copyright and ISBN registration. Either way, you have a considerable up-front investment and you must do all the selling.

You may choose to use the traditional route of becoming a small publisher and printing a limited number of copies to sell. The downside is that publishing in itself is a demanding occupation which requires considerable time and marketing savvy. There is a great deal to know about "buying print," as dealing with printers is called, and other aspects of the business. You have to manage all the legal and manufacturing details. You get full control over your book, but it is also up to you to produce a professional product and market it.

Print on demand is today's hybrid between vanity publishing and traditional publishing. It is the self-publisher's wish fulfilled by advances in computer technology. Given that it has become axiomatic that the author has to get out and sell the book, it's a good option for an unknown writer who wants to get out there quickly. You have less clout in the bookstore, but that may not matter if you see your book as having a narrow target market or a special distribution channel, or if you see advantages to doing it immediately.

Print-on-demand publishing is rapidly becoming the route of choice to reaching the market with a self-published book. This is a method of book production which provides book production services to an author and as few as one copy at a time to a buyer. Copies are usually sold on the Internet and may be available through bookstores, and you can sell them yourself. Advantages of this route include control over your work, low cost compared to small press runs, and quick availability. Since inventory does not have to be maintained, the author is able to keep a work in print for a long time. Print on demand is especially appropriate for works that may sell steadily over time but never be best-sellers. It is also good for writers with chutzpah and impatience to become known, as stories are occasionally picked up by the big publishers from POD services. Study the matter and decide what is best for you.

Print on demand

POD "publishers" are book manufacturers, but with a difference. Because books are stored in electronic form and because computer driven printing and binding equipment is used, books are printed as they are ordered, usually in trade paperback form. These printers can print one or a hundred books after the order is placed, and ship them with a turnaround of hours or days. There is no inventory tying up cash and space.

POD evolved in response to the opportunity to provide books for fast distribution by electronic means through the Internet. Most of them offer e-books in one downloadable form or another as well as paperback books. Some offer to set your book up for hardcover also. They generally take little or no responsibility for content. Not only the quality of the book, but its marketability becomes entirely your responsibility. Most have an online presence and will sell your book through their website.

A POD published book can be made available in a bookstore or sold through any other normal distribution channel. Your ISBN insures that anyone in the industry can order the book, and POD houses will list the book with book distributors and search engines. Your favorite independent book dealer is your best bet to carry your book on her shelves. Major bookstores will not generally store POD books in the store but wait for customers to order them, so the plan is not as strong if you want a bookstore presence. In contrast to traditional publishing, POD houses usually do not allow returns from bookstores, which considerably simplifies the whole matter of determining how many books are actually sold and what royalties are due. The business is changing daily, check to see what options are now available to you.

POD books may also be delivered electronically to your customer's email box. This can also be accomplished directly through a website without making the paper version available through POD. The customer may print his copy or not. Problems with security and print quality exist due to the nature of the medium, but these are being addressed. Generally, the system works amazingly well; however, you must look out for yourself and be sure that you have the security, the quality, and the guarantees you need in your contract and in reality.

With POD you don't wind up with a garage full of expensive books. You get the number you order, and you get going on your marketing plan to sell them. POD publishers can print copies in a few days, so you can always get more. You don't shop for years for an agent and a publisher; you move forward on your own schedule. From manuscript to bookstore takes between six weeks and a year—far less time than traditional publishing.

How POD Works

Basically, a print on demand publisher takes your camera-ready book layout and prints it. They have a cover done and manage distribution for you. They also handle standard publishing tasks like registering copyright, securing an ISBN, and so on. They can generally do a better job for less expenditure than you can of these routine publishing tasks. Books are generally perfect bound—the standard softcover binding–with hardcover, mass market and online options available.

Print on demand publishers generally take no responsibility for content. It is up to you to have your work edited, illustrations prepared, and have good marketing copy for the cover. All of these things can be learned, and there are many people available to help you for a fee. Find someone you trust for each step of the project. Your POD publisher may offer referral for some of these services.

POD plans differ considerably. They charge for different services separately or offer package deals. Read the contracts very carefully. You may or may not be listed as the publisher. You may or may not have control of the title and cover. A good cover is very important in a bookstore–not so important if you sell the book in your classes only.

While there are several strong POD publishers, the winner in the POD growth wars seems to be 1st Books, now known as AuthorHouse. They have a large number of titles in their list, and offer many options for you to choose from. They operate in a very fast-paced environment with a lot of personnel change, I think, from my personal contact with them. Also check out iUniverse and Trafford. Trafford, a Canadian company with a US presence, claims to be the original POD publisher and offers a very clear set of options. Operating in a chaotic marketplace, they have demonstrated steady growth and continuity while systematically introducing improvements and innovations.

You will find other POD publishers if you look online or for ads in writer's magazines. Some specialize in one type of work such as books on sci-fi, books for writers, or other specialized markets. Only you can determine who can best meet your needs. Your goals for your book will help you to make that decision. Pay attention to how you like to work and relate to people, as well as to the type of book you want to produce. Choose a company you are comfortable with, and read your contract carefully.

Afterword

Having added the chapter on publishing to this material, I feel that there is something that should be said to round out the book.

There is a lot of material in this book; I hope that it has been helpful. I hope that you have gone back over earlier pieces of work and improved them as well as written new ones on a regular basis. I hope you have an overflowing notebook of stories and ideas. I hope you will continue to work with these until you have a memoir that satisfies you.

I've been asked what people who are not in a group should do with their assignments.

Obviously (I thought), if you are in a group or have a writing buddy, you would share them with each other at your meetings. A large percentage of the time in my classes is devoted to having students read their work. I give suggestions which I hope are helpful. I meet with clients individually and/or by email to go over their work. Unfortunately I can not do that with readers. Getting together with others who share your interests is a good plan. Try bookstores, libraries, civic and religious organizations, and community colleges to find a group – or start one.

If you read your work together in a group, do not criticize; and don't help each other to death, either. You all have different styles and purposes. Keep in mind the purpose and project that the individual has when they read. Give the reader your full attention. After someone reads, thank them. Thank each other for having the courage to try something new, to share your efforts, and to keep trying to improve your writing.

If you as a group agree to give each other some feedback, have someone who is even-handed be the moderator. Then try the "3 X 3" plan: One person reads. If that person wants comments, a person gives three things that work about the piece (or three people can each give one different thing that works well.) Then someone makes up to three suggestions for improvement. Thank that person and let someone else read. Do not spend time as a group shredding or reworking someone's whole story—you can see why.

But what if you are not in a group? My first choice is that you find a writing buddy or a group, or start a group and work through it together. You be the leader, and take them through this book. You will learn a lot.

If you are determined to work alone, I recommend that you write new pieces regularly so that you always have some that you are working on and some "in the drawer" and a growing pile of stories you have finished. It's a good idea to put a piece of writing away for a while before you edit it. When you take it out, you will get a fresh view of it. From time to time, take one or two of the stories that have been waiting in the drawer out. Review them, edit them and finish them. Apply the things you have learned from your own exploration and reading as well as from your writing practice.

If you have a considerable stack of material and you want to see how far you have come, get it all out, put it in order according to the date it was written, and reread it. You will be surprised. Writing is truly a field where you learn by doing. Do any editing you want to, then share your work with someone you love.

It has been a great challenge and a great pleasure to write this book and share it with you. Thank you for your time and attention. Peace and joy go with you.

Glossary

This is a glossary of technical terms, defined as I am using them in this book where I am applying them to memoir writing. You will find different interpretations and further information in dictionaries and other books about writing; please avail yourself of as many other sources and ideas as you can to broaden your understanding of the concepts you are interested in. My purpose here is to give you a quick look-up for a term as you come across it.

There are many other words in this book that are not used every day. If you don't own an up-to-date and extensive dictionary and you are serious about writing, buy one. Also, have a current atlas, an encyclopedia, and a general grammar reference available as you write. If you use a computer, you will find that many reference materials are available on disk or on line. Not all of these are high quality, but they may be kept up to date in a way that no printed source ever can be. Things are changing. Use whatever references work best for you, and don't just let them take up space. Words are our tools; keep them in good order.

Antagonist	Villain
Audience	The typical reader of a work; the person you have in mind as your reader.
Autobiography	One's own life story.
Back story	Background material, story background. The story behind the story, the back story is the repository of reasons why things are as they are and details about the characters Back story is important to the writer, but should be sprinkled gently into your story.
Biography	Written account of another person's life. Also general term for the genre including biography, autobiography, memoir and reminiscence.
Character	A person playing a role in a book.
Character flaw	Weakness or blind spot that a character has. The character flaw serves to make a character seem more real, and may provide a major obstacle to his success.
Creative non-fiction	True reporting with added non-factual detail; a true story told in a way to make it more interesting. Also called true fiction and true-life story.
Dialect	An accent, or non-standard usage of spoken language. Writing dialect implies writing with phonetic spelling or markings to indicate the way the spoken language sounds.
Dialogue	Quoted speech between characters in a book.
e-book	Book published in electronic form, delivered through e-mail or other digital means to the buyer.
Fiction	Stories of various kinds that are made up by writers.

Flow of story	The flow of your story is its path from beginning to end. It is also the sense that the story is moving along, happening, getting somewhere.
Genre	A specific, recognizable type or category of books. Examples are detective stories, contemporary romance, literary fiction. For memoir writers distinguishing different types of biography such as autobiography, adventure, tell-all or historical biography can be useful.
Hook	An opening line or paragraph that entices the reader to read more.
Inner Writer	That portion of the mind or self which provides words to the writer. Muse.
Lead, lead in, lead sentence	Opening line. Journalistic term, implies importance of the content.
Memoir	Book or story written from the point of view of memory or reminiscence; may be an account of one's own or someone else's life. A written memorial or appreciation for a person's life, honoring that person.
Mind Map	A tool for diagramming associations to a word or central concept. A mind map is particularly helpful for creative thinking.
	If you don't know how to do one and your problem seems very circular, look up "mind map" on the Internet or in a library. You will find easy-to-follow resources which will help you sort it out. See bibliography for references.
Narrator viewpoint	Story told through the eyes of a narrator who is a participant in the events of the story.
Non-fiction	Reports and writings that are said to be factual or true. Non-fiction includes narrative works which deal with opinions as well as facts and truth. Poetry and drama are generally excluded from non-fiction. All works which are not specifically fiction are considered non-fiction, including critique and works about fiction as well as most biography and memoir.
Omniscient narrator viewpoint	A viewpoint in which the narrator knows all. Omniscient Narrator Viewpoint is particularly useful for memoirs written from a retrospective stance or perspective.
Omniscient viewpoint	The viewpoint in which the author knows all.
Pace of story	Pace refers to the rate of movement within the story.
Protagonist	Hero or heroine.

Resolution phase	The portion of a scene, sometimes called the "sequel," in which the scene is ended and the next scene is set up; resolution deals with the internal motivation of a character, particularly the clarification of the scene's meaning in the story or the character's next intention.
Role	Part that a person plays in the story.
Scene	Segment of a story that contains an incident or event. "Scene" is used at two levels; first to designate the event or action itself, and second, to encompass both the action and resolution phases of the segment.
Sidebar	A box or set-off portion of text that relates to the subject but is not part of the flow of the piece; examples are found in this book.
Slant	Shaping your writing to present a certain viewpoint.
Story elements	Bits and parts out of which a story may be constructed; e.g., a character, a motivation, an objective, an event, an object, a location, etc.
Story ladder	A series of questions and answers underlying the story, the answers to which comprise the skeleton of the story
Story problem	Core problem of a story. Motivational issue for the protagonist or problem to be solved by the core characters
Story question	Question, the answer to which is fundamental to resolving the story. The question, or many questions, the reader wants to have answered in order to feel satisfied with the story.
Structure	Underlying design, plan, formula or plot of a story.
Target audience	The typical buyer of a book; the potential market for a book
Theme	Refers to the underlying message of a story, the line of reasoning that the author explores in an essay or book, and the underlying values of a person's life. Theme implies continuity over time of a message or value statement. Related to voice.
True fiction	Fiction work based on a true story. True-life story. See also creative non-fiction.
Viewpoint character	The character who is the lead character at least for the purposes of the scene. Character from whose perspective the story is told.
Viewpoint, point of view	The perspective or standpoint from which the story is told.
Voice	A writer's special style or particular way of communicating. A writer's underlying philosophy and perspective on life
Warm up	Practice of writing quickly, without conscious thought, to waken the Inner Writer and get the mind into the groove for writing.

Endnotes

Preface

[1] If you don't know how to do some of these things, that's what this book is about.

1 Life as Story

[2] Jimmy-Neil Smith, president of the International Storytelling Center, quoted by Marcianne Miller. To Wit, Storytellers gather to salute a legend, *Mountain Express*, p40, September 5-11, 2001.

[3] Women Who Run with the Wolves; Myths and stories of the wild woman archetype. New York, Ballentine, 1992.

[4] M. Willard, private conversation.

[5] Pearson, Carol S. Awakening the Heroes Within; Twelve archetypes to help us find ourselves and transform our world. San Francisco, HarperSanFrancisco, 1991. P. 223.

[6] Frank B. Gilbreath, Jr and Ernestine Gilbreath. Cheaper by the Dozen. (Available in reprint version; also see the movie.)

[7] Oates, Joyce Carol. New York: Dutton, 1996.

2 Let's Write

[8] Dyer, Wayne W. You'll see it when you believe it; the way to your personal transformation. NY, William Morrow, 1989.

[9] Fuller, Rebecca. Personal communication. Fuller is a well-known maker of models for museums, national parks, and other venues. She specializes in tactile models providing accessibility to these experiences for all people. She has developed her career and her niche while raising three boys.

[10] Ueland, Brenda. If You Want to Write: A book about art, independence and spirit. 2d. ed. St. Paul, Graywolf Press, 1987.

[11] Asimov, Isaac. I. Asimov; A memoir. NY., Doubleday, 1994.

[12] A mind map is a tool for diagramming the associations you have to a word or central concept. Look in the glossary for a fuller explanation and references.

3 Finding Stories

[13] "Ode: Intimations of Immortality from Recollections of Early Childhood." *William Wordsworth, Selected Poetry.* Ed. Mark van Doren. NY, Modern Library, 1950.

4 Warm Up

[14] This one is thanks to Natalie Goldberg

5 Writing Letters

[15] Those were the days

[16] Shakespeare. Julius Caesar (Cassius)

[17] I'm thinking 500 to 1000 words. Any length you want to write is OK.

[18] Rent the movie and watch it if you haven't

6 Setting

[19] Old Chinese proverb

[20] Smithsonian. January, 2004

[21] Spielberg, Stephen. Close Encounters of the Third Kind; movie. Columbia, Pictures, 1997. Star: Richard Dreyfus. Data from SciFlicks.com

7 Viewpoint

[22] Trigiani, Adriana. Big Stone Gap; Big Cherry Hollar; and Milk Glass Moon form a wonderful trilogy set in West Virginia.

[23] Greeley, Andrew M. The Bishop and the Missing L Train. NY, Tom Doherty Associates, 2000.

[24] Holman, Virginia. Rescuing Patty Hearst; Memories from a Decade Gone Mad. NY, Simon & Schuster, 2003.

[25] Viewpoint in fiction—best refs

[26] Card, Orson Scott. Characters and Viewpoint. 1988. Cincinnati, Ohio. Writer's Digest Books.

8 Unforgettable Characters

[27] Shute, Neville On the Beach. NY, Ballantine, 1983.

[28] Piercy, Marge. He, She and It. Fawcett, 1993.

[29] Lukas, George. Star Wars.

[30] Block, Lawrence. Write for Your Life; The book about the seminar. Ft. Myers, FL, 1986.

[31] I had a book when I was a tiny child that I think was called "True Zoo Stories" I suppose it got lost after making its way through the family. In any case, there are many books about zoo animals which are early favorites with toddlers. The *Life of Pi* by Yann Martel (NY, Harcourt, 2001), a recent novel for adults and winner of the Man Booker prize, is an entirely different kind of story about zoo animals.

9 Journaling

[32] Johnson, Alexandra. Leaving a Trace, On keeping a journal; the art of transforming a life into stories. Little, Brown, 2001.

[33] Read up on this in Sheila Bender's A Year in the Life; Journaling for Self-Discovery. Cincinnati, OH; Walking Stick Press, 2000. Or check out your dictionary.

[34] Song—Alfie From *Georgie Girl*, a movie from the 1960's.

[35] Morning pages are the core exercise of Julia Cameron's *The Artist's Way* (NY, Jeremy P. Tarcher/Putnam, 1992) The idea is to get up and start writing before doing anything else.

[36] Johnson, A. op cit.

[37] Progoff, Ira. Originally quoted in The Write to a Fulfilling Life: An interview with Ira Progoff. The New Times magazine, January, 1993, Vol. 8, #8. Dialogue House Associates. www.intensivejournal.org 2/5/2004 2:11 PM.

[38] Dialogue House Associates; 80 E. 11th Street Suite 519, New York, NY, 10003

[39] Progoff, Op.cit.

[40] Cameron, Julia. NY, Jeremy P. Tarcher/Penguin, 1999.

[41] Taylor, Cathryn L. The Inner Child Workbook; What to do with your past when it just won't go away. Los Angeles, CA; Jeremy P. Tarcher, 1991. John Bradshaw and Charles Whitfield are probably the most prominent authors in this field.

[42] NY, Warner Books, 1998.

[43] NY, Warner Books, 1999.

[44] NY, Warner Books, 1995.

[45] Lewis and Clark's journals are unusual in having been kept by more than one individual, but fascinating, and available in various editions.

[46] Fulghum is the author of *All I Really Need To Know I Learned in Kindergarten; It Was On Fire When I Sat Down On It;* and other books. *Maybe (Maybe Not)* is a favorite of mine.

[47] Bender, Sheila. A Year in the Life; Journaling for Self-Discovery. Cincinnati, OH; Walking Stick Press, 2000.

[48] There are many. Eric Maizel's Deep Writing; 7 Principles that Bring Ideas to Life. (NY, Tarcher/Putnam, 1999) teaches seven basic principles of creativity. Also see The Creativity Book: A Year's Worth of Inspiration and Guidance.

[49] Johnson, A. Op cit.

[50] Mayes, Frances. Under the Tuscan Sun; At home in Italy. San Francisco, Chronicle Books, 1996.

[51] Breathnach, Sarah Ban. Something More; Excavating your authentic self. NY, Warner Books, 1998.

[52] Johnson, A. Op cit.

[53] Mayes, F. Op cit.

[54] Frank, Anne. The Diary of Anne Frank.

[55] Ten Boom, Corrie with John and Elizabeth Sherrill. The Hiding Place. Old Tappan, NJ. Fleming H. Revell, 1971.

10 Research

[56] Walters, Barbara. How to Interview Anybody on Anything.

11 Story Structure

[57] Campbell, Joseph. Hero with a Thousand Faces.

[58] Vogler, Christopher. The Writer's Journey: Mythic Structure for Writers. 2d ed. Studio City, CA, Michael Wiese Productions, 1998.

[59] Pearson, Carol S. The Hero Within; Six archetypes we live by. 3d ed. San Francisco, Harper/SanFrancisco, 1998; also Awakening the Heroes Within; Twelve archetypes to help us find ourselves and transform our world. San Francisco, Harper/SanFrancisco, 1991.

13 Editing

[60] Stein, Sol. Stein on writing; A master editor of some of the most successful writers of our century shares his craft techniques and strategies. New York, St. Martin's Griffin, 1995.

15 Theme

[61] Greeley, Andrew M. Furthermore! Memories of a parish priest. NY, Tom Doherty Associates, 1999.

Writing the Stories of Your Life

[62] Downing, Christine. Ed. Mirrors of the Self; Archetypal images that shape your life. Los Angeles, CA. Jeremy P. Tarcher, 1991.

[63] See Pearson, Carol S. The Hero Within; Six archetypes we live by. Awakening the Heroes Within; Twelve archetypes to help us find ourselves and transform our world. The Female Hero in American and British Literature. The Fuzzy Red Bathrobe; Questions from the heart for mothers and daughters. And a number of other works.

16 And They Rode Off... Finishing

[64] Ellison, Ralph. Invisible Man.

[65] Heyerdahl, Thor. Kon Tiki. available in reprint. The Ra Expeditions. Translated by Patricia Crampton. Garden City, NY, Doubleday, 1971.

[66] Put in *"first lines" + biography* OR *stories + first lines* and you will find websites with thousands of published story openings. There are also websites with story starters for practice writing.

[67] Dickens, Charles. A Tale of Two Cities. Found on the website: www.biblomania.com/fiction, 06/20/2004. Check it for many other famous first lines.

[68] Sebold, Alice. The Lovely Bones. Little, Brown; 2002.

17 Publishing

[69] Publisher's Weekly, Estimated Annual Publisher Sales of Trade Books. © 2003 Reed Business Information, a division of Reed Elsevier Inc. Information retrieved 11/3/2003 from Website: www.reedbusiness.com.

[70] Grabois, Andrew. U.S. Book Production Statistics, 1992-2002 Information retrieved 11/3/2003 from Website: www.bookwire.com.

[71] Publisher's Weekly Online, 10/03/03

[72] Turner, Walter. Paving Tobacco Road; A century of progress by the North Carolina Department of Transportation. Check www.nctrans.org for a preview.

[73] If you have no experience with marketing, you may want to find a consultant or take an introductory course. Small business assistance organizations provide courses which may be helpful in thinking this through. Check with your local community or technical college or Chamber of Commerce for possibilities. In addition, check my bibliography for books on marketing.

[74] First made available in 1948 as the index to Publishers Trade Manual, Books in Print is now available on-line with restricted access. You can learn more about that through your librarian or at the website: www.bowker.com, which is provided by R.R. Bowker LLC, the corporation which provides ISBN and other services to the book industry.

[75] Writer's Market. Annual from Writer's Digest Books, an imprint of F&W Publications, Inc., Cincinnati, Ohio. You will find current editions in bookstores or check it out online at www.writersmarket.com. Beware of using older editions; things change very fast in publishing today. The dated years run ahead a bit like auto model years.

[76] See website by John Kremer www.bookmarket.com for lots of great information on self publishing and independent publishers.

[77] U.S. Book Production Tops 150,000 in 2002, Trade Publishing Down, University Presses Up. Publisher's Weekly Online, 10/03/03

[78] Ross, Tom and Marilyn H. Ross. The Complete Guide to Self-Publishing; Everything you need to know to write, publish, promote and sell your own book. 3d ed. Cincinnati, OH, Writer's Digest Books, 1994.

[79] SPAN may be accessed online at www.spannet.org, or write to P.O. Box 1306 Buena Vista, Co, 81211-1306

Bibliography

This list is neither fully systematic nor random, and it's not a syllabus designed for instructional use. It is not representative in any way except that the writing has come to my attention and interested me somewhere along the way to completing this book. I own a great many of these, which has me use them rather than look for others which may also be good. Some of the most recent I have come upon in the process of finishing up this work and found kindred spirits.

I have included works on self awareness, journaling and writing, myth and folklore, culture, some anthologies of writings from ordinary and extraordinary people, and a few favorite memoirs. After some thought I left out the novels; there are hundreds of first-person and other novels that it would be appropriate to include. Some of these books are simply my favorites. I am sure that not everyone will agree with my tastes and choices; I share my preferences as I encourage you to; you will find what you need.

I hope this list is helpful. If you can't find some them because they are out of print, I apologize. Perhaps your librarian can suggest something on the same topic.

Asimov, Isaac. I. Asimov; A Memoir. NY., Doubleday, 1994. One of Asimov's last writings, a fascinating collection of 166 short essays on various people, books, and events in his life. There's a lot about being a writer and being an individual.

Auster, Paul, Ed. I Thought My Father Was God: And Other True Tales from NPR's National Story Project. NY, Henry Holt, 2001. A well-known novelist, Auster took on the NPR Story Project thinking there would only be a few responses. There were thousands. This book of 179 short pieces written by all kinds of people, sharing themselves, shining a light on what it is to be alive in the USA at the end of the twentieth century, is the result.

Baer, Ulrich, Ed. 110 Stories; New York Writes after September 11. NY, New York University Press, 2002. Poignant stories from 110 people who experienced New York, September 11, 2001.

Bender, Sheila. A Year in the Life; Journaling for Self-Discovery. Cincinnati, OH; Walking Stick Press, 2000. An invitation to journaling from a respected writing teacher.

Block, Lawrence. Write for Your Life; The book about the seminar. Ft. Myers, FL, 1986. A well-known writer of mysteries, Block wrote for Writer's Digest for many years. This book, if you can find it, provides an introduction to techniques for writing, and a lot of encouragement for the beginning writer.

Bradshaw, John. New York, Bantam, 1990. Available in paperback and as a reissue.

Breathnach, Sarah Ban. Something More; Excavating your authentic self. NY, Warner Books, 1998. A system for journaling from the author of Simple Abundance.

> I have found the insights in this book very helpful in my life. There is a companion volume: The Illustrated Discover Journal, Creating a visual autobiography of Your Authentic Self, which provides guides and ideas, beautiful blank pages and pockets for creating your own book.

Browne, Renni and Dave King. Self-editing for Fiction Writers; How to edit yourself into print. NY, Harper Perennial, 1994. All you need to know about editing, especially at Phase 2, with plenty of examples.

Cameron, Julia. The Artist's Way. NY, Jeremy P. Tarcher/Putnam, 1992. Cameron has become famous for this course in creativity, self-awareness and art. It is a demanding road, but one worth the effort.

Cameron, Julia. The Right to Write; An invitation and initiation into the writing life. NY, Tarcher (Putnam), 1998. A book on enhancing creativity specifically for writers,

Campbell, Joseph with Bill Moyers. Betty Sue Flowers, ed. Joseph Campbell and the Power of Myth. (Also known as The Power of Myth.) Princeton, Princeton University Press, 1972. Conversations between Moyers and Campbell on the stories that guide us even in a "mythless" age.

Campbell, Joseph. The Hero with a Thousand Faces. 2d ed. Princeton, NJ, Princeton University Press. 1972. Campbell presents his ideas about the underlying pattern of the hero's journey, an archetypal path that is available in virtually all times and places. This classic work has laid down a solid core for generations to follow in discovering their bliss.

Card, Orson Scott. Characters & Viewpoint; How to invent, construct, and animate vivid, credible characters and choose the best eyes through which to view the events of your short story or novel. Cincinnati, OH. Writer's Digest Books, 1988. A writer of distinction, Card is also a good and caring teacher.

Carrera, Phyllis. A Journey of My Choosing: Traveling the creative path of life. Humanarts; 2003. I plan to actually read this one as soon as I get this book in!

Coles, Robert. The Call of Stories; Teaching and the moral imagination. Boston, MA. 1989. A beautiful book by a formidable mind on the relationship of life and story.

Conway, Jill Ker, Ed. Written By Herself: I: Autobiographies of American Women: An anthology. II. Women's Memoirs from Britain, Africa, Asia and the United States. Vintage, 1992, 1996. Conway, a historian and former president of Smith College, has edited this excellent collection of writings from women who were pathfinders in their lives.

Writing the Stories of Your Life

Conway, Jill Ker. When Memory Speaks; Reflections on autobiography. NY, Alfred K. Knopf, 1998. Insightful and beautifully written study on the writing of memoir. This one is deep and personal.

Crichton, Michael. Travels. NY, Ballentine, 1988. Crichton, the author of Jurassic Park and many other novels, tells stories from his medical school years and vacations–trips he took in search of rejuvenation, but learned about himself.

Downing, Christine. Ed. Mirrors of the Self; Archetypal images that shape your life. Los Angeles, CA. Jeremy P. Tarcher, 1991.

Dyer, Wayne W. You'll see it when you believe it; the way to your personal transformation. NY, William Morrow, 1989.

Esquivel, Laura. Between Two Fires; Intimate writings on life, love, food & flavor. Tr. S. Lytle. NY, Crown, 2000. One of my favorite books, a collection of writings on family, food, and living in two cultures from a great writer of our times. Laura Esquivel is the author of Like Water for Chocolate.

Feinstein, David, & Stanley Krippner. The Mythic Path; Discovering the guiding stories of your past—creating a vision for your future.. NY, Tarcher (Putnam), 1997.

Fulghum, Robert. Maybe, (Maybe Not). NY, Villiard Books, 1993. What can I say? Robert Fulghum must be one of the most loved story tellers alive. He brings compassion and humor to the most everyday situation.

Greeley, Andrew M. Confessions of a Parish Priest; An autobiography. NY, Pocket Books, 1987.

Greeley, Andrew M. Furthermore! Memories of a parish priest. NY, Tom Doherty Associates, 1999.

Greeley, Andrew M. Why Can't They Be Like Us? Facts and fallacies about ethnic differences and group conflicts in America. NY, Institute of Human Relations Press, 1969.

> This is the same Andrew Greeley who gave us Blackie Ryan and all the imaginary (and maybe not so imaginary) clan of Irish Catholics of Chicago. I was introduced to Why Can't They Be Like Us? as required reading for my fellowship in ethnic studies. About that time his novels began to appear. Greeley's ability to track the complex web of family relationships among his characters is beyond me; I confess, however, that my favorites among his novels are still the early and complex ones. What I see in Greeley's novels, besides a good read (which is enough) is love and compassion for people and his application of a brilliant intellect to the real social issues of our time.

Johnson, Alexandra. Leaving a Trace, On Keeping a Journal; the Art of Transforming a Life into Stories. Little, Brown, 2001. An encouraging book on journaling and writing.

Johnstone, Barbara. Stories, Community, and Place; Narratives from Middle America. Bloomington, IN, Indiana University Press, 1990. This one is the result of linguistics field research in the Midwest. Scholarly. Interesting.

Klement, Alice M. and Carolyn B. Matalene. Telling Stories: Taking Risks; Journalism Writing at the Century's Edge. Belmont, CA. Wadsworth Publishing Co., 1998. Intended as a reader for journalism students, this collection of powerful stories focuses on telling true stories from the inside—at depth—getting to a true expression of human being. Read it for the wonderful stories, if not for the models they form.

Lamott, Anne. Bird by Bird; Some Instructions on Writing and Life. NY, Pantheon, 1994. A gentle and delightful book on writing and life. Prize winning author of novels and women's inspirational books, Lamott has a fine sense of language.

Levinson, Jay Conrad, R. Frishman and M. Larsen. Guerrilla Marketing for Writers: 100 Weapons for Selling Your Work.

MacLaine, Shirley. Dance While You Can. NY, Bantam, 1991. While I would recommend any of MacLaine's books as models for writing from life, I chose this one because it deals with working out family stories, conflict and programming.

Mayes, Frances. Under the Tuscan Sun; At home in Italy. San Francisco, Chronicle Books, 1996. A poet's memoir.

Mitchell, Edgar with Dwight Williams. The Way of the Explorer; An Apollo Astronaut's Journey Through the Material and Mystical Worlds. NY, G. P. Putnam's Sons, 1996. A modern day hero's saga, Mitchell's memoir tells the story of his inner path as well as his external success. Mitchell is one of twelve human beings who have walked on the moon.

Mountain Dreamer, Oriah.. The Invitation, San Francisco, HarperSanFrancisco, 1999. A call to courage and creativity in self-expression.

Pearson, Carol S. Awakening the Heroes Within; Twelve archetypes to help us find ourselves and transform our world. San Francisco, HarperSanFrancisco, 1991.

Pearson, Carol S. The Hero Within; Six archetypes we live by. San Francisco, HarperSanFrancisco, 3d. ed. 1998.

Pinkola Estes, Clarissa. Women Who Run with the Wolves; Myths and stories of the wild woman archetype. New York, Ballentine, 1992.

Phillips, Kathleen C. How to write a story (Speak Out, Write On). Franklin Watts, 1995.

Writing the Stories of Your Life

Remen, Rachel Naomi. My Grandfather's Blessings; Stories of Strength, Refuge, and Belonging. NY, Riverhead Books (Penguin Putnam), 2000.

Rogers, Fred. The World According to Mister Rogers; Important Things to Remember. NY, Hyperion, 2003. I have many happy memories of glancing into the living room while my two soaked up the truth about life from "Wogers." We even made up an opera in our kitchen one day with the back door open to be the audience.

Ross, Elizabeth Irvin. Write Now! Surprising Ways to Increase Your Creativity. NY, Barnes & Noble Books. 2003. Can you write while you sleep? A writer and stress therapist's approach to using the subconscious mind to improve your time management and your writing.

Ross, Marilyn H. and Tom Ross. Jump Start Your Book Sales; A money-making guide for authors, independent publishers and small presses. Buena Vista, CO, Communications Creativity, 1999.

Ross, Tom and Marilyn H. Ross. The Complete Guide to Self-Publishing; Everything you need to know to write, publish, promote and sell your own book. 3d ed. Cincinnati, OH, Writer's Digest Books, 1994.

Schumacher, Michael. Creative Conversations: The Writer's Complete Guide to Conducting Interviews. Cincinnati, OH, 1990. Written for reporters, this book covers many types of interviews clearly and simply.

Selling, Bernard. Writing From Within; A guide to creativity and life story writing. Almeda, CA, Hunter House, 3d ed. 1990. A 4th edition is now available. This is the best book I have ever seen on its subject. Had it been in print when I started writing, I might not have pursued the project. My book has turned out to be quite different, however. I recommend this for the examples and astute comments. Selling seems to be able to coax genius from his students.

Stein, Sol. Stein on writing; A master editor of some of the most successful writers of our century shares his craft techniques and strategies. New York, St. Martin's Griffin, 1995.

Steinem, Gloria. Revolution from Within; A Book of Self-Esteem. Boston, MA. Little, Brown and Company. 1993. Steinem, the editor, the writer, the quintessential feminist, knowledgeable seer—writes about herself, her struggle and her search in this collection of deep and fascinating essays.

Taylor, Cathryn L. The Inner Child Workbook; What to do with your past when it just won't go away. Los Angeles, CA; Jeremy P. Tarcher, 1991.

Tobias, Ronald B. 20 Master Plots (and how to build them). Cincinnati, OH. Writer's Digest Books, 1993. Take a look at this if you want to write a novel or adventure story from your life, but you don't exactly have a quest plot.

Ueland, Brenda. If You Want To Write; A Book about Art, Independence and Spirit. 2d. ed. Saint Paul, MN, Graywolf Press, 1987.

Underhill, Daryl Ott. Ed. Every Woman Has a Story: Many Voices, Many Lessons, Many Lives; True Tales. NY, Time Warner, 1999. There should be many more collections like this. Stories from women, sharing lives—suddenly you are among friends, and this is the deep stuff, and you find peace.

Underwood, Kim. Dope on a Rope: Oddments from the Mind of Kim Underwood; A collection of columns by Kim Underwood as published in the Winston-Salem Journal. Winston-Salem, NC, Piedmont Publishing, 1998.

Vogler, Christopher. The Writer's Journey: Mythic Structure for Writers. 2d ed. Studio City, CA, Michael Wiese Productions, 1998.

Walters, Barbara. How to Talk With Practically Anybody About Practically Anything. Bantam Dell Pub Group, 1970. Available as reissue.

Whitfield, Charles L. Healing the Child Within: Discovery and recovery for adult children of dysfunctional families. Atlanta, Health Communications, Inc., 1987.

Index

A

Archetype	7, 144, 199
Audience	46, 47, 50, 232, 242
Memoir	49, 63
target	244
Autobiography	100, 242
Strategy	208

B

Back story   10, 113, 117, 126, 160, 184, 212, 213, 214
  and beginning   212
  and characters   90
  and structure   204, 211, 213
  and viewpoint   78
  Fiction   10
  How much   210
  Research   117, 125, 138
  Story opening   214
  Use of   51, 65, 183, 212, 213, 214
  Why questions   214
  Writer   213
Beginning
  Getting started   14, 15, 20, 205, 211
  Hook   14, 113, 155, 206, 214, 215, 229
  Story opening   211, 212, 214, 216
Benefits
  of book   233
Biography   242
Book manufacturers   230, 237

C

Change
  as a way of life   60, 99
Character
  and plot   138
  Details   91
  Development   64, 87, 109
  Dialogue   148
  Flaw   86, 242
  Goal   136
  Narrator   76, 82
  Tag 69
  Viewpoint   71, 75, 78, 79
Characters   13, 38, 66, 70, 136, 142, 146, 210
  and setting   59, 61, 64, 65
  and story   136
  Fictional   10, 23
  Memoir   16, 86
  Personal quirks   149
  Who don't talk   153
Children   5, 26
  Stories for   18
  Thinking   6
Computer   7, 13, 111, 183, 209, 242
Copyright 120, 122, 224, 230, 236, 238
Copy shop   175, 226, 227, 230
Creative non-fiction   4, 9, 11, 134, 139, 244
Creativity   22, 24, 36, 100, 102
Culture
  and folktales   4, 5
  and story   4, 5, 6
  Setting and   59, 65, 66, 67, 70
  Thinking patterns   36

D

Dialect	156, 157, 158
Dialogue	
Characteristics of	146
Functions of	146, 147
Diarists	112
Diary	113

E

Editing
  Clarity and focus   173
  Content and structure   170, 171, 177
  Details   174
  Phases of   171
  Separate from writing   169, 170, xii
Editing versus Writing   xii
Emotion   108, 113, 114, 159, 182, 186, 187, 189, 190, 191, 214
  and details   68, 181
  and viewpoint   72, 81

Language of	181
Reader response	182
Tone	68, 154, 186
Ending	172, 173, 209, 217
Twist	76
Equipment for writing	16

F

Family history	10
Fiction	
Biographical	11, 134
Memoir	11, 133, 181
Technique	11, 134, 181, 182, 184, 186, 187, 190, 209, 212
Folktale	4, 5, 7

G

Genealogy	1, 119
Goals	
and story	136
Memoir writers	167, 218, 223, 227, 229
of book	xiv
Publishing	225, 235
Writing the Stories of Your Life	229, xiv
Your book	228

I

Ideas	
Finding	5, 24, 25, 31, 52, 53, 54, 55, 119, iii
Tracking	28
Writing	21, 22, 24, 25, 31, 52, 53, 54, 119
Your story	33
Inner Writer	14, 23, 35, 36, 38, 39, 41, 54, 99, 102, 104, 186, 189, 243, 244, xii
Internet	7, 8, 86, 99, 122, 219, 225, 231, 233, 234, 237, 243
Interviewing	122, 123, 128
Family	124
ISBN	230, 236, 237, 238

J

Jack tale	4, 7, 8
Journaling	97, 99
and memoirs	104, 112
for personal growth	100
Inner Child	100
on computer	98
Sketchbook	102
Story Notebook	104, 116
Writers	101
Journey	6

L

Languages and Memoir	157
Legacy	1, 10, 145, 166, 223
Letters	
in memoirs	51, 120, 177, 178
Libraries	119, 219, 234
Life Theme	200, 225
Listening	46, 123, 124, 125, 139

M

Market	
Target	233
Marketing	36, 121, 200, 225, 227, 229, 230, 231, 232, 233, 234, 235, 236, 237, 238, 244
Memoir	68, 104, 113, 115, 204, 232, 234
Book-length	203, 216
Collections	8, 32, 62, 114, 115, 130, 176, 204, 208, 209, 226
Distinction	9
Fiction	10
How to organize	130, 176
Multiple sources	131
Strategy	18, 115, 131, 208
Structure	5, 204, xii
Theme	193
Viewpoint	71, 72, 77, 243
Memoirs	
Celebrity	8, 10, 73, 115, 122, 229, 243
Collaboration	73, 80, 208
from journals	112

    Idea based   114
Memorabilia
   116, 130, 176, 177, 178, 179, 226
Memories
    Accessing   16, 17, 18, 23, 28, 52, 53, 54, 92, 104, 119, 157, 195
    Childhood   54
Memory   117
Middle   111, 209, 211, 212
My friend Susan   89

N

Narrators
    Multiple   73, 80, 176, 208
Non-Fiction
    Memoir   133

P

Personal growth
    Story   9
Plagiarism   121, 224
Plot
    and memoir   133
    Quest or journey   143, 205
    Subplot   138
Print on demand
   227, 236, 237, 238, 239
    Advantages   237
    Break Even   227
    How it works   238
Publish
    Self   226, 230, 237
    Your memoir   223
Publisher
    Finding   229, 230
    Responsibility   237, 238
Publishers
    Small   236
Publishing   223, 225, 226, 229, 230, 232, 233, 234, 235, 238
    Business   231, 236
    Goals   225, 227, 228
    Plan   225, 235
    Print on demand   227
    Self   226, 236
    Special interest   235

R

Recollection   9, 14, 105, 113, 114, 208
Recollections on a theme   115
Remembrance   8, 130
Research
    How to write from   118, 120
    Resources   118
    Types   117
Rewrite
   39, 40, 113, 170, 173, 183, 208

S

Scrapbooks   1, 51, 104, 225
Secret Formula   55, 141, 143
Setting   137
    Elements   66
    Influence of   59
    in memoirs   61
    Place   61, 65
    Social   65
    Social environment   65
    Time   64, 119
    Twentieth century   60
Sharing yourself   115
Space
    for writing   17
Stories
    and culture   4, 5, 7
    Emotional impact   61
    Family   78, 123, 126, 157, 158, 226
    Finding   117
    functions   2, 4
    Organizing principle   23, 27, 32, 115
    teaching   4, 5, 9, 143
Story
    Development   30, 112, 142
    Distinction   8
    Middle   64, 111, 156, 203, 205, 209, 211, 212, 216
    Personal growth   9
    Shaping   142
Storyteller   1, 81, 125, 132, 151, xiii
Storytelling   1
Story elements   133, 135
Story flow and pace   13, 36, 39, 41, 113, 148, 163, 166, 187, 203, 209, 211, 243, 244

Story formula 141, 142, 144
Story ladder 133, 138
Story notebook 21, 30, 61, 66, 88, 90, 97, 98, 102, 104, 110, 112, 116, 138, xviii
    Tips 29, 111
Story opening 14, 113, 155, 211, 212, 213, 214, 215, 229
Story problem 244
Story question 138, 212, 244
Story strategy 115, 213
Story structure 133
    Approaches to 135

T

Teaching stories 5
Theme 8, 14, 115, 193, 197, 208
    Identifying 194, 197
    in life 14
    in memoir 199
    in title 225
    Life 194, 196, 197, 200
    Literature 194, 199
    Meaning 194
Thinking skills 36
    Culture 6
    Emotion 182
Time
    for writing 16, 17, 19, 42
Tips
    Memoir writers xvii
Turning point 105, 115, 143, 147, 148, 150, 152, 198, 207, 209, 216

U

Urban myth 7

V

Viewpoint
    Child 11, 31, 75
    Depth 72
    Memoir 72, 243
    Multiple 73, 76, 80, 208
    Narrator 74, 176, 243
    Omniscient 71, 72, 75, 76, 77, 78, 79, 176
    Omniscient Narrator 72, 76, 77, 78, 176
    Purpose 71
    Test for 78
Viewpoints
    Multiple 208
Voice 33, 80, 148, 159
    Finding 82
    Storyteller 82, 150
    Whose story is it 18

W

Warm up 35, 36, 39, 46, 77, 244, xviii
    Example 35, 169
Word choice 126, 150, 154, 171, 174, 181, 184, 186, 190
Writing
    and personal growth 109
Writing Groups 66, xiv
Writing Process xiii
Writing versus Editing 38, xii

Y

Your story
    Organizing 115, 199, 203, 208, 225
    Writing 52, 72, 81, 105, 109, 115, 150, 203, 207, 209, 216, 217

About the Author:

Funny, how hard it is for me to write about myself. You'd think it would be easy—as much as I have written about memoir writing. I have lived with this book for several years now. There have been times when it took up all my waking hours; yet I find it difficult to figure out what to say here. It is that very knowledge—how difficult it is to write autobiography–that has driven me onward to complete this project. Because it is worth it. Because I couldn't let my students down by failing to do what I have pushed them to achieve. Because when someone writes from the heart, she makes the world a better place.

My first adult job was as a library clerk; I narrowly missed becoming a writer then because the newspaper didn't call back until I had agreed to the library position. I've been married to the same handsome man since I was almost 19. We put ourselves through college and I earned a Ph.D. in psychology from the University of Pittsburgh, which allowed me the joy of making a difference in mental health administration for a few years. Since then I've worked as a secretary, writer, and editor. I'm a natural coach and teacher, which sometimes comes out as bossiness.

I am a mom and a feminist. I am passionate about painting, books, classical music, education, and travel. When I travel, I visit the art museums. I am working on another novel. I am thrilled to be finishing this book, and eager to meet new people interested in stories.

Elsa Eysenbach McKeithan

Order form

Know someone who should write a book?

Give the gift of story!

Check your favorite bookstore, or order here!

YES! I want ___ copies of Writing the Stories of Your Life; How to Turn Memories into Memoir.

US orders at $24.95 each. Canadian orders $31.00. Shipping is extra (please call number below and inquire). Allow 4–6 weeks for delivery.

Check or money order for $ _____ is enclosed

Name _____
Organization _____
Address _____
City/State/Zip or code _____
Phone _____
Email _____

Card Number _____ Expiration _____
Signature_____

Order by phone or online:

Phone: 252-633-3690

Toll Free: 1-888-240-3723

Fax: 252-633-4816

Online: www.trafford.com

Or send to:

Trafford on-demand Publishing Service™

Suite 6E–2333 Government Street

Victoria, BC CANADA V8T 4P4

Check our website for information about discounts for bookstores, schools, libraries and groups.

ISBN 1412035287

Made in the USA